# Form, Space, and Vision

DISCOVERING DESIGN THROUGH DRAWING

# Form, Space, and Vision

DISCOVERING DESIGN THROUGH DRAWING

SECOND EDITION

# Graham Collier

FOREWORD BY SIR HERBERT READ

PRENTICE-HALL, INC., ENGLEWOOD CLIFFS, NEW JERSEY

© 1963, 1967 by Prentice-Hall, Inc.,
Englewood Cliffs, New Jersey.
All rights reserved. No part of this
book may be reproduced in any form
or by any means without permission
in writing from the publisher.

Library of Congress catalog card
number: 67-12189

Printed in the United States of America

current printing (first digit):

1  2  3  4  5  6  7  8  9  10

designed by Herbert M. Rosenthal

PRENTICE-HALL INTERNATIONAL, INC. *LONDON*
PRENTICE-HALL OF AUSTRALIA, PTY. LTD. *SYDNEY*
PRENTICE-HALL OF CANADA, LTD. *TORONTO*
PRENTICE-HALL OF INDIA (PRIVATE) LTD. *NEW DELHI*
PRENTICE-HALL OF JAPAN, INC. *TOKYO*

TO MARY

foreword

I am often asked if it is possible to teach "modern art"—by which the questioner means whether there is a short cut to skill or efficiency in such contemporary styles as the abstract or non-figurative. My first inclination is to evade the question—I do not like being responsible for other people's destinies. But if I am compelled to answer, I murmur something about "contact with things," "immersion in physical materials," "the discipline of the senses." Go to the potter's wheel, I have sometimes said, and when you can throw a bowl with a perfect outline, you will be ready to indulge in action painting. Spontaneity is not enough —or, to be more exact, spontaneity is not possible until there is an unconscious coordination of form, space, and vision.

These are the three elements which Mr. Collier has chosen as the prime concern of the teacher of art; and, good teacher that he is, he knows that the nature of these elements cannot be realized conceptually, but must be discovered experimentally. This is a book of "exercises," and is not only clear and practical, as every manual must be, but is throughout informed by the author's awareness of the limits of art and of the dangers of dogmatism. He knows also that art involves imagination as well as skill, and that even imagination cannot be left to chance, but has laws of its own origination, as Coleridge called them. It will be said that imagination is a gift and cannot be taught—turn then to Part 2 of this book and you will find such a superstition refuted. This is the most original contribution that Mr. Collier has made to the teaching of art, and I know of no previous treatise that has dared to define the laws of visual imagination, and to build an educational method on them.

Mr. Collier is not unknown to me. For a few years we were neighbors in England and I had an opportunity then of observing the inspiring character of his teaching. We have lost his physical presence in our schools, but I am happy to find that he can express himself so clearly that teachers everywhere can now adopt and adapt his methods to the needs of their pupils. This is an illuminating book and will help even the general reader to a better understanding of art.

HERBERT READ

preface

The second edition of this book is largely new material. The basic concepts are the same as those treated in the first edition, but the text is completely rewritten and expanded, and the chapter sequence is changed. The illustrations also have been widely supplemented.

I must, therefore, make several new acknowledgements for this edition, without prejudice to my gratitude to those who helped me prepare the first book.

I should first express my appreciation to the galleries, collectors, and artists who have so willingly supplied the new illustrations, in many cases at very short notice. I am indebted to the staffs of the Museum of Modern Art in New York and the Avery Memorial Library of the Wadsworth Atheneum, Hartford, Connecticut (Mr. Richard Tooke and Mrs. Elizabeth Hoke respectively); to my colleagues, Professors Robert Kiley and Kenneth Forman for their criticisms and suggestions (their belief in the book has been an important endorsement for me); to Professor Joe Reardon at the State University of New York at Buffalo for allowing me to use three examples of his calligraphy oriented method; and to several fine art students at the University of Connecticut for their interest and help.

The faculty of life sciences at the University of Connecticut have been most tolerant both of my ignorance and my frequent invasions of their domain. The snake skeleton (Fig. 3-1) is a typical example of my borrowing from the Department of Zoology. But I would especially like to acknowledge my debt to Dr. Howard W. Pfeifer of the Department of Botany. He has not only provided illustrations (the magnificent bladderwort in Fig. 3-18), but has also initiated me into the art and science of botany in a most beguiling manner. He has given freely of his time and his friendship.

John Albaugh, teacher and artist, contributed many fine photographs of nature to the first edition. Although I am no longer on the West Coast, we have still been working together, he taking photographs and I selecting them. His new contributions to this edition of the book are numerous and varied. Where no specific acknowledgement is made for an exciting nature photograph, it comes from John Albaugh; the more ordinary examples are my own. Someday I would like to do a book in which I merely make a painter's comments on his photographs.

I am indebted to the University of Connecticut Research Foundation for their generous help in the preparation of the manuscript, and to Mrs. Selma Wollman for her patient and skillful typing, not to mention her occasional editing.

Finally, we come to Prentice-Hall. Robert B. Davis was responsible for coaxing the first edition out of me, and, in a way, he is still lurking behind the scenes. His enthusiasm and support can span a continent, and I feel that this new book is as much his as mine. I shall always be grateful to Bob Davis. Jim Harris has also kept me up to the mark in Connecticut—he is a great man for boosting an author's morale. But without the controlling hand of a series editor like James M. Guiher, all our efforts might not be realized. His judgment, impeccable sense of style for a book of this sort, and his considerable background knowledge of art and the function of art in university education, ultimately determine the nature of the transformation from manuscript to book. The production editor's job is less glamorous and, in this edition, has been a tedious one. Layout and text have undergone constant modification during the production stages. William R. Grose has displayed the patience of Job in controlling it throughout, and I have constantly relied upon his efficiency in keeping all the many threads together. And then it is up to the designer to physically bring the book to life and create its "personality." I am grateful to Herbert M. Rosenthal for all his hard work. He identified himself with the spirit of the manuscript from the very beginning and set out to produce a book which handles well, is visually exciting, and provides an example of first-rate design in itself.

**GRAHAM COLLIER**
*Storrs, Connecticut*
*1967*

contents

CONTENTS

introduction

The opportunity to take introductory courses in drawing and design is open to most undergraduate university and college students, irrespective of whether or not they intend to specialize in art. In a 12- or 15-week period it is hoped that the student will develop new sensitivities and skills and take on an artist's view of life and the world. Possibly, he or she will proceed to take further courses, but even so, it is a slight introduction to the complex activity of art. Even a student who majors in fine art has only started to nibble at the surface of it, for as any artist knows, art expects a lifetime's apprenticeship.

I have never thought that art books of the "how to do it" variety were much help either to the student or the artist-teacher. For I believe that one becomes an artist through a drawing response to a live situation, and then through experiencing the dialectic interchange resulting from live criticism of one's efforts. On the other hand, we must recognize the limitations of time suffered by the average studio course. In academic subjects the lecture period is supplemented by vast library resources, and the student can do a great deal of independent study. In writing this second edition I have tried to provide a book that will supplement the studio period in art, as other literature supplements the lecture in academic courses. I hope that it will enable the keen art student to continue the development of his potential skill, and his perceptual, emotional, and imaginative responses, outside the studio, in his own time. Therefore this is not a book of instruction, intending to guarantee the production of conventional, academic, "nice" drawings. Instead, it is the student's attitude I want to influence—to make him look, think, and enthuse before finally losing himself in the act of drawing—and to ensure that when he does draw, it should be from an inner compulsion. Drawing is a tool to serve insight and expression, and therefore we are not concerned merely with proficiency in handling materials. For skill is less important than awareness, the surface appearance of things is less important than their meaning and aesthetic significance, and mental and imaginative reality is at least as important as physical reality.

What is it that the universities want from studio courses in art? And what do the artists themselves—those who do the studio teaching—see as the justification for their work? This question is crucial to an expanding university population who can experience art both as a general educational requirement and as specialized professional training. This book represents my own answers to the question. As such, it is a statement of belief as well as a manual of the basic grammar of drawing and design. I believe that the function of art in university education is to help the student to:

1.
Conceive the world in plastic, visual terms.
2.
Graphically express his own inner needs and attitudes.
3.
Develop a strong sense of self through heightened mental and emotional experiences.
4.
Discover the spiritual significance of formal order, proportionate harmony, and over-all unity, which we call beauty.
5.
Develop a sensitivity to great works of art through undergoing the frustrating ordeal of trying to draw.
6.
Penetrate to the essence of things and develop a scale of values.

These statements attempt to define the higher function of art, the function that Sir Herbert Read describes as "the mental processes which lead to the creation of the most permanent achievements of mankind. . . ." [1] Therefore the philosophy of this book is that drawing should be used by beginning students to record their personal reactions to all kinds of stimuli, and that in so doing the senses will be sharpened and the mental life quickened, through the exercising of intellect, intuition, and feeling. We also maintain that drawing is the *first* means of expression; that a piece of sculpture, a work of architecture, a painting, a contemporary table lamp, more often than not, takes shape first as a drawing—hence the subtitle, *Discovering Design through Drawing*. If "design" means *bringing into being*—the graphic or otherwise concrete realization of mental images—then drawing and design are inextricably linked, though we may draw without any intent to design. Rather does design grow inspirationally out of the act of drawing.

The drawing experiments in the book will attempt to involve the student in a series of fundamental experiences. He will be asked to look intently at many things and to search and analyze rather than tacitly to accept. First, he will be confronted with many problems of form and the omnipresent context of space. After concentrating on visual sensations and so intensifying his perception, he will develop a greater

---

[1] Sir Herbert Read, *The Forms of Things Unknown* (New York: Horizon Press, 1960), p. 28.

understanding of both form and space. (Actually we are incapable of perceiving either one separately.) Second, the reader is asked to consciously examine and be aware of his attitude to the motif, and to respond to the object's aesthetic significance (or lack of it). But these experiences alone cannot produce a work of art. There must also be the compulsive force of the imagination, for only the imagination has the power to turn fact into art. We say a person has "vision" when he experiences a moment of heightened perception accompanied by an all-pervading mood, both of which trigger the transforming processes of imaginative development. Part 2 of the book introduces the student to the imaginative reality of art.

The chapters are conceived as a sequence for both reading and drawing, for the later work builds on the understandings gained in the earlier sections. But there is nothing rigid about this format; the instructor or the student can elect to complete the work dealing with families of form before he becomes involved with space—or vice versa—should he so desire.

It is my hope that this book will provide the reader with a vocabulary of art and with an insight into its workings that will enable him to place greater reliance on the creative, rather than the imitative, act of drawing. And he should gain some personal standards of aesthetic judgement that will help him distinguish the genuine from the fake, the instinctive from the contrived, art from craft.

In conclusion, I would echo Paul Valery's comment, "We must always apologize for talking painting . . . ," for words convey but poorly the quality of communication achieved by the plastic arts. Yet, I suppose we must suffer words if we believe that art is one of the great transcendent experiences of human life, and therefore should be part of our educational system. The Welsh artist, David Jones, made the following comment on the occasion of his seventieth birthday: "One is trying to make a shape out of the very things of which oneself is made. . . ." And the statement which sums it all up for many artist-teachers was made by Max Scheler when he said that the purpose of art is "not to reproduce what is already given (which would be superfluous), nor to create something in the pure play of subjective fancy (which can only be transitory and must necessarily be a matter of complete indifference to other people), but to press forward into the whole of the external world *and* the soul, to see and communicate those objective realities within it which rule and convention have hitherto concealed." [2]

---

2 Max Scheler, *The Nature of Sympathy*, trans. P. Heath (London: Routledge & Kegan Paul, Ltd., 1954), p. 253.

# Form, Space, and Vision

# Part 1

We have no visual knowledge of any kind except that of form and space. The dimensions of space determine the world in which we move and live; and space, in turn, is established and defined by the objects or forms that occupy it. The artist, concerned with giving graphic expression to his perceptions and his creative imagination, cannot avoid re-creating form in space, for there can be no visual communication that is formless and spaceless—there can be just nothing at all.

If this point seems very obvious, it is insisted upon because the reader must be impressed with how fundamental the concepts of form and space are in art. The practice and philosophy of art must start with them. The thirteen chapters in the first half of this book are designed to involve the reader with certain aspects of form and space, and with the interrelationship between the two. The experiments are not meant to be comprehensive, but merely to introduce two of the three basic factors underlying the whole structure of the visual arts. The third, the element we call "vision," is the concern of Part 2.

The five aspects of form with which we shall be concerned are its structural, aesthetic, organic, tactile, and dynamic qualities. Each experiment is only a starting point for further discoveries about these qualities. Involving the student in a personal awareness of space is more difficult. As you will see, space must be approached through an awareness of form and through a perception of tonal values in the ground (surface) which is used. Consequently, the experiments dealing with space also involve form and the perception of tonal values. The operation of forces in space, our intuitive sensitivity to space, and our intellectual ability to structure it precisely are the prime concerns of the experiments involving spatial awareness.

First, we must introduce the graphic factor itself, for this is the actual impressing of marks and lines on a ground—it represents the act of drawing. Therefore the first chapter is called "Drawing Marks."

# Form and Space

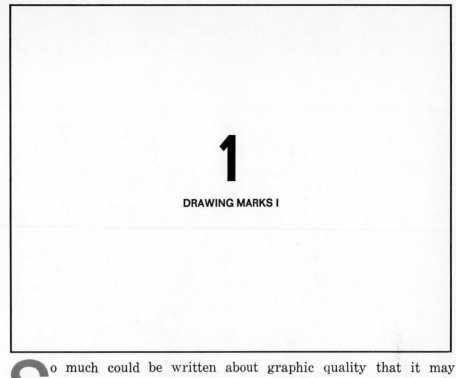

# 1

## DRAWING MARKS I

So much could be written about graphic quality that it may seem presumptuous to discuss it so briefly, in one chapter. But as this whole book deals with drawing in one form or another, and as constant references will be made to "the line" and "the mark," we must present at least a brief introduction to the graphic element.

What is a graphic statement? It is the impression of marks on a ground or surface. In drawing, the marks may be lines, dots or points, or areas of tone. Once drawn, such marks can be as personal to the artist as his own fingerprints. A line or a smudge of tone is a person's direct, graphic response to an experience. It may or may not be a sensitive response, for the degree of sensitivity is largely governed by two factors: first, the nature and quality of the individual's attitude to the experience; second, the ability of his kinesthetic drawing action to exploit the medium chosen, and to correspond to his total attitude. The kinesthetic element constitutes the craft of drawing, and ultimately must become unconscious in its operation—the artist must not have to think about how he is doing what he does. The subtle, tactile relationship of the drawing instrument to the surface, and the nerve-muscle coordination that effects the movement of arm and fingers, must be-

**Fig. 1–1**
**Student Drawing Sheet 3**

# The

# graphic

# experience

3

come instinctive, for only then can the drawing be truly *expressive* of mood or attitude, a sort of spontaneous combustion springing directly from the excitation. Jackson Pollock's *Number 32* (Fig. 1–3) is an excellent example.

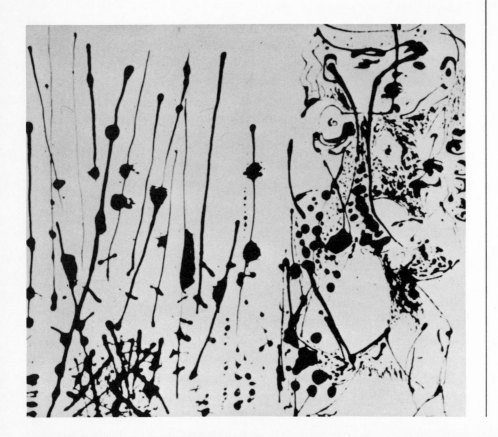

**Fig. 1–2**
Jackson Pollock
**Number 10**
*(Collection, Mr. Alfonso Ossorio,
Long Lsland)*

**Fig. 1–3**
Jackson Pollock
**Number 32**
(Collection Kunst-
sammlung Nordrhein-
Westfallen,
Düsseldorf, Germany;
*photograph by Hans Namuth, New York)*

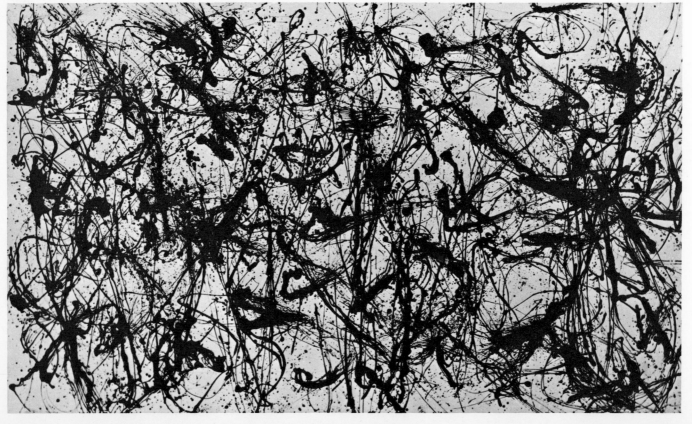

But not all graphic responses are as expressive as this. The lines, dots, and tones of some drawings may be more mechanical, more regular, and more consciously controlled. Images of this sort may lack the emotional vitality and the spatial definition of an expressive drawing, but they do something else. They can give us precise, structural information. For example, the drawings called for in Chapter 3 are basically diagrammatic, intended to give information which has been gathered about structural essentials by a visual analysis of an object. As such, you will find that these are *perceptual* rather than expressive drawings.

**Fig. 1–4**
Paul Klee
**Botanical Gardens**

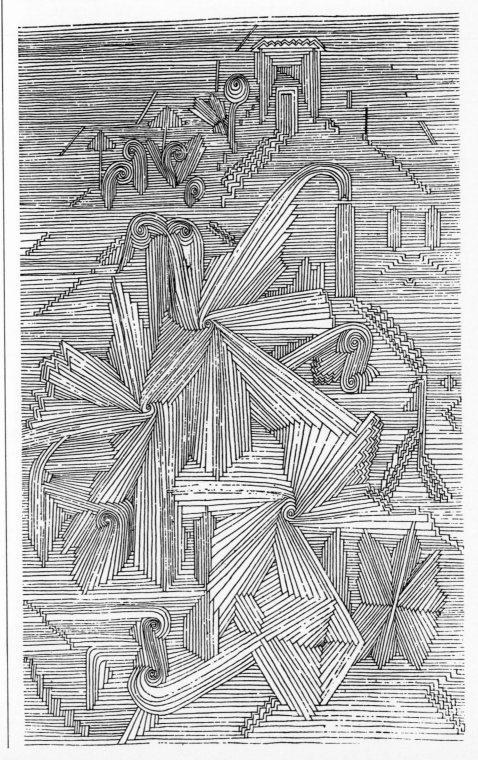

Because of this dual nature of drawing, the graphic experiments in this chapter will be concerned particularly with the two kinds of lines —expressive and perceptual. The first category serves our feelings and our more intuitive attitudes; the second serves our more rational mental processes which tend to analyze and order form, and is more tied to an act of perception. The two categories of lines may be thought of as inductive and deductive, respectively. An analytical or structure drawing may be as sensitive in its own right as an expressive drawing. The constancy and clarity of a structure line, as well as its positive directional movement, indicate a refinement of perception and a controlled sense of touch which result from an alerted consciousness—and therefore may be termed "sensitive." See Paul Klee's drawing, Fig. 1–4.

In following the suggestions made by the experiments, your personal response will differ from that of your neighbor. Your concepts, ideas, and feelings are not likely to be identical; and certainly the reactions of your sense of touch to the medium and the ground will be your own. There is no reason why your marks should not have a unique graphic quality. If you sing to yourself while drawing the line, the line will reflect your mood; if you mutter angrily beneath your breath, then the line, even though describing the same object, will be a different kind of line. Some people are almost hypnotically relaxed in drawing, while others feverishly bite their tongues. And as you draw, the paper, de-

**Fig. 1–5**
Jean-Dominique Ingres
Study for **La Grande Odalisque**
(Courtauld Institute of Art, London;
Collection, Mr. Charles Morgan)

pending on the type of surface, will set up a resistance to the pen or brush or finger or piece of wood. How you overcome this resistance will obviously also play a part in determining the quality of your line. If you will mentally contrast for a moment the sensations you would experience in using soft charcoal over a coarse paper surface or in using a hard, spiky nib over velvet-smooth paper, you can *feel* the kind of line that will result, without having to draw it. These tensions are kinesthetic and tactile, but when you move from studio exercises to drawing seriously for yourself, a different and more powerful tension is present—a psychological tension, which is both dynamic and compulsive. It results from the attempt to graphically re-create a form after perceiving an external object; or from the attempt to create a graphic image which corresponds to images internally initiated and experienced in the self. In either case, the marks of drawing evolve from difficulties of resolution—from using an experience which is personal and real to make an image which is artificial. Kinesthetic tension and psychological tension are important dynamic forces behind the graphic existence of art. Look at the varying qualities of line and movement in Fig. 1–4 and try to feel the sensitive touch-sense involved in their making.

Throughout this book we treat drawing as a catalyst between perceiving and imagining—between knowledge and invention. There may be an object to draw or there may not, but whether the created images are objective or non-objective, we hold that to draw is to *know*. For the graphic images of art, once accomplished, give meaning and value to the experiences which stimulated them, and meanings and values are important constituents of knowledge. From the illustrations, you will see that more importance is placed on the direct, personal drawing that is the spontaneous result of the artist's attitude, or that results from a refined act of perception, than on a technically good, but dead, imitative or representational drawing.

Fig. 1–6
Eugène Delacroix
Figure Studies for **Sardanapalus**
(Collection G. Aubry, Paris)

(Fig. 1–7), we follow every change in direction made by the lines of the structured form. The building is exposed skeletally, and we respond conceptually to the mechanics of thrust and counterthrust and swell. The point-to-point movement is hardly disguised.

Using the pen or brush, start firmly, anywhere on the paper, with a graphic point. Deliberately move in a certain direction, keeping the pressure constant so that the weight of the line will be uniform. Stop and allow the instrument to make a point. Move off in another direction. Stop. Move again. Observe the rhythm of line lengths and the directional counterpoint of one movement answering another. This is a very positive articulation of space by line. In the kind of non-objective drawing you are making it becomes a dynamic structure—an ambiguous representation of either form or space. You should exploit this emerging dynamic as you move over the remainder of the sheet. This can be done quite non-objectively. Curved or straight lines may be used; they may be long or short in movement, and the dots or points which reveal where you stopped to change direction, need not be disguised. Stop at any point and "read" the sheet. Finally, compare the sheet with Drawing Sheet 1, previously completed. The graphic result is quite different, for the lines serve completely different functions and reflect completely different attitudes. It is not frivolous to suggest that Sheet 1 may be likened to the magnificent hysteria of Wagnerian sound, Sheet 2 to the structural counterpoint of Bach.

**Drawing Sheet 3—Free Experiment**

In this final exercise, the aim is to discover as many varieties of graphic marks as possible—both lines and tones—through free experiment. A tone is an indefinite area of "color" value. Our color here is, of course, monochromatic, ranging through the grays between the extremes of black and white. Use the paper space freely. First, however, assemble as much drawing "equipment" as possible, from the conventional pen and brush to more unorthodox materials such as rubberbands, pieces of twig or wood, edges of paper, the edge of a thumbnail, hair grips and curlers, and so on—as varied a range of things as can be dipped in dark ink to make a line of drawing. Experiment with every single piece—metal, wood, bone, paper, or plastic. As the lines go down, be aware of the quality of the mark produced—sharp or dull, gray or black, firm or broken—and try to remember the particular "feel" of the instrument that made the mark as it was moving over the paper surface. You will probably remember some that particularly suited you, producing a definite feeling of control and satisfaction while the line was being made.

After this, try a few lines which will have a completely different character, lines which you will *print* rather than draw. For example, ink the edge of a ruler, press the ruler onto the paper, and see what you have; repeat this ruler line, but this time dampen the paper area beneath the ruler. Compare this line with the first. You might even print a line from a piece of string. Each of these variations—and there

are many more you can invent— produces a different line quality (see Fig. 1–1). Printed marks on dampened surfaces will appear grayish, varying from black to lighter tones, depending upon the printing pressure and the dilution of the ink by the damp paper. When making some of these printed marks, pull the instrument slightly to the side and observe the dark-light value of the resulting smear of tone. Print from leaves or any other surfaces. Make areas of tone by inking your thumb and rubbing in marks with different pressures. When there is nothing more to do, regard the sheet. Notice the varieties of lines and dots, the differing tonal values and textures; notice how they all relate to each other when singing in unison on one sheet of paper. Remember that every mark is capable of use in a drawing. This is true for the lines and marks on all three of the drawing sheets. Ultimately you may find yourself selecting and exploiting some of the graphic qualities you have discovered here. Yet keep the linear images of Pollock and Klee firmly in mind: for here are two modern masters giving us the extremes of the graphic line—Pollock expressive, Klee structural.

Fig. 1—9
Student Drawing Sheet 1

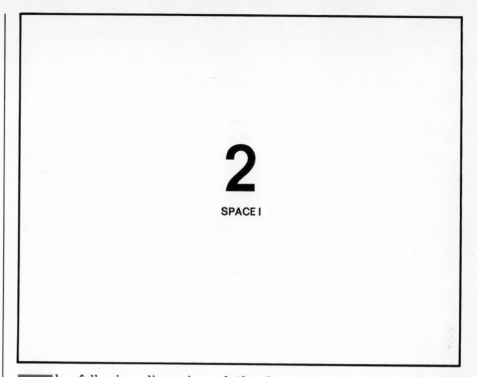

**2**

SPACE I

The following discussion of the figure-ground relationship follows naturally from the material covered in Chapter 1 and serves as an integral link to the introduction of skeletal (linear) structure in Chapter 3. In the previous series of graphic experiences, we discovered that as soon as a series of lines or marks develops on a white ground, we perceive a spatial relationship in depth between the lines and the ground. Perception depends upon the fact that the ground has become a "space," a three-dimensional area. *At any moment in perception there is a figure on a ground.* A psychologist describes it in this way:

The perceptual properties of figures and grounds have been extensively discussed in the psychological literature (especially by the Gestalt psychologist), and the nature of stresses induced by various patterns of figure and ground can be summarized—although it rarely is. Some painters show off a perceptual virtuosity by exploiting figure-ground tensions: Ben Nicholson in one way, Mondrian in another. One aspect of the struggle between the various "schools" of art opinion centers in the nature of the figure-ground relationship. The more representational artists want the ground to stay in its place behind the figure. The decorative artists like figure and ground to stay much on the same plane. Other painters want

Fig. 2–1
Broken window screen

# The figure-ground relationship

a *struggle* in perception between figure and ground—what at one moment is figure, at another becomes ground; and vice versa. This shift produces a perceptual, and presumably an aesthetic, stress.[1]

In the light of these statements, look again at the Pollock and Klee drawings in Chapter 1 and clarify your perceptions of line to ground relationships. The area of an unmarked sheet of paper is meaningless, apart from an awareness of the paper itself; we have no perception of it as a space-field. Yet put a few random lines or marks on it, and our eyes begin to search for depth, and to find it. Even one blob made with the end of the brush is enough to create a perceptual situation. For perception, and particularly for space perception, there must be a figure (blob) on a ground. Then a tension is created between a positive and a negative—the blob and the emptiness—and we perceive. This tension is probably a mental one, resulting from the different meanings we give to things we see, but until there are *two* things to see, namely figure and ground, we have no perception. We obviously live our lives "in depth"—that is, we move physically in space, and our ability to do this in daily experience depends on the same figure-to-ground perception which informs our experience of art, except that the "ground" is now actual space. The ability to comprehend this depth, and to adjust our bodily actions to a three-dimensional environment is an optical, mental, and kinesthetic (muscle-limb control) faculty we use constantly. Every time you put out your hand to grasp a door handle you make an automatic appraisal of the distance your hand should travel in order to make contact with the handle. If this combined optical, mental, and kinesthetic apprehension of space were upset, you would find yourself misjudging the distance and either hitting the door hard with your hand or stopping short in mid air before reaching the handle. If you close one eye and then reach out to pick up a book, you will find it surprisingly difficult to judge the depth of space involved. Some people are afflicted with a more limited depth perception than others, and such misjudgment of depth can be a frequent cause of highway accidents; a driver making a left-hand turn in front of oncoming traffic may have a collision because he considered the approaching cars far enough away to allow plenty of time for the turn.

In Chapter 3 it will be specifically pointed out that when we isolate

---

1 Robert Miller, in a letter to the author, November 30, 1965.

Fig. 2–2
Victor Pasmore, **Relief Construction in White, Black,
and Maroon** (*Victor Pasmore*)

any skeletal object in order to look at it more closely, we must realize that the space immediately around the form is just as important an aspect of our perception as is the solid fact of the object itself. We perceive the *shape* of the space as significantly as the shape of the form. Just look at your own hand with the fingers stretched and extended, and see this.

Ever since the development of perspective techniques in the early Renaissance, the illusion of depth over a flat surface has been created by establishing an artificial horizon, vanishing points, and disappearing lines. This perspective has been the traditional means of taking the onlooker into the picture. But this mechanical illusion, by becoming merely a formula, can blind the artist to an intensive personal experience of space, to the natural experience of depth perception. However, it would be well to point out that when the illusion of perspective is used creatively rather than automatically, the result can impart a genuine and personal experience of space. A great authority on Italian Renaissance art, the late Bernard Berenson, had this to say about the work of Perugino (1445–1523), the Umbrian (central Italian) painter who was a master of perspective:

Space-composition ... can take us away from ourselves and give us, while we are under its spell, the feeling of being identified with the universe, perhaps even of being the soul in the universe. ... For those of us who are neither idolaters nor suppliants, this sense of identification with the universe is of the very essence of religious emotion—an emotion, by the way, as independent of belief and conduct as love itself. ... The religious emotion—for some of us entirely, for others at least in part—is produced by a feeling of identification with the universe; this feeling, in its turn, can be created by space-composition; it follows then that this art can directly communicate religious emotion—or at least all the religious emotion that many of us really have, good church-members though we may be.[2]

This statement exposes a great truth about our experience of art, and one which is so relevant to our day as man ventures further out into space, for Berenson implies that the microcosmic area of a drawing or a painting can move us imaginatively and perceptually into the infinite, macrocosmic space of the universe. When this is achieved by a design, as in the case of Perugino, we identify ourselves with the universe: our instinctive links with the great systems of space, matter,

---

[2] Bernard Berenson, *The Italian Painters of the Renaissance* (London: Phaidon Publishers, Inc., 1952), p. 122.

and energy are more consciously realized, and we lose ourselves in the mystery. Architects shape space, and religious architecture creates a spatial environment which encourages us to make the link with universal space. Today painters and sculptors, even though they work in abstract forms, are tremendously preoccupied with space and our feeling for it. We are creatures of space, and art uses it to symbolize our human need for freedom, both physical and spiritual. Perhaps when man knows more about the space which surrounds him and its relationship to time, both the artist's attitude to it and our general sensitivity for it may be modified. But at the moment it still remains a vital constituent of our aesthetic response to the world, and to our own condition within it.

Although this chapter is not concerned with perspective as such, it is concerned with the *natural* way of depth perception via figure-ground relationships. Victor Pasmore's construction (Fig. 2–2), and Tōhaku's painting (Fig. 2–4), the one totally abstract, the other partially so, provide examples of figure-ground tensions which initiate a natural per-

**Fig. 2–3**
**Photographs of tree trunk spacings**

**Fig. 2–4**
Hagesawa Tohaku
**Pines** (detail from a screen)
Late sixteenth century. Ink on paper, 61″.
*(National Museum, Tokyo)*
*(Photograph courtesy, Exhibition Delegation,
"Art Treasures from Japan," 1958)*

ceiving of three-dimensional space. The Pasmore construction is totally
devoid of any perspective, yet one perceives that each of the lines and
forms superimposed on the ground stands in a different spatial relationship to it, although, in fact, these forms are equal in thickness and
actual projection. The rectangle at top left and the lines at bottom right
and middle right are almost part of the ground—yet one perceives some
ambiguity in determining their exact position and relationship. This
is certainly not true of the large maroon rectangle which is frontal
and dominant. The other lines project themselves from the ground in
differing frontal degrees. There are two conclusions which can be derived from a heightened three-dimensional experience of this nature:
1.
That projection is achieved when the tone (dark or light) of an area
or line (called "the figure") is in strong contrast to the tone of the
ground.
2.
That the *sharpness* of an edge of tone or of a line produces a stereo-
scopic-like projection from the ground.

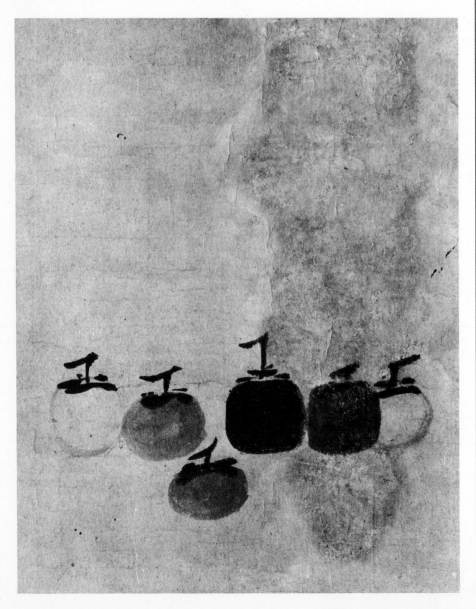

Fig. 2–5
Mu-Ch'i
**Persimmons**
*(Daitoku-ji, Kyoto)*

THE FIGURE-GROUND
RELATIONSHIP

**SPACE I**

These two facts will be used and developed in the drawings which are suggested for this chapter.

Although the Japanese painting (Fig. 2–4) is a landscape and not an abstract construction, the artist does not employ the perspective system to secure depth. As was the case in the Pasmore, depth is achieved by intensities of tone, varying from those which are uniform with the ground in value to those which are antithetical and contrasting. The central pine stands forward in the painting because, as a dark notation in the over-all misty vagueness of the ground, its perceived surfaces are more antithetical to the empty space than are those of any other tree. If one looks carefully, it will be noticed that the incisive sharpness of the line at the tree's base is also responsible for bringing the object forward. As a consequence, the vaguely toned trees behind melt away into the ground. Both Pasmore and Tōhaku produce dominant frontal forms, together with receding and ambiguous forms and areas. There is *ambiguity* between form and space (figure and ground), and there is also a sharp distinction made between form and space. By these means both men produce depth over a surface without utilizing the techniques of perspective.

**Fig. 2–6**
**Squares of tree groupings**

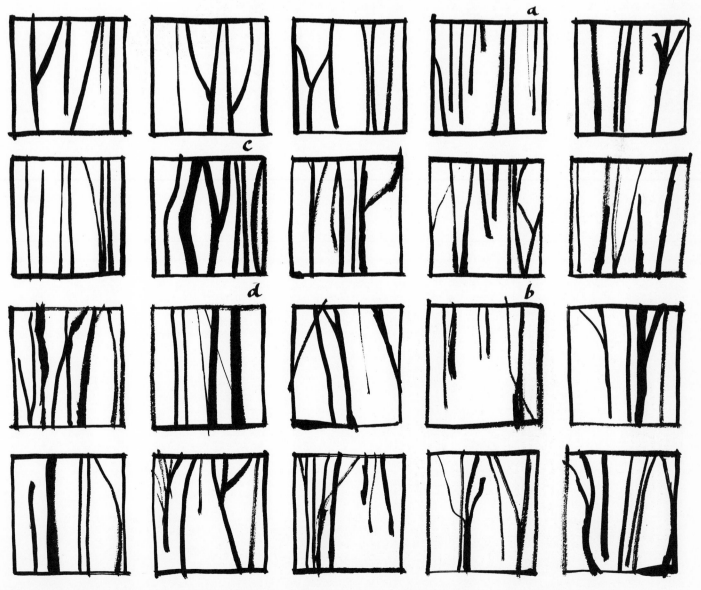

Fig. 2–7
**Hunters Shooting Deer**
Fragment of fresco from Alpera, Spain.
*(The American Museum of Natural History)*
*A spatial situation created without recourse
to perspective. Line quality and the relative
size of areas of black tone create the spatial
sensation. The deer are the largest objects,
irrespective of their space position in the
design, because they are the most
important objects.*

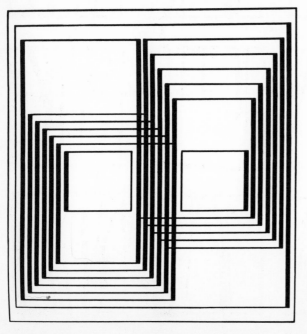

Fig. 2–8
Josef Albers
**Seclusion**
*(From the book* Despite Straight Lines
*by Josef Albers and Francois Bucher,
Yale University Press)*

**THE DRAWINGS** In the drawings that follow we are to illustrate *space in depth* without having recourse to the more mechanical disappearing lines of perspective—to discover, in fact, how a natural depth perception operates. The first drawings will be made quite objectively by observing tree formations, for this will ensure a variety of free sketches from which to work; it will also create a situation in which your spatial perceptions are exercised. Fifteen minutes outside with a sketch pad and a soft, black drawing crayon will be sufficient. Look at a clump of tree trunks (Fig. 2–3) and note how they are grouped together in bunches of three, four, or five trunks. As you look around, notice the different grouping arrangements of other clumps of trees. On your pad, draw about a dozen small squares, freehand, about 2" x 2". In each square, make a simple and direct line sketch of vertical trunks, using a different formation in each square for the different clumps you see. These visual notes, as in Fig. 2–6, are drawn quickly and are basically notes or diagrams of spatial organization; they are not meant to be pictorial views of trees. Your first perception when looking at groups of trees and making such drawings will probably be of the *sideways* distance between each tree. Then you will notice the directional movement of each tree, straight or curved, and draw your lines accordingly. The operation of your depth perception may be simultaneous with these observations, or it may be sequential. But at some stage you will observe that some of the trees (the vertical lines) are farther back than others, and the natural way to indicate this fact is to start these lines higher in the square—as squares *a* and *b* in Fig. 2–6. This produces a certain suggestion of depth in the square. Finally, before leaving, select any two of the "views" and make the following additions. Thicken the lines which represent the nearest trees in both squares, thus giving these lines more weight and tone—as squares *c* and *d* in Fig. 2–6. Then look for one or two very distant trees, which were not included in the sketch, and add them as very *thin* lines in their proper positions. This has been done in square *d* in Fig. 2–6.

**CONCLUSIONS** What significant conclusions are to be drawn from such spontaneously produced diagrams of tree groupings? The three most important ones are:

1.

When an area is not completely contained by lines—that is to say when there is relatively little *definition* to the area—the area recedes. Compare square *b* with square *c* in Fig. 2–6. The general openness of the area in the former suggests depth and recession—whereas in *c* all the areas are enclosed and appear frontal. The infinite suggestions of space in Tōhaku's painting (Fig. 2–4) are achieved in the same way.

2.

The heavier the weight of line, and the stronger the tone, the more frontal dominance it *and the space it encloses* will have. Squares *c* and *d* in Fig. 2–6 show how frontal the thick lines with their contained areas become. The Pasmore construction (Fig. 2–2) works perceptually on the same principle. Conversely, thin and delicate lines move to the rear together with their contained area. Observe this in square *d* in Fig. 2–6.

3.

The quality of a line may also relate to depth. Examine the drawing sheets previously made in Chapter 1. Sharp, incisive lines come forward (study the quality of lines and surfaces in Fig. 2–4); broken, blurred, or gray lines recede. You will notice that even a heavy line that is grayish and "spongy" will appear to be farther back than a much slighter line possessing sharpness and the quality of a biting edge.

These three points are borne out when they are applied to any visual experience, whether the field of vision be a drawing on a flat piece of paper or an actual spatial situation among the trees. The *graphic* description of a space field works in just the same way as does an actual perceptual experience in the environment. Look at the Rembrandt drawing, *Christ and the Woman Taken in Adultery*, Fig. 2–13. Every point this chapter has made about our natural depth perception is illustrated here. Check every one of our conclusions, including those made earlier concerning Tōhaku and Pasmore, against Rembrandt.

By way of contrast, see the application of these principles in architectural interior design, as exemplified in Fig. 2–9. Here, the designers have created spatial illusions by exploiting the three principles of line weight, enclosed space versus open space, and varying degrees of tone. Full practical use is made of the wall for the typewriter tables, yet the visual barrier of the wall is diminished, for its precise position is somewhat ambiguous. The sharp, black frame of the table projects forward from the wall, while the heavy, black "O" on the wall seems to stand in front of the mosaic design. Thus three regions of depth are suggested, and the wall is neither visually nor psychologically oppressive. Study the drawing by Josef Albers (Fig. 2–8) and notice how this artist graphically creates spatial illusions not unlike those illustrated in Fig. 2–9.

**CONCLUDING DRAWING** To reinforce this elementary lesson in depth perception, we will present a more developed and more consciously organized problem. In the studio make a larger and more finished drawing in pen and ink of one of the simple tree trunk studies, along the following lines. (About 8″ x 8″ is a good size for this new square, which should be enclosed with a good firm pen line.) Redraw any one of the small sketches in the larger square, with thin, delicate pen lines all of equal weight. This now gives you a design of vertical lines, the special arrangement of which has been taken from an observed source in nature, and in which you have some totally enclosed (frontal) areas and some space-penetrated (receding) areas. But since the lines are all of equal weight, the drawing will not appear very three-dimensional. Now, with a pen or brush, thicken two lines which almost, or

Fig. 2–9
**Offices for British Olivetti Ltd., London**
*Misha Black and John Diamond, designers*
(The Architectural Review, *London*)

THE FIGURE-GROUND
RELATIONSHIP

**SPACE I**

totally, enclose an area, in order to achieve a stronger frontal dominance for that area and for those particular lines. Look over the design again (remember you are no longer thinking about tree trunks) and decide which verticals should be thickened only slightly in order to produce some frontal dominance but not as much as in the area already defined. In other words, you will be making these lines and their immediate area appear behind the first. After these two operations, the design is now composed of three different weights of line—the forward-thrusting heavy lines, the medium lines in the middle distance, and the thin lines of the original drawing which now appear well recessed. One more thing remains to be done. From the page of line experiments made in Chapter 1 choose one type of line of some definite quality, either very sharp or very diffuse, and insert a similar line anywhere in this design. Does this specific line appear near or far away in relation to the other lines? Figure 2–11 illustrates this experiment. The last line added was the thin but sharp line in the center of the drawing, which seems to hover somewhere in the middle distance. Figure 2–10 indicates how this last drawing may be developed. The left-hand drawing is similar to the one described above—it is the abstract linear diagram of tree positions in space, in which line weight and quality aid three-dimensional perception. It is the natural scene reduced to the linear abstraction. The right-hand drawing is the natural scene re-created from the abstraction, and it owes its depth to the analytical breakdown of the first drawing.

**Fig. 2–10**

**Fig. 2–11**

23

**SOME FINAL CONCLUSIONS** While discussing space in depth, it is interesting and I think necessary to draw attention to some approaches to art that achieve a three-dimensional realization of the world through apparently flat, two-dimensional design.

I am referring, of course, to Eastern art and to the art of children the world over. Japanese woodcuts, Chinese scroll painting, Mogul and Rajput paintings in India, and a six-year-old's drawing from anywhere all have one thing in common—namely, a lack of formalized perspective depth. During the last sixty years, art in the West has finally broken away from the stranglehold of perspective and is now free to utilize the tonal, linear, and spatial principles which this chapter has described. Think of a Mondrian or of a Matisse such as is shown here in Fig. 2–12. Observe how Matisse attracts you to certain dominant shapes by the weight of line and the total enclosure of a space. One's eye moves in and out of the picture; one experiences depth where an area lacks enclosure and definition, and where the tone is ambiguous and vague. And then the black blob of a man's head pulls almost violently to the front. In 1908, the French painter Henri Matisse wrote:

Expression to my way of thinking does not consist of the passion mirrored upon a human face or betrayed by a violent gesture. The whole arrangement of my picture is expressive. The place occupied by the figures or objects, *the empty spaces around them,* (my italics) the proportions, everything plays a part.

There is little conscious use of perspective in the painting of Matisse, but depth is created naturally through the organization of his design in the manner we have discussed. The idea that space, empty space, can be expressive was quite a perceptive statement to make in 1908,

Fig. 2–12
Henri Matisse, **The Joy of Life**
©*1967 by the Barnes Foundation, Merion, Pennsylvania)*

even though the Japanese print had then been in vogue for some time.

Let us conclude by looking at *Persimmons* by Mu-Ch'i (Fig. 2–5). Our spatial perception of this painting is more natural and subtle than it is in much Western art. In fact, its great spatial qualities may not be immediately obvious to Western eyes, which are so accustomed to the converging lines and diminution of perspective. The space of the painting, and the disposition of forms within that space, work on our perceptions in the natural way without need of perspective. The painting poses many visual problems, for although the five fruits are disposed along the same horizontal line, each fruit possesses a differing degree of frontality. This is achieved by the weight of tone and by the graphic

Fig. 2–13
Rembrandt
**Christ and the Woman Taken in Adultery**
*(Collection, Kupferstichkabinette, Dresden)*

quality of the brush mark. Yet the stalks remain curiously detached, almost on the same plane.

Before leaving this chapter, study the two photographs, Figs. 2–15 and 2–1 respectively. They are good photographic "diagrams" of tone and line as they make a three-dimensional experience of a two-dimensional surface. Figure 2–1 is the more complex of the two. See how many layers of depth your eye discovers in this photograph. Which is the most distant space? Every theory we have put forward to account for depth perception over a graphic surface can be discovered in these photographs, but in terms of the creation of spatial illusions by means of lines alone—which has been part of our theme—it is difficult to find an example more sophisticated and active than Josef Albers' *Transformation of a Scheme* (Fig. 2–14). A three-dimensional field is created almost entirely by the perceptual play engendered by the weight of a line, the sharpness of its quality, the intensity of its white or gray tone value, and its directional movement over the ground. You should read again points 1 to 3, which are stated under the heading Conclusions in this chapter, and relate each point to the Albers drawing.

**Fig. 2–15**
**Pilings in Puget Sound**

**Fig. 2–14**
Josef Albers
**Transformation of a Scheme**
*(From the book*
*Despite Straight Lines*
*by Josef Albers and*
*Francois Bucher, Yale University*
*Press)*

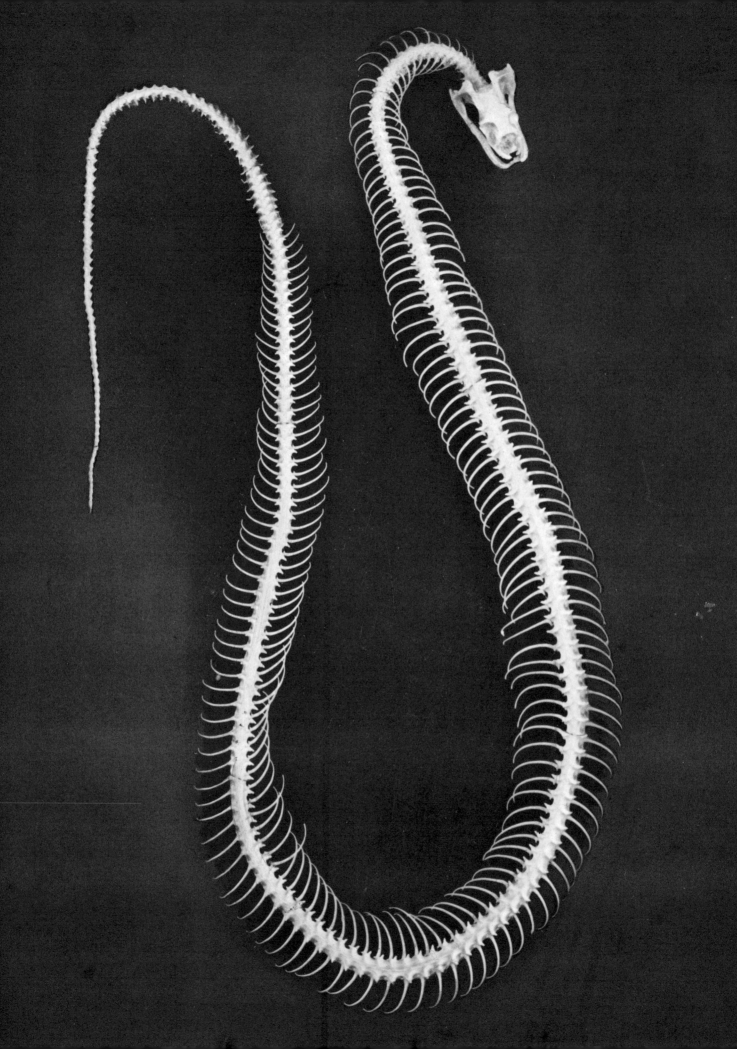

# 3

## FORM I

We now draw your attention to form itself—to the countless variations of shape designed by nature and by man. In order to distinguish between structural types, it is obvious that some fairly general classification of objects should be made. For this reason we suggest that it is realistic to postulate two basic family groups, based upon structural characteristics. One family is composed of *skeletal* objects, and the other of objects of *mass*. This chapter will attempt to introduce the former, and Chapter 5 will treat the latter.

It should be understood that these two categories are not mutually exclusive, for forms which are predominantly skeletal also possess mass or volume while objects of mass may result from complex skeletal structures. A postscript to Chapter 5 deals with this structural duality of form in more detail but here we are concerned with primary structural characteristics. How would one define "the form of an object"? A straightforward definition would be that the form of an object is *its shape determined by its structure*. Hence it is important for an artist to understand structure. The aims of this book are to develop perception, to induce confidence in drawing, and to stimulate a personal attitude toward design. As the emphasis of this chapter is on the ex-

**Fig. 3–1**
**Skeleton of a water snake**

# Structural families: the skeletal object

amination of form-structure, it is obvious that demands will be made on your powers of both observation and analysis of form, which will serve the interest of developing your perception and cause you to realize that there are structural implications to design.

Some artists would not agree that observation is crucial in the work of a mature painter or sculptor; and in the sense that we are using the word, implying a self-conscious looking, they would be justified. But if it is true that a capacity for observation is vital for the student, it is equally true that at any stage of development, the memory of a thing seen is a prototype image on which the artist's imagination will build. Even the non-objective artist is immersed in the world of things seen, from which he gathers much of his knowledge of form. There are many ways of regarding an object, from a superficial glance to a penetrating scrutiny, either casually and disinterestedly or with intent and involvement. When we look with intent we try to see beyond the immediate, apparent shape of the object into its true and essential structure in order to understand "how" it is. Looking with intent also yields an understanding of "why" it is, what is its function, and what part it plays in its particular setting. It is this type of looking which enables us to see the design potential of the object and to reveal its form through a drawing. We are led to the essential, permanent nature of the object.

Obviously, external appearances do not tell the whole story about an object. Asked to describe a tomato, the average person would say that it is a small, round, and reddish object. Some might go further and describe its softness to the touch, but relatively few would cut it open and describe its internal cross section. Yet the tomato's cross section is as much an aspect of the tomato as its roundness and redness. When purchasing a new automobile, few people decide to buy solely on the basis of the "looks" of the car; they want to know how it performs and perhaps how well it is built. Similarly, to make a significant drawing of any object, one should know about its structure and function as well as about its external appearance.

An inquiring person is alive with all his senses, restless with curiosity, eager to know more about himself and the world beyond himself. He tends to regard objects much as the prospective automobile purchaser views his gleaming new model—as objects which are *his* to respond to with feeling and to explore visually and intellectually. Through drawing he may express these several attitudes to objects. Such a person tends to identify himself with the natural world and does not restrict his curiosity and interest to the comparatively few objects he calls his own, or to products of human workmanship; he develops an awareness of the entire range of natural phenomena. In the twentieth century man has come to accept that phenomenologically he is a part of nature. He lives in a dynamic universe and must find room in his system of values for the "man-made" and the "natural" object, for that which is finely engineered by man as well as for that which grows by its own law.

Analysis of the principles of structure provides a basic experience of form, and leads to three important aspects of perception. First, a knowledge of form-structure helps us to understand *how* the shape we see is made. Second, seeing how structure determines shape, and ultimately function, enables us to give more *meaning* to the object. And third, a structural analysis of form leads us to discover that the spatial context of an object—the space in and around it—is very important. For when we are aware of the shape of the surrounding space, we heighten our perception of the concreteness of the object, of its *reality*. Following closely on these perceptions comes our inevitable aesthetic response to form, and this is discussed in Chapter 13.

Leonardo da Vinci is the exemplar of the attitude to drawing which we have been discussing. He pursued structure ruthlessly, stripping away externals until the bones of the form were laid bare. The drawings in the Notebooks are masterpieces of structural statement, whether they be of flowers, rocks, or human anatomy. Leonardo's eye was like a microscope. Do not be deceived by the apparently easy beauty of such

Fig. 3–3
Leonardo da Vinci
**Anatomical Drawing (Shoulder)**
*(Royal Collection, Windsor Castle;
Reproduced by permission of Her Majesty
Queen Elizabeth II)*

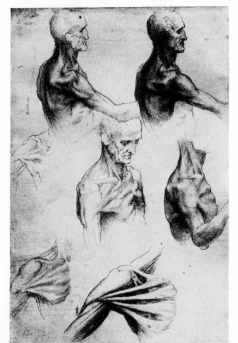

Fig. 3–2
**Skeletal form of a twig**

paintings as *The Virgin of the Rocks*, or the famed *Mona Lisa*. Beneath that soft patina of the face Leonardo reveals all the structural thrusts which shape and form the skull. Observe his drawings of the shoulder which we reproduce in Fig. 3–3. These drawings are a part of the anatomy studies, and Leonardo writes:

The painter who has acquired a knowledge of the nature of the sinews, muscles, and tendons will know exactly in the movement of any limb how many and which of the sinews are the cause of it, and which muscle by its swelling is the cause of this sinew's contracting, and which sinews having been changed into most delicate cartilage surround . . . the . . . muscle.

Leonardo reveals the purpose of discussion that follows. But before we can expect our looking "with intent" to reach this level of acuteness, we must train ourselves in the more elementary aspects of visual analysis, in such things as proportions, directional movements, rhythms, and organic growth—to mention just a few. In so doing, we are led inevitably to the object's structure. The aim of this first experiment is to initiate you into the processes by which simple observation can grow into the greater understanding of perception and perhaps, finally, into the full imaginative significance of "vision."

**Fig. 3–4**
George Stubbs, **Anatomical Exposition of Tiger**
*(Victoria and Albert Museum, London) This eighteenth-century British artist displays a Leonardo-like preoccupation with structure as a means to understanding the articulation of the animal's movements.*

## THE FIRST STRUCTURE DRAWINGS

In this first drawing experiment, our principal objectives are:

1.
To train your powers of *observation* so that you can better analyze the structure of form.

2.
To develop your ability to *make a drawing* on the basis of this observation and analysis.

3.
To expand your *knowledge of form* through drawing of this kind.

4.
To enhance your ability to see the *creative potential* in a drawing based on analysis of structure.

5.
To point out that form is entirely *dependent on structure.*

These are five basic statements about drawing. If the words in italics are extracted from each statement, we can summarize the objectives in this way: observe and analyze the object to make a drawing based on your knowledge of form, keeping an eye on the creative potential of the drawing. The final drawing should reflect the fact that form is dependent on structure. These words represent a basic vocabulary which can aid the student in eventually speaking the language of art. But you must remember that although they sum up the aims which are behind most beginning students' work, they do not tell the whole story about art, for in the last analysis, it is the transforming vision of the the artist that creates a masterpiece.

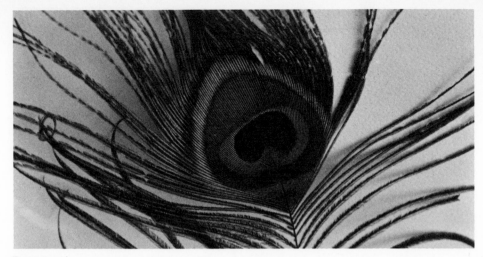

Fig. 3–5
Skeletal form of a peacock's feather

Fig. 3–6
Skeletal form of a leaf

The student should now collect four or five specimens of objects with a skeletal structure: grasses, twigs, seed-head formations, leaves, the backbones of fishes, and the bony skeletons of small animals are some possibilities (Figs. 3–1, 3–2, 3–5, and 3–6). Once engaged in the search, you will be amazed at the variety of skeletal forms at hand. Skeletal structure may be defined as structure which can be represented by a number of lines moving in different directions, all connected to a main stem by a series of joints in what is known as an "articulated system." It is form possessing a discernible skelton.

That discernible skelton is what we are looking for now. Our purpose is to make a strong black-line diagram that reveals how the object "holds together" through its skeletal limbs. In the case of a leaf, we are concerned with only the central skeleton, ignoring the flesh of leaf area (Fig. 3–6). A straightforward sketch representation of its appearance is not our purpose.

To make these drawings, it is best to use a black grease pencil or a broad-nibbed drawing pen and black ink. It is also a good idea to make some tentative line diagrams on a rough newsprint pad, in order to get to know the object before producing the finished black drawing on a good quality offset paper. To make these drawings effective, ignore secondary detail and the outlines or edges of the form: an X-ray approach is required. A glance at Figs. 3–9 and 3–10 will show how these drawings appear. In the drawing, you could make a distinction between principal and secondary skeleton lines by means of

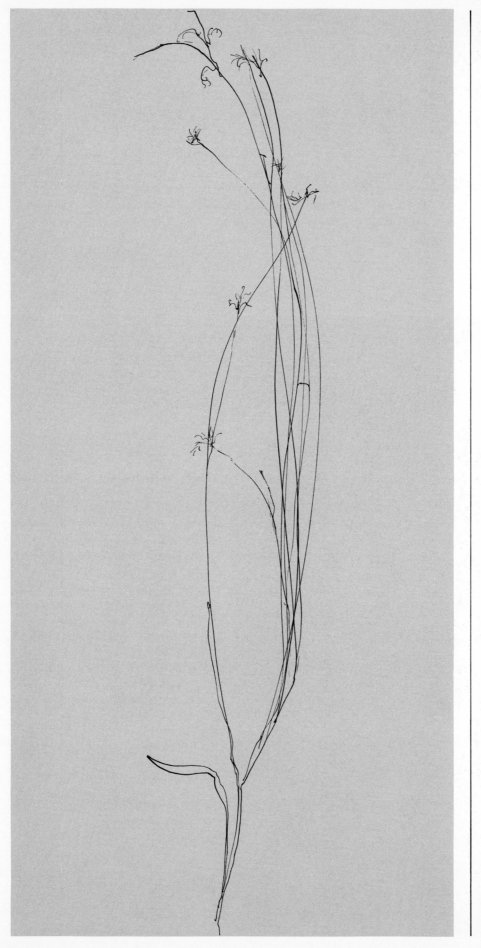

thick and thin lines—that is, make the main growing stems or central limbs with a thicker line than you use for the subsidiary veins. Where the skeleton limb makes a change of direction, indicate the joint by means of a dot before moving the drawing line off in the new direction. Watch for proportionate lengths of the lines in relation to other lines of the structure and also for the subtleties of the varying angles in changes of linear direction.

The drawings so far, as we have described them, are of strongly

**Fig. 3–7**
**Grass skeletal form**

STRUCTURAL FAMILIES:
THE SKELETAL OBJECT

**FORM I**

*articulated skeletal* systems, in which changes of linear direction are sudden and angular. Now, find and draw a skeletal object which is more curvilinear, where the line is more continuously flowing. In representing such an object of *continuous skeletal* structure, there will be less need to show joints by means of dots, and the line will flow rhythmically and freely over the page (see Fig. 3–7). The sculpture illustrated in Fig. 3–11 is free flowing in the movement of its main lines. The only angular joints are where the small twig lines join the principal stem, but even these do not interrupt the flow of the primary skeleton. If you compare the lines of this sculpture, and those of Fig. 3–7, with the drawings of angular systems (Figs. 3–9 and 3–10), you will notice how much less "tight" is the movement of a continuous skeletal form. Figure 3–8 is a drawing of continuous skeletal structure where both the line itself, and the spatial regions defined by the line, are altogether more curvilinear and less static than would be found in an angular form. The drawing results from a study of skeletalized sea-weathered rock (Fig. 3–14).

**Fig. 3–8
Drawing of weathered rock forms**

**Fig. 3–9
Skeletal form of weed**

**Fig. 3–10
Skeletal form of fern**

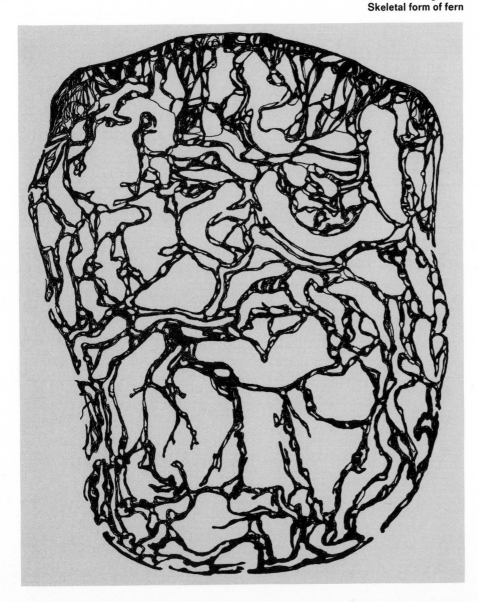

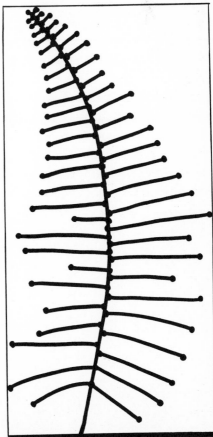

**CONCLUSIONS** Look at the drawings as they now appear side by side (Figs. 3–7 to 3–10). You will notice perhaps for the first time that the divisions of space between the limbs of each drawing make almost as much visual impact as the limbs themselves. One's eye is drawn to these spaces and notices their respective dimensions and their dynamic characteristics—whether they flow and move or are static. For example, in Fig. 3–10 the space seems to flow in from the sides to between the limbs, whereas in Fig. 3–9 the space is static by comparison, caught in small pockets between the limbs. An important point emerges: that skeletal form is always perceived *together with its ground*. That this is true for sculpture no less than for drawing is borne out by examination of Theodore Roszak's *Rite of Passage* (Fig. 3–17). The space (air) between the limbs is as important a part of the sculpture as the limbs. The reason for this is obvious. The limbs of a skeletal form, by their very nature, divide up space, and thus give it a shape we perceive. Paradoxically, this induced perception of space aids our fuller perception of the object. In the drawings of skeletal forms, figure and ground stand in a complementary relationship—they tend to stay on the same plane. It is this which gives a certain decorative "flatness" to the drawings.[1] The second point to realize is that in drawing or observing a skeletal form, merely following the apparent edges of the object is not sufficient. Volume is not as important as linear extension. Consequently, one should note the linear proportions of the parts of the object, the joints and directional movements of the limbs, and perceive the dynamic shape of the space in and around the limbs.

Look again at your own sheet of drawings. Which of the structures appears to provide the most interesting visual arrangement of jointed or curved lines and areas of space? You will probably find that the structure having the least symmetrical and least regular space divisions and the fewest parallel lines has the most appeal. This is another crucial point: sameness or regularity tends to produce an inanimate and mechanical structure—a dull thing not enlivened by a variable element. On the other hand, a linear structure composed of diverse and opposing elements, if held together by a structural unity, compulsively holds the interest of mind and eye. (A sense of structural unity is imparted

---

[1] Remember, however, that in Chapter 2 it was pointed out that depth *will* be suggested as soon as areas of space become completely enclosed, or when some lines are made heavier.

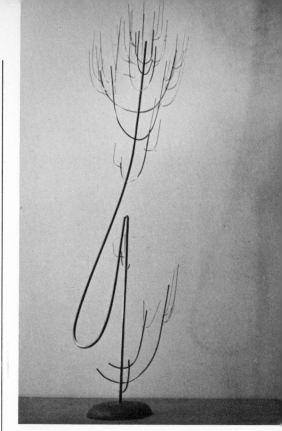

**Fig. 3–11**
Ernest Mundt
**Tree Broken by Storm Decides to Live**
*(Courtesy of the artist)*

**Fig. 3–12**
**Bare trees in spring**

Fig. 3–13    Rapid twig sketches

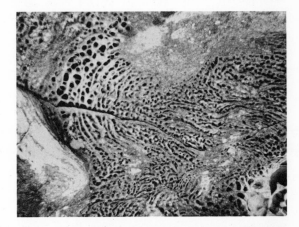

Fig. 3–14
Rock corroded by the action of the sea and weather

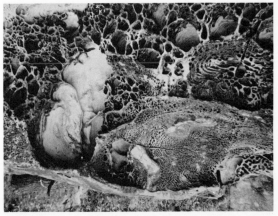

when the organic movement from limb to limb is intrinsically a characteristic of the structure—it has *grown* that way apparently, rather than having been contrived artificially from a series of parts. Regard the fantastic organic engineering of the snake's skeleton in Fig. 3–1.) Now to summarize the essential characteristics of a skeletal object.

**1.**

A skeletal object, unlike an object of mass, constitutes a number of parts jointed or flowing together as a series of limbs.

**2.**

The linear structure of the object defines the space which the object occupies. A skeletal object breaks up the space around it very considerably through the extension of its limbs. Consequently, we are aware of the space immediately surrounding and penetrating such an object, and this helps us to comprehend the form. (Extend your fingers and notice the shape of space between them. Close the fingers and their form is less positive.)

**3.**

An object with a skeletal structure can be represented by a number of lines moving in different directions, but all connected to a main stem. The connections may be jointed in what we might call an "articulated system," or free flowing in a "continuous system." A drawing of such an object should effectively realize the structural form of the object.

Opposed to the skeletal object is a second family of objects composed of mass. A boulder, a pebble, a loaf of bread, and a cloud do not possess limbs. They are objects of volume or mass and will be discussed in Chapter 5 (Form II).

It should be stressed that a close analysis of objects from nature will enable you to solve many different types of design problems which may call for either predominantly skeletal or volumetric forms. We have been working here with relatively small-scale items, but the structural principles remain the same even with objects of gigantic size. A great deal of contemporary architecture is basically skeletal and makes no effort to hide the structure. The church illustrated in Fig. 3–15 is an excellent example of large-scale articulated skeletal form in architecture; skeletal complexity resulting from a standard joint unit is illustrated in Fig. 3–16.

**Fig. 3–15**
**Presbyterian Church, Stamford, Connecticut**
*(Architect, Wallace Harrison;*
*Photograph, Anthony Mauer)*

Keeping one of our initial aims in mind—to heighten the ability to perceive nature through this search for structure as exemplified in Leonardo da Vinci's drawing (Fig. 3-3)—it is important to realize that we have made these skeletal structure drawings from actual objects, that the information has come from outside one's self. Too often the layman imagines that the artist and designer are suddenly struck by a flash of inspiration from nowhere. Usually, however, such "inspiration" derives from a sharpened faculty of observation and an acute perception which triggers the imaginative vision. A twig structure can suggest a tubular steel chair frame or the movement of a figure in action. Look at some of the skeletal structure drawings upside down and see how they change their character completely, suggesting new objects and uses. When we see a photograph such as Fig. 3-12, a complexity of skeletal lines cutting up space, we realize that

**Fig. 3–16**
Konrad Wachsman
**Servicing Hangar Project**
*(Designed by Konrad Wachsmann)*
*An example of structural, skeletal engineering using one standard unit of construction—a joiner unit with three diameters of steel pipe in 10' lengths.*

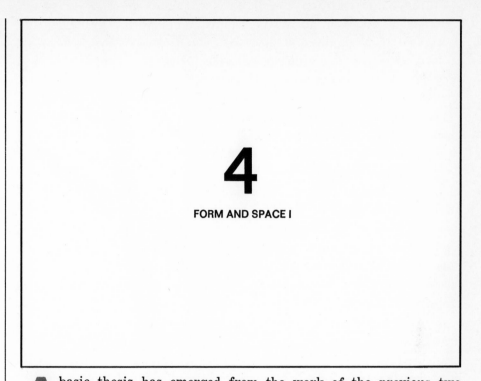

# 4

**FORM AND SPACE I**

A basic thesis has emerged from the work of the previous two chapters. It is, simply stated, that any perception of both form and space depends upon the presence of a figure on a ground. Almost every chapter in this part of the book develops this theme, until it emerges at its most sophisticated level in Chapter 9. At this point we should consolidate the work of Chapters 2 and 3, for they have overlapped in some areas. In the discussion of figure-to-ground relationships in Chapter 2, we introduced the three-dimensional factor and the natural perception of depth. In the last chapter we saw that a characteristic of skeletal form was to cut up and define space, thus aiding our perception of it. Inevitably, we conclude that form and space stand in a complementary relationship in a perceptual situation. It has been noted in working with skeletal structures, that an awareness of the space immediately surrounding the object is necessary to fully comprehend the object itself. With a piece of furniture the ins and outs of space (between the legs, through the arms, and so on) contribute very substantially to our perception of the form of the object, a fact that every designer must take into account.

In this chapter we want to foster a more positive awareness of the

**Fig. 4–1**
**Tree form**
*(Herbert M. Rosenthal)*

# Positive
# and
# neutral space

43

treatment of space or ground as an integral part of drawing—to understand the "designing" of space as complementary to the drawing of form. The drawing problem will take for its motif a skeletal twig form—one of the twigs previously used in Chapter 3—and will suggest how this object may be treated imaginatively to serve our needs.

Look first at the twig photograph in Fig. 4–3. Here the ground is black and the figure of the twig is white, thus reversing the normal situation of a black figure on a white ground. Any suggestions of depth in this image come from the graphic quality of the twig itself. Sharp lines are in front of blurred lines, white lines are in front of gray lines, and lines of weight stand before lesser lines. The ground itself, because of its over-all black tone, would be on one plane only, were it not for the various twig lines marking it. All of these factors have been discussed previously. Now imagine how much *more* depth would be produced in this image if the ground also varied in tone from light to dark.

It is not generally a good thing to compare a photograph with a drawing or painting, but it will serve a useful purpose here. Mondrian's painting, *Horizontal Tree* (Fig. 4–2), makes a strong skeletal design. It is a twig form writ large. The graphic qualities of his drawing lines—heavy, blurred, sharp, pale, intense—are similar to those of the twig lines in the photograph. But then observe what Mondrian has done with the ground or space. He has continued the rhythmic, skeletal structure of the tree over the ground laterally and vertically, and into the ground in depth. We might say that the space has become "tree'd." However, the space is not treated uniformly. There are some areas which are part of the tree—that is, they are shaped positively by the limbs and are immediately *part of our perception of the tree form.* Other spatial regions are not concretely defined, and are not immediately part of our perception of the tree, but are detached from it and are thus neutral. These regions tend to vibrate in the space enveloping the tree, making "tree to ground" vibrations. (The mental tensions created by the ambiguous neutrality of these areas probably cause the visual vibrations.) There is a similar sort of vibration in the photograph, set up in the space between those parts of the twig which are not in focus and those which are; for again there is a tension developed between a positive and a neutral region of space. Mondrian achieves this distinction between positive and neutral regions of the ground, first by

44

**Fig. 4–2**
Piet Mondrian
**Horizontal Tree**
*(Munson-Williams-Proctor Institute*
*Collection, Utica, N.Y.)*

totally enclosing positive areas with heavy or incisive lines, and second by giving contrasting tonal values to the differentiated spaces. The positive areas are given a stronger tonal value; their value is *forte,* to use a musical term. (They are bluish in the painting.) The neutral areas of vibration are lighter in value (blue-gray and pink-gray in the painting), or *piano* to *pianissimo.* In the photograph, on the other hand, there is no suggestion of any tonal variation. The ground is uniform. Consequently, there is less ambiguity between figure and ground, and no varied planes of depth in the ground itself. In the Mondrian there is constant tension and movement. It occurs because the ground is never still as a result of the three-dimensional play between the positive and neutral regions. The tree form is also in movement because it is connected structurally to the positive space and moves with the space. And then, as the structural shape of the neutral areas is defined by tree-like lines, there appears to be an "out of focus" tree in the background which produces tension and ambiguity between it and the main form.

**Fig. 4–3
Twig form**

**THE DRAWING** The purpose of this work is to allow the student to discover how he can manipulate space for perceptual and aesthetic ends— for the perceptual act and the aesthetic experience are bound together. That image which is whole or complete, beautiful or perfect, is neither recognized nor understood without the clarification of perception.

There should be no mere imitating Mondrian here, for this would defeat our ends. The problem must therefore be an individual one, so we will start with an individually selected skeletal twig form which will "cut up" the ground in a unique way. The object will automatically suggest possibilities for developing the ground as a region of positive and neutral areas. A useful size for this drawing is about 9″ x 7″. First, use a single, pure, line to draw the skeletal form in pencil. Let the drawing nicely fill the area. Using a brush or pen, ink or black paint (or combinations of both), draw over the pencil lines. Give weight and intense tone to the primary limbs, sharp and incisive quality to the secondary limbs which are frontal and obtrusive, and gray, broken, or half-tone lines to the least important incidental limbs.

It is possible that the skeletal form

**Fig. 4–4**
E. R. Weiss
**Bookpaper design**

chosen may be rather "flat" and not sufficiently complex to create varied and interesting spatial regions over the ground. If you think this is the case, draw in a vague second image —a shadow almost—behind the primary form. This does not need to be a complete duplicate, merely a repetition where the space calls for it. (Note the vague, out-of-focus shadow form in Fig. 4–3.)

With these linear developments complete, we come to the treatment of the space itself. We cannot begin this aspect of our study without looking hard at the drawing to analyze the figure to ground relationships. Each skeletal form will produce its own problems in space perception. You must observe which of the spatial regions are positively defined by the limbs and are therefore inseparable from the form in your perception of the total image. As we have already said, a strong awareness of these areas produces a heightened awareness of the form which shapes them. These positive regions of space will tend to be juxtaposed to the basic and central parts of the skeletal structure. Yet it may be that the incisive end-line of a secondary limb may suddenly curl and define a positive circle of space which intrudes strongly upon one's perception, although it is out toward the edge of the ground. For this particular experiment it is best to work with a black to gray range of tone for the treatment of the ground. Any black and white gouache or tempera paint will suffice. The same problem could be worked again later using a range of color values.

We shall work on the assumption that when a light tonal value (pale gray to white) is given to a more open area of the ground, that area will not immediately engage our eye. Conversely, when a dark or strong tone (black-gray to gray) is applied to an enclosed or partially enclosed area, that area will dominate our perception; we will see it first and it will persist in holding our attention. It is easier to start with these strong areas. You should avoid using a dead, heavy black; wash in a dark gray with the brush and let it be fluid and variable, according to the way the paint settles and dries. Do not try to smooth it out to produce a uniform, flat tone. Select the region which you see as the most positive space and wash in the dark tone. This area should remain the most dominant and positive despite any other development of the image. From now on, work up the scale of tone to lighter and lighter values. Adjust the tone value to the positive or neutral role of the space with each painting step. The more neutral the space, the lighter the applied tone becomes. It is not necessary to paint all the ground. The white paper can represent the lightest tone and so become the most neutral space.

A final differentiation can be achieved as follows. Some neutral areas can be rendered more negative by blurring or breaking down the lines which vaguely shape them. Scumble gray or white paint over the lines to achieve this effect. The converse will hold for the heavy lines of the positive areas: the limbs of these regions can be

strengthened with black. By this constant modulation of the tonal value of both line (figure) and space (ground), an image is created in which object and ground become inseparable and mutually dependent. The result (Fig. 4–5) is no longer a drawing of a twig form on a white piece of paper. The organization of the space field is perceptually as interesting and as important as the skeletal object. We have already stated the significance of such totality in a drawing, and although we have laid the emphasis here upon a *heightened perception* of the complementary nature of spatial and figurative elements, two other factors emerge from this experiment. The image takes on a dynamic pulsating movement through this treatment, and it also gains in three-dimensional quality—that is to say, in depth. These latter aspects of figure-to-ground relationships are dealt with more specifically in other chapters. Chapters 6, 7, 8, and 9 are concerned with dynamics, while Chapter 5 discusses relevant facts concerning mass and volume. We have also discussed figure and ground perception in Chapters 1 and 2, but we have not yet shown an illustration in which figure and ground are almost impossible to separate visually. The term "positive and neutral space" makes little sense with an image of this kind. The bookpaper design by E. R. Weiss (Fig. 4–4) represents the peak of the syle known as Art Nouveau in Germany in the late nineteenth century. The style's characteristics of flowing lines and organic, undulating, bulbous forms which extend into stalk-like extremities moving in a breeze, are all present.

**Fig. 4–5**
Barbara Raney
**Tree and Space**
*(Courtesy, Professor K. Forman)*

But *flatness* is the essence of the pattern. All suggestions of light, shade, space, and volume are avoided. Figure and ground are on the same plane, juxtaposed with hard edges. In fact, one cannot tell which is figure and which is ground in this design.

What is "in front" and what is "behind"? The dark gray shapes may be form-figure, or may be ground-space. The same may be said for the light gray shapes. Art Nouveau presents extreme examples of figure-to-ground ambiguity. By comparing Mondrian (Fig. 4–2)

with Fig. 4–4, one sees how Mondrian "carves" the ground almost like a sculptor in order to treat it as a positive and complementary environment of several planes of depth, which penetrate the form and are penetrated by it.

# 5

**FORM II**

The second family of objects to concern us differs in every way from the skeletal forms discussed above in Form I. Experience there showed us that when we can determine structure, we must do so if we are to draw with complete understanding; and we also learned that since space often intrudes between the parts of the skeleton, we must take account of the space surrounding an object if we are to draw successfully its significant proportions, movements, and structure.

There is an element of discovery in all drawing. Either as a conscious reaction to an objective stimulus (that is, in a face to face confrontation with an object), or as an act of spontaneous creativity (the invention of forms from the artist's own resources), the act of drawing is concerned with knowing. In the first case, the knowledge gained tends to be objective, revealing the physical nature of the object. In the second example it is more subjective, revealing personal attitudes and states. This is a pretty general statement and dichotomies of this sort do not always hold in the great world of art. Think how personally we know the emotional intensity of Vincent Van Gogh through his treatment of such a mundane object as a little wicker chair. Ob-

**Fig. 5–1**
**Stairway in Berlin**
*(Ullstein, Berlin;
photograph by Fritz Eschen)*

# Structural families: objects of mass and the structure of volume

jective and subjective discoveries are the warp and the weft of art. But in a training scheme designed for beginners, it does help to make a distinction between objective and subjective aspects of discovery. It is the general aim of Part 1 of this book to develop the former, and of Part 2 to treat the latter.

We have seen that an objective analysis of skeletal structure provides knowledge of one aspect of form. However, objects that are composed of mass—a pebble or a loaf of bread—have no such skeleton (see the definition of skeletal structure under the heading "Conclusions" in Form I) and thus form a second family of object types which may be called the "mass" group (Fig. 5-3). Such objects are not made up of a jointed series of skeletal parts; they are gently swelling or inert in comparison with the tremulous vibrancy of skeletal limbs, and may even have a lumpy, awkward quality about their form (Fig. 5–2). It is not easy to perceive how the structural characteristics of a large pebble determine its form, and how such characteristics are to be revealed in a drawing. It is much easier to do this with a twig. The basic characteristics of these solid objects are their mass and space displacement, together with the planes and curved surfaces of their volume. These aspects are not easy to comprehend structurally, for they are the antithesis of skeletal characteristics. Nevertheless, we must set out to determine a graphic means of expressing mass and volume. Most artists dislike systems and methods which suggest "how to do it," and in making the following suggestions, this is not what we are trying to do. We want to lead the student to a beginning point, through sharpening his perception, and then let him find his own way.

Objects of mass and volume possess a major characteristic which tends to intrude first on our perception. This is the movement and shape of their surface areas. Regard the wooden form illustrated in Fig. 5–6 and the pebble in Fig. 5–4. In the first, our perception of the mass of the object is aided by the linear relief of its surface. These lines and channels are the result of the worm eating the wood, and they move all around the object. They show us the curves and planes of the mass, and as it is obvious to our eye that they continue around the sides that we cannot see, our appreciation of the object's volume is increased. It would therefore be feasible in drawing an object of mass to make use of such a line to help express volume, even if the surface of the observed object is quite smooth. A line used for this purpose

**Fig. 5–2**
**A warty gourd**

**Fig. 5–3**
Constantin Brancusi
**Muse**
*(Portland Art Museum, Oregon;
photograph by Eliot Elisofen)
Bronze on stone base. An object of mass,
the highly polished surface of which invites
your hand to experience its swell, and
exploits the reflections to suggest both
concave and convex characteristics. It is
the very antithesis of the skeletal object.*

could be called a *continuous surface directional line*. Henry Moore makes use of this surface-describing line in his *Four Grey Sleepers* (Fig. 5–5). And what a heightened suggestion of volume these forms take on as a result! Look also at how Titian uses surface directional lines to hack out and shape the mass of the two figures in the drawing *Jupiter and Io* (Fig. 5–14). In both drawings, but particularly in the Moore, these lines move almost without any break over and around the surfaces of the mass, constantly describing volume.

When we turn our attention to the pebble (Fig. 5–4), we note that the highly smoothed and polished surface of this object seems to rule out the use of the continuous surface directional line. Rather, it is the change of tone—light and shade—over the swelling curved surface area that bespeaks the object's volume. This movement of light and shade over the surface reveals the main directional planes or curves, as does the continuous surface line. Thus, tonal values used to express mass may be called *continuous surface directional tones*. Rodin uses tone in this way to reveal the solidity of form in his drawing *The Peach* (Fig. 5–10). Although the values of his light and shade are not so dark as in the photograph of the pebble, his tone, following the surface direction of the figure's swell, performs the same function.

The relationship of planes and curved surfaces, as well as the plane or curvilinear directional inclination of the surfaces, are primary aspects of our perception of mass and volume. Many people, as their eyes travel over the surface of a heavy, solid form, trace imaginary lines relevant to the surface under observation, rather as if the tips of the fingers were stroking the form. In some cases, the visual sense is so closely attuned to the tactile that it is possible to "feel" a surface merely by intensive looking. This imaginary surface directional line continues to be "felt" even when it disappears from view around the other side of the object. The following illustration is a good example of this interoperation of the senses. If you were asked to estimate the weight of a watermelon placed before you, your eyes would travel over the surface, appraising the swell and form of the surface in order to judge the total mass or weight. They would repeat their assessment on the side that is out of sight; and at the same time, you would be imaginatively "feeling" the heaviness of the melon in your hand. The continuous surface directional line, or tone, the former as used by Moore and the latter by Rodin, does all this with an object of mass entirely

Fig. 5–4
Pebble

Fig. 5–5
Henry Moore
**Four Gray Sleepers**
*(War Artists' Committee, London)*

Fig. 5–6
**Worm-eaten wood form**

through drawing. It is the nearest we can get to a structural realization of these forms in drawing.

At this stage a complication occurs, inasmuch as the title of this chapter refers to "the Structure of Volume," for volume has a dual role. Volume denotes the space occupied by solid form or mass but it also signifies defined regions of space. Volume may refer to a solid like a pebble or to emptiness like a hole in the same pebble (Fig. 5–8). There is no real contradiction here: there are two kinds of volume that exist independently of each other or can exist side by side as properties of the same object. A stone is mass volume; an egg or a snail shell is space volume. But volume must be defined; and this is another important function of the continuous surface directional line or tone. Separately or together, they will define the mass volume of a rock or the space volume of a hole. It will be easier to understand this by referring to Fig. 5–8, where mechanically moving lines create this illusion. The continuously revolving line suggests now a hole, now a mass. The technique is more diagrammatic and self-conscious than we find in Henry Moore's drawing of the shelter sleepers (Fig. 5–5), but the principle of graphically expressing mass and space volume is virtually the same in both cases. It is important to note how the weight and tone of line in Fig. 5–8 influence one's perception of the form. The darker and heavier lines bring the curved surfaces and their apparent "edges" forward; the converse is true with the lighter and grayer lines, as we would expect from our discussion in Chapter 2. The same perception results from the same means in the revolving line of the stairway in Fig. 5–1, which defines an architectural hole in a building.

We now come to the important question of how we perceive the difference between "hole" and "solid" in volumetric objects, and how we translate this perception into the drawing of such forms. In this respect, one can really make only fairly general statements, for common visual experiences suggest different things to different people. For clarification, let us regard two illustrations, Figs. 5–9 and 5–19. In the first of these there is a black stone with a white spot, and in the second a white piece of wood with a black shadow. At first glance this shadow appears to be a hole in the wood, and it is only after continued observation that one realizes it is just a dark tone on the surface. Conversely, it is immediately apparent that the white spot on the black stone is the forward projecting end of the mass. There is obviously

Fig. 5–7
Pebble with holes

a psychological factor operating in perception of this sort. Black suggests recession because we associate darkness with the depth of a hole or the darkness of a long passage, whereas we associate the projecting high point of a mass with light reflection because it catches the light.

So we have four graphic elements which help to express the "structure" of mass and volume:

1.
Continuous surface directional *line*
2.
Continuous surface directional *tone*
3.
Dark tone for receding space volume (holes)
4.
Light tone for projecting mass

These elements may be used in any combination. Points 3 and 4 above apparently reverse the suggestions for natural depth perception that were made in Chapter 2. There it was stated that dark lines and tones came forward, while the lighter ones receded. This is an example of the difficulty of postulating rules of perception, for so much depends on the *context* of the tone or line, where "meaning" plays an important role. In the context of holes and mass the roles are reversed because of mental associations and experiences. If you look again at Fig. 5–7 you will see that the middle hole in this stone appears the deepest. It obviously isn't, for it does not go right through to the other side as does the bottom hole where we can see the "white air" behind. The intense darkness gives the illusion of great depth for this middle hole.

**Fig. 5–9**
**Pebble with white spot**

**Fig. 5–8**
**Study in optical illusion**
**from the Bauhaus**
*(Museum of Modern Art,*
*New York)*

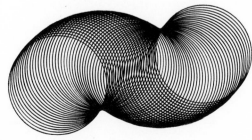

**THE DRAWINGS** Lines that are continuously exploring either surface or space volume demand a free, unforced movement. The whole arm, rather than just the wrist or the fingers, must move, and a rhythm should be built up while drawing. The first drawings may help to achieve this rhythmic freedom by trying to construct a few holes and a few mass projections. Figure 5–20 is a photograph showing a complexity of holes and projections over a large rock surface. Dark and light tone operates to reveal the holes and the high points. A close scrutiny of the print will also reveal that fine lines trace the curvature of the volumes over the surfaces. This combined effect of line and tone expressing surface curvature and recession is beautifully illustrated in Andreas Feininger's photograph of a decaying pine (Fig. 5–7). The hole appears almost "threaded" as the space volume is defined. Try to develop these structural characteristics as you draw holes and projections on your paper. Figure 5–21 shows a few randomly selected attempts by students to construct holes and projections. This is the first experiment. The experience of perceiving a hole—that is, space—in a solid form reinforces the thesis that form and space complement each other perceptually. Solid form may be drawn with a sense of its structural mass in terms of surface, just as space may be drawn structurally in terms of the surfaces that provide its boundaries. The painting, *Der Grosse Weg* (Fig. 5–15), shows all the structural characteristics of mass and space volume which we have

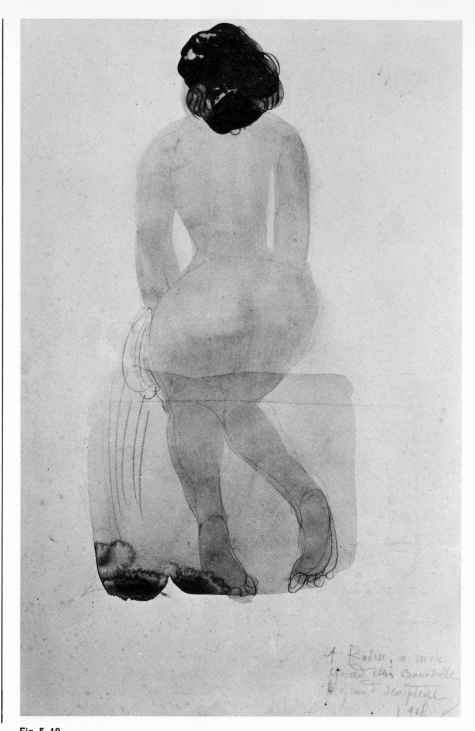

**Fig. 5–10**
Rodin, **The Peach** *(Courtesy of the Bourdelle Museum, Paris; Photo Bulloz)*

discussed, as does Albers' drawing, *Seclusion* (Fig. 2–8), which you will recall from Chapter 2. The Albers drawing is more geometric and does not possess the organic variability which has been the keynote of this chapter, but it works in the same way.

Finally, we should attempt to make some drawings of solid form objects, using these theories in as personal a way as possible. Search for some interesting stones or pieces of wood—driftwood often possesses some exciting forms—and draw them in any medium. But do make a conscious attempt to heighten their surface characteristics of movement, their holes, and their projections, and thus emphasize their weight and their space containment. Figures 5–13 and 5–16 are student drawings made of objets trouvés. Pen and ink, pen ink and washed tone, and pencil, are the mediums used. Each drawing makes a different use of the four graphic elements which we have previously listed as helping to express the "structure" of mass and volume. Figure 5–13 depends upon the revolving surface line and bears comparison with the photograph illustrated in Fig. 5–17. The drawings in Fig. 5–16 make more use of tone values which follow the direction of the surface; the drawing of the large piece of driftwood is the "loosest" of the three and makes the most use of the varying line qualities which we discussed in Chapter 1. All the objects chosen (or found) are complex forms of hollows, ridges, and swelling surfaces, for it is this type of complexity that the continuously moving surface line or tone is most suited to describe.

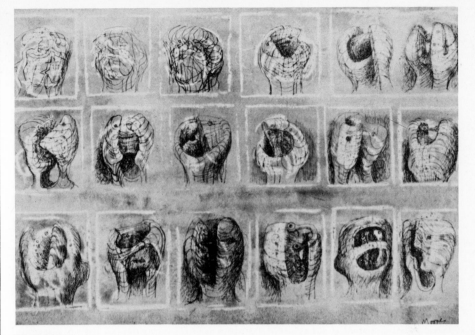

**Fig. 5–11**
Henry Moore, **Page of Heads—Ideal for Sculpture 1940** *(Collection, Peter Watson Esq.)*

**Fig. 5–12**
Eugène Delacroix, **Study of Horses** *(Collection G. Aubry, Paris)*

CONCLUSIONS Objects of mass and the dual nature of volume have now been tentatively explored through structural drawing. If we add skeletal objects to objects of mass and volume, we have examples from each of the two principal families of form. It is very difficult to think of any kind of form—from the substantial object, or the shell which is merely a defined region of space, to the hairlike thread—which does not take its place in either of these families.

This emphasis on structure is not just a frill. In Form I, an attempt was made to relate structure to the process of comprehending form, for without structure drawing is meaningless. Leonardo da Vinci and many lesser artists have attempted to establish that art (and drawing is the foundation of art) is a mental activity and a science, searching for objective reality. On the other hand, we also admit that art is an expressive act, relating directly to the subjective experiences of the artist, springing from an "inner necessity" as Kandinsky says,[1] or corresponding to the *vie intérieure* as described by Eric Newton.[2]

Searching for the structural rendering of an object is an intellectual part of the objective processes of perception. Eventually, the revealing of the structural aspects of form becomes almost an unconscious faculty of the good artist—it is an integral part of the total experience of drawing, but I believe it takes a long time for this to happen to the average student. Therefore, in a book of this sort, separations such as these between the conscious and unconscious aspect of perception are necessary. One hopes they are not misleading, for the reader should realize that the world's great works of art embody a complete marriage of diverse elements. A visual impression may be wedded to structure, feeling may be integrated with knowing, objects of the world may be changed through the artist's own visual invention. The phrase "unity in diversity" is often used to explain this curious completeness of a work of art. And yet when one tries to explain the phrase, the result is never very satisfactory, for when one explains art there is no art left. Here lie the difficulties for the teacher of art.

Knowledge of this family of form—of objects which have mass and space volume defined by mass—has wide application. The cylindrical

[1] Wassily Kandinsky, *Concerning the Spiritual in Art*, Documents of Modern Art, No. 5 (New York: George Wittenborn, Inc., 1947).
[2] Eric Newton, *The Romantic Rebellion* (New York: Schocken Books, 1964), p. 11.

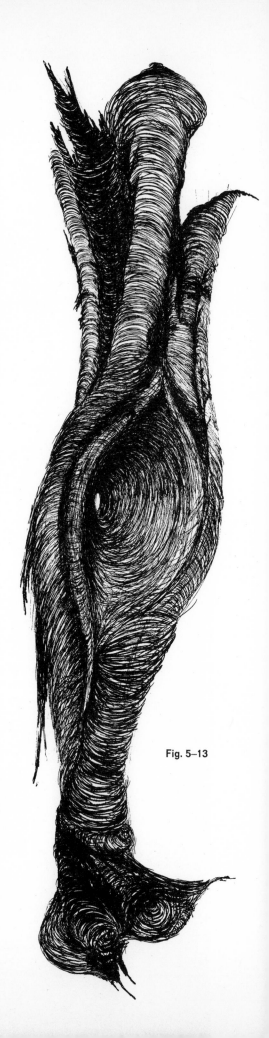

Fig. 5–13

STRUCTURAL FAMILIES: OBJECTS OF MASS
AND THE STRUCTURE OF VOLUME

**FORM II**

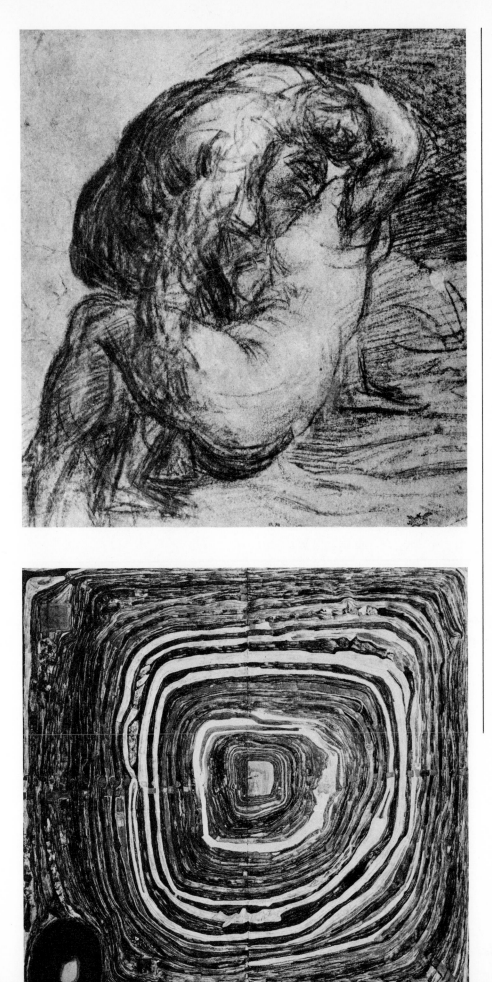

**Fig. 5–14**
Titian
**Jupiter and Io**
*(Cambridge, Fitzwilliam Museum.
Reproduced by permission of the Syndics
of the Fitzwilliam Museum, Cambridge)*

**Fig. 5–15**
Fritz Hundert-Wasser
**Der Grosse Weg**
*(Courtesy Hundert-Wasser, Giudecca,
Venice)*

61

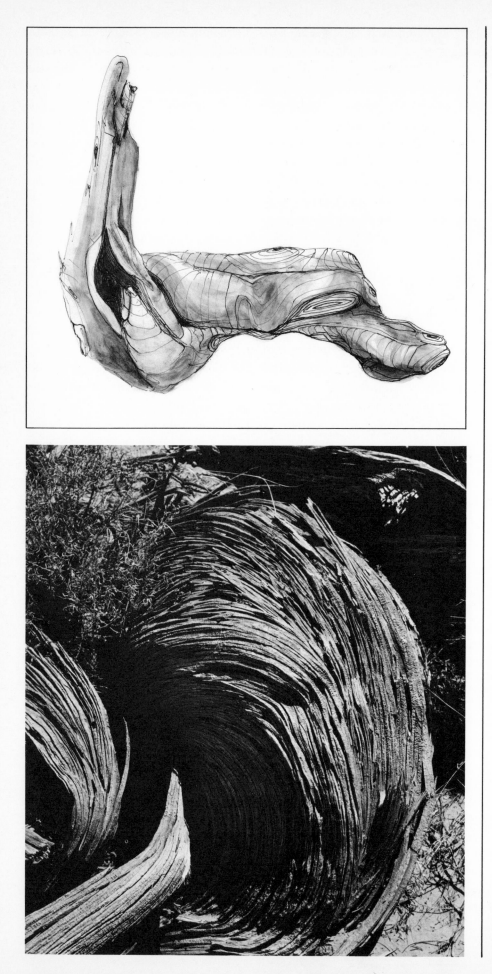

Fig. 5–16

Fig. 5–18
Henry Moore
**Shapes in Bone—Drawing for Sculpture 1932**
*(By kind permission of the artist)*

Fig. 5–17
Andreas Feininger
**Decaying Pine**
*(Courtesy of Crown Publishers, Inc.,
New York)*

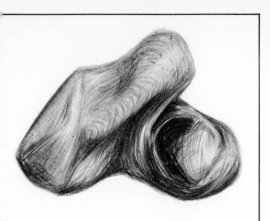

Fig. 5–19
Nail in wood

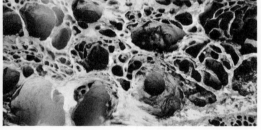

Fig. 5–20
Holes in rock

stalk of a plant, clouds and holes in clouds, eyes situated in sockets, the mass of a boulder, the volume of the human thigh—these forms may be realized in drawing through this emphasis on following the movement of surface by means of line or tone. Look at the drawings of Henry Moore for a final confirmation. Figure 5–11 shows a series of ideas for sculpture, and Fig. 5–18 a number of drawings for sculpture made from shapes in bone. These drawings say more than all the words of this chapter. Would these forms be as compellingly massive or hollow without the drawing's insistence on surface movement over both the convex and concave aspects of the objects?

**A brief note on a drawing theory of Eugene Delacroix** Delacroix has taught, ". . . ne pas prendre par la ligne, mais par le milieu," which may be freely translated as, "take hold of objects by their centers, not by their lines of contour." The obvious implication is to treat objects as *masses*. There are undoubtedly two ways of drawing visible things—by using outlines to define them precisely, or by treating the planes and curved surfaces of their mass. We have previously suggested that skeletal forms not having any dominant mass may be treated as outlines, purely. But in this chapter we have taken the view of Delacroix, using a multiplicity of surface directional lines and tones to shape mass and volume.

Delacroix states the case against pure outline as a means of shaping mass, as follows: "The contour [outline] accentuated uniformly and beyond proportion, destroys plasticity, bringing forward those parts of an object which are always most distant from the eye—namely, its outlines." [3]

We have previously discussed how objects which are uniformly outlined on the paper tend to lie flat on the ground and do not reveal their volume (see Fig. 4–4). The dominant idea behind Delacroix's drawing is to use lines to express masses, not edges; to take the fundamental volumes and planes of an object *first*, when making a drawing, and to come to the contour edge last. In so doing, he was also concerned with a gradation of lines in terms of weight and quality, in order to bring some masses forward and cause others to be less distinct. And this, after all, is how we perceive a solid object. Consequently, pay special attention to his *Study of Horses* reproduced in Fig. 5–12, and observe how Delacroix constructs the animal by shaping the

---

[3] Kurt Badt, *Eugene Delacroix Drawings* (Oxford: Bruno Cassirer, 1946), p. 59.

basic areas of a horse's mass, showing their rhythmic, organic relationship. What a fine *plastic* sense is realized in this drawing!

**Postscript—skeletal and mass form** We have to recognize that all skeletal objects possess mass and volume. Even the slenderest twig has mass. Although predominantly linear and skeletal in appearance, its mass may be seen if we cut through it and expose a cross section. However, the reverse is not true; objects of mass do not automatically have a skeleton. What, then, is the point of dividing objects into two families if fundamentally they all possess volume? The reason is that we want to bring out the *dominant* structural characteristic. Hold a hair from your head in the palm of your hand and see if you find yourself concerned with its volume or mass. No, the dominant perception is of its length and directional linear movement. Thus the division of objects into structural families is based on our perception of the dominant structural aspect of the object—whether linear and skeletal, or mass and volume. And I have tried to suggest the approaches to drawing which best reveal the skeletal or the mass object.

A glance back to Fig. 5–20 will show that it is not always easy to discover a visually dominant characteristic. Is it the mass, the hollows, or the skeleton which is perceived as the primary characteristic in this image? And how would you draw it? Would you use a combination of continuous skeletal structure lines (there is no articulated skeletal form), with revolving surface lines and tones? There is no reason why you shouldn't, and I would think it a good solution to the problem. It would be an intelligent application of the principles behind structural drawing.

**Fig. 5–22**
**Goldzack Elasticized Fabric Plant
at Gosseau, Switzerland**
*(Architects: Danzeisen and Voser, 1955)
The voluminous form of this building is
visually and structurally heightened by the
linear emphasis given to the curved surface
of the shell. One might use similar lines
and tones in drawing a great seashell.*

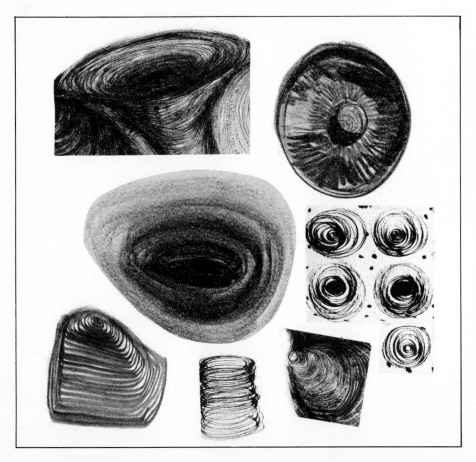

**Fig. 5–21**

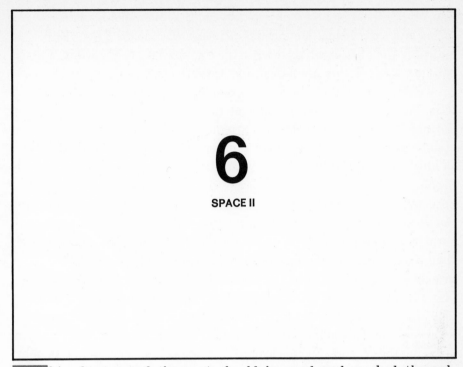

# 6

**SPACE II**

Thial chapter and the next should be read and worked through as one chapter. Both are concerned with the ways the painter, sculptor, and architect approach the handling of space. The difference between this chapter and Chapter 7 is explained by the difference between the words "spontaneous" and "deliberate" used in the chapter titles, for this chapter will initiate some spontaneous drawings which will then be treated more deliberately in Chapter 7.

At first we shall try to deal with space per se. And I do not think we can do this without going a little more deeply into the psychology of perception, albeit somewhat summarily.

It has been repeatedly stated that the perception of objects or images is dependent upon the presence of a figure on a ground. The ground for the general observer is the spatial environment; for the artist it is his two-dimensional paper or canvas; for the sculptor it is three-dimensional physical space itself; and for the architect it can be either a two-dimensional wall surface similar to the painter's flat ground, or actual physical space as it is for the sculptor. The ground, therefore, is the spatial environment in which the artist's shapes and surfaces exist. In Chapters 2 and 4 we have tried to suggest how our percep-

**Fig. 6–1**
*In this illustration the student drawing is reversed (white on black) in order to reveal more forcefully the graphic qualities of the calligraphic line.*

# The spontaneous
# creation
# of space

tion of the artist's forms is affected by the relationship between the forms and the ground. Mondrian's painting *Horizontal Tree* (Fig. 4–2) indicates that his creative interest in the spatial environment was almost as great as his analytical and inventive attitude to the tree. So we would suggest that the image created by an artist is a dual thing. It is, on the one hand, his material forms and their surfaces, and on the other, the spatial field (or ground) in which these shapes concretely exist. Consequently, our concern in these two chapters is not so much with creating form as with allowing the spatial aspect of the problem to remain the central issue. As the experiments with spatial perception continue throughout Part 1 of the book, this emphasis on the vital role played by the constant intervals between the surfaces of form will be reinforced. You may recall that it was suggested earlier that if you observe the outstretched fingers of your hand intently, the intervals of space between the fingers, being empty space, become visible only because the surface of your fingers is visible. Paradoxically, one result of the "visibility" of empty space is a heightening of the awareness of the surface of the forms disposed in space. We therefore come to the important conclusion that an act of perception is more than just a visual sensation of form. It seems to be abstracted from the series of sensations experienced by the blinking eye—from the time-sequenced impressions of objects seen in a vague spatial field of flux as one moves around. Perception appears to be a recognition of the constant disposition of surfaces of objects in relationship to the spatial intervals which separate them. Surfaces possess a directional movement; they may be rough, smooth, reflective, opaque, angled, curvilinear, concave, or convex. But it is because these surfaces give visible shape to empty space that we have a heightened awareness of the object which the surfaces represent.

There is, apparently, a static element to perception, for the multifarious and ambiguous surfaces of objects appear seemingly fixed in a rigid and specific relationship with their spatial context. Contemporary sculpture is extremely interested in these aspects of perception, and the best visual illustration of our argument is a work like Barbara Hepworth's "Curved Form," Fig. 6–2. The vertical plinth, the horizontal base, and then those space-defining planes and curved surfaces provide a multi-dimensional experience of space for the viewer. The sculptural form itself suggests a great space-cradle. How impor-

**Fig. 6–2**
Barbara Hepworth
**Curved Form (Trevalgan)**
*(British Council, London; Photograph Studio St. Ives Ltd.)*

tant these surfaces are for our perception of the sculpture's ground—namely, three-dimensional, physical space! Sense impressions alone tend to be kaleidoscopic and blurring, distorting the phenomenal world. Perception however, tends to rigidity. Hence the clarity of spatial definition in Fig. 6–2. The case is stated as follows by a pioneer psychologist in visual perception:

Historically, the central problem of perception has been taken to be how we see depth and distance, the so called third dimension of space. The psychologist and the painter have been led to ask what the clues or cues may be for tridimensional perception as distinguished from bidimensional sensation. It begins to be evident, however, that the heart of the problem is not so much how we see objects in depth as how we see the constant layout of the world around us. Space as such, empty space, is not visible but surfaces are.[1]

The point I am trying to make here, perhaps much too superficially, is that when a sculptor begins to create surfaces (which we should take to mean aspects of form), he perceives the three-dimensional development of his image in much the same way as he perceives the layout of the world around him. He perceives the created space of his ground because he is making surfaces of a specific kind, which in themselves are visible.

Figures 6–4 and 6–5 are reproductions of monochromatic Chinese paintings. Look at them for a moment without considering their title. See each painting as a series of spontaneously brushed surfaces. Each surface is characteristically rounded, pointed, linear, or volumetric, moving in this plane or that. Notice how this disposition of brushed surfaces fixes three-dimensional rather than two-dimensional intervals between the surfaces. These intervals possess depth because the brush marks suggest varieties of surface movement, of light reflection or absorption, and thus they shape space in depth. Certain surfaces are

---

[1] James J. Gibson, "Constancy and Invariance in Perception," in *The Nature and Art of Motion*, Gyorgy Kepes, ed. (New York: George Braziller, 1965), p. 60.

Fig. 6–3

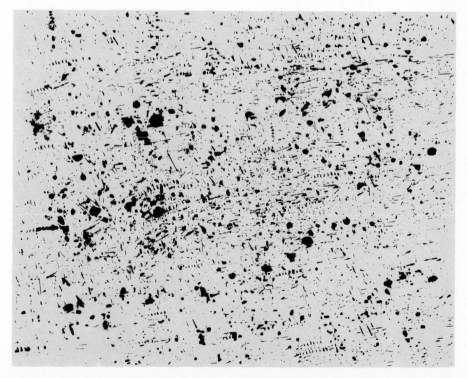

more dominant than others and provide focal points which take on fixed positions, as do objects in the phenomenal world. The paintings appear remarkably unforced, free, and natural; although each brush mark seems so surely placed, they do not appear premeditated. Like all apparently simple wonders, however, these paintings result from a profound distillation of perceptual experience. I would like to quote Vernon Blake's remarks about them, because they are so relevant to our own brush-drawing experiments in this chapter:

The infinitely subtle play among themselves of the smallest number of irreproachable brush strokes, varying in value, in width, in hasty rhythmic movement or in perfect repose; the hinted mastery of fully extended means, from which with rare reticence just the few units essential to the theme were chosen, such was the aim of artists who have striven far more than all others to fix on silk or on paper a symbol of the intangible human perception of the universe, of its seeming laws.[2]

We cannot remain unaffected by the dimensions of space in which we live, and I believe that the creation of space in a work of art can often be quite unconscious. The line between conscious and unconscious motivation in art is difficult to determine, as are the conscious and unconscious elements of an act of perception. Yet over the years experience in teaching art has led me to believe that if the student can relax sufficiently to gain a new sense of balance and poise, and can escape the constant run of thoughts and ideas through his mind, he can move freely over a ground with a brush, and achieve a spatial design which is a direct expression of space perception experiences. I would call this kind of ideationless action-drawing of space *spontaneous,* in order to distinguish it from the more deliberate and conscious attitudes which are to be developed in Chapter 7.

The three main objectives of this chapter are: (1) to establish that some of us have an instinctive or unconscious tendency to create a layout of marks (surfaces) which establish a deep three-dimensional ground; (2) to show that we tend to see linear relationships, both two-dimensional and three-dimensional, between such marks on a ground; (3) to establish the realization that rhythm and movement, freely and spontaneously rendered in drawing, produce significant spatial designs.

---

[2] Vernon Blake, *The Art and Craft of Drawing* (London: Oxford University Press, 1927), p. 197.

**THE DRAWINGS** There are three drawing experiments, each of which serves these three objectives. It is advisable to perform them in the order given, for they are designed as a sequence in order to fully develop the theme.

**Drawing 1**

This first experiment is short and has to be carried out on a white sheet of paper, not less than 20″ x 15″ in dimension, pinned to a drawing board and then erected on a semi-vertical easel at about shoulder height. You will need a regular sable water-color brush of medium size, the handle of which should be lengthened by tying it to a piece of dowel stick about 12 inches long. The lengthening of the brush handle by this means insures a lack of deliberation in handling the brush and maintains a distance between you and the paper which helps to preserve the detachment necessary for inducing an intuitive response. Now, standing at least three feet from the easel and holding the brush right at the end of the dowel stick, dip the brush into a saucer of black ink and proceed to dab the paper with the brush point. It must be stressed that there should be no attempt to *draw* with the brush: the movement should be just a touch with the point before moving back. You should be completely relaxed, both physically and mentally, with your mind as completely blank as you can make it, and your whole body loose as you move rhythmically backward and forward making the dabs. When there is an automatic reaction against continuing to dab, then stop. Don't think about when to stop;

just stop on some such automatic impulse. Figure 6–3 is a sheet of dab marks resulting from such an exercise; it should be studied closely in the light of what is written below.

This drawing will take only about three or four minutes, so when you are finished, put up another piece of paper and do another; and possibly another one after that, in order to make comparisons between the three drawings. In studying the results you will notice that some of the dabs were made with a stronger impact than others, and so a pattern of dominant and minor marks has been produced. These differences suggest a variation in the force of movements involved in making the marks. As the backward and forward movement is repeated, a rhythm builds up which corresponds to a stimulus which is partly emotional and partly perceptual, for as the ground becomes more crowded, perceptual and emotional responses are called into play. It is difficult to separate movement, emotion, and perception in an exercise such as this. They appear to operate simultaneously, and to be partly unconscious.

At this point we have a direct link to Chapter 2, for you will notice that the strong black dabs project forward over both smaller and grayer dabs, thus making areas of depth where the eye penetrates. As you allow your eye to wander freely over the paper, it will probably come to rest at one particular region where there is a confluence of dabs, a concentration of dominant marks. This represents the major focal point. There may be other minor areas of concentration, or there may be no such point of concentration

**Fig. 6–4**
Su Kuo
**Bird on Bamboo Stalk**
*(Reproduced from "Kokka," Kokka Co., Tokyo)*

written form of language—of individual letters or lines of script—has been traditionally treated in the Far East as an elegant and rhythmic form of art. The brush is the traditional instrument of Eastern calligraphy, and it is the brush mark which gives Eastern art generally its grace and style. Letter forms, though varying from culture to culture, possess common *linear* characteristics, the lines being either curvilinear or angular in movement. Circles, triangles, rectangles, and their variations combine to make up letter forms. The sensitivity of Eastern brushwork is recognized not only in the context of writing, but also in painting and ceramic decoration (Fig. 2–13), and has inspired a use of the brush in Western action painting which is stylistically oriental.

A flat, one-stroke, half-inch lettering brush and a bottle of black ink are required for this drawing. (This is not the type of brush used in China or Japan, but it gives a beginner the chance to make greater contrasts in line width, which this drawing calls for.) Cut your paper or board into 8″ squares and work on one square at a time. Before pinning the square to the drawing-board, place a larger white piece of paper beneath it. The reason for this is to help you to work on the square without thinking of its edges as boundaries or limits to your brush movements, for the flowing movement of the line to be made in this drawing may need to be carried off the square onto the white backing paper, before returning to the square in one continuous, flowing movement. This flow of the line without any break is an essential characteristic of Eastern

brushwork. If the student is aware of the edges of his paper as a limit to his movements, the brush marks are usually hesitant and broken in flow. Moreover, this freedom to disregard the sides of the ground will allow you to think of the "edges" of the drawing surface in a new way—not as a limiting boundary cutting off the design it encloses, but as an integral part of the design allowing spatial areas to move in and out. Thus, the continuity of the spatial flow is established beyond the confines of the edge or "frame."

Figure 6–8 is an illustration of Chinese brush work, and gives an indication of how the brush is used, spontaneously yet under complete control. The constant transition from fullness of line to delicacy, is not merely the result of changes in pressure. The brush is also *turned* between thumb and forefinger as it moves over the surface, and it takes a lot of practice to accomplish this while retaining full control. The angle of the brush to the surface is maintained at approximately 90°. In using the flat half-inch brush

Fig. 6–7
*(Courtesy, Professor J. Reardon, State University of New York, Buffalo)*
*Again the drawing has been reversed for calligraphic forcefulness.*

that is recommended for this drawing, bear in mind that it is possible to draw with the chisel-edge of the brush and make a thin line, or with the full half-inch width to make a full half-inch line. These are the two extreme possibilities, but in turning the brush from the chisel-edge to the full width, the line produced will vary from thin to thick relative to the width of brush being brought into use. You will have to practice this turning motion on some scrap paper before starting the finished drawing. Figure 6–1 illustrates a practice attempt by a student, using a ¼″ flat brush.

The drawing itself is simple enough, and, like the others, depends upon a spontaneous response to the empty ground, expressed through a certain type of action. Think vaguely of letter forms—an "i," an "a," a "j," an "n," etc. These forms are to influence the general character of the brush flow, but it is not intended that you should choose one letter specifically and draw it. Charge the brush with ink carefully, for the delicate line of the chisel-edge will be lost if the brush is dripping with ink; likewise, the full half-inch width line will not materialize if it contains insufficient ink. Start the movement anywhere, on or off the square itself, with a thin line or a thick, and make a sweep over the square turning the brush as the line changes direction. The brush itself possesses a natural inclination to turn with the movement of the arm, and this should merely be assisted by the thumb and forefinger. After making one "run" over the square, start a second as quickly as you can. Don't try to think it out. Make the movement instinctively. Let the brush hover over the square, continuing to describe its angles and arabesques in the air, before bringing it down again to leave the trace of its motion on the square. This second run may complete the first by joining lines, adding loops, dotting "i's" or crossing "t's". You can make a third approach, and a fourth, if you wish. This must be your decision and depends upon your attitude to the spatial design all ready initiated. But bear in mind that you should exploit the characteristics of letter form as spontaneously and as naturally as possible. Try to avoid forcing the forms—let them come with the action and with the feeling of the brush sweeping on and off the ground. You can work with the drawing board horizontal, inclined, or nearly vertical. See which suits you best.

Figure 6–7 shows a student drawing made in this way. What special spatial qualities do you see in it? First, I believe most people would be aware of relatively "flat" spatial areas which are in a lateral, vertical, or diagonal state of movement. Our significant perception in this case is bidimensional, which is not to say that a natural depth perception does not operate dependent upon the mass, value, or quality of the line—the openness or enclosure of ground—as was discussed in Chapter 2. The sweeping action of the brush is so related to the two-dimensional area of the ground, exploring length, breadth, and diagonal distance, that great depth is not revealed. And letter forms themselves tend to be two-dimensionally simple, rather than three-dimensionally complex, because of functional considerations such as legibility. Nevertheless, this image is dynamic;

the space is on the move. It moves in and out, unrestricted by any boundary. The shape of an area is related to its movement, and there is a certain homogeneity of spatial shape over the whole design because the various directional movements are so rhythmically integrated. There is no "cluttering" of the ground; all the ground shapes are bold and clear. The swelling and thinning of the brush lines seems to affect our space perception in two ways. First, these linear variations affect the two-dimensional movement of the space they describe. The space appears static where contained by the broader lines, but gains momentum and rapidly accelerates as it follows the direction of the thinner lines. Second, this linear change also induces a depth perception. As the front surface of the line changes to what is apparently a thin side, we perceive that the frontal plane of the line has *turned in space* to reveal its edge. This suggests the potential depth of the regions where

this linear change occurs.

It is difficult to "read" an image spatially. Our rational culture, with many hundreds of years behind it, trains us to be interested in the concrete, not the intangible. We look for form, not always realizing that what we see as form is really space. The "forms" in Fig. 6–7 are spatial forms; the marks of the brush become physical surfaces which give us a layout of space. We have relied up on *instinctual action* rather than deliberation in making these drawings, but in the following chapter this calligraphic experiment will be repeated to involve a series of deliberate operations intended to produce more depth as well as two-dimensional dynamics.

We set out in the beginning to draw space, not form. We now have three different results which should be compared side by side. Try to perceive the varied dynamic aspects of space which they present, rather than considering their formal aspects.

**Fig. 6–8
Chinese brush
work and script**
*(Courtesy of the
publishers, Faber
and Faber Ltd.,
London)*

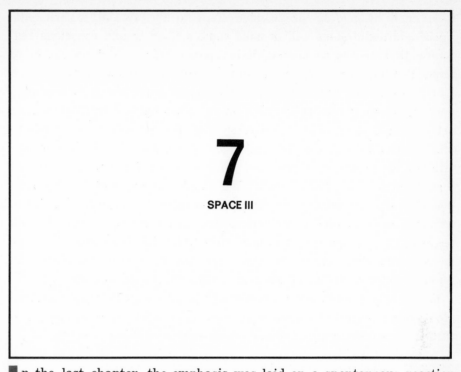

# 7

**SPACE III**

In the last chapter, the emphasis was laid on a spontaneous reaction to empty space (the ground) by marking it with a brush. As far as possible we abjured mental processes and rational ideas. Instead, we depended upon differing rhythmic patterns of brush movement to release intuitive, natural, and dynamic responses in order to create a spatial design.

Chapter 6 commenced with a brief attempt to suggest an explanation of the way we perceive space in depth in our world. It is difficult for an artist to make positive statements about how we perceive our environment, especially when science has only partial answers for the phenomenon. For, as we have seen, the artist creates images intuitively in which his space perception seems to operate in the same way as it does in his involvement with the natural world. There is no point in repeating these arguments in this chapter, but it should be remembered that the exposition on perception in Chapter 6 holds as a basic thesis for this chapter also. Chapters 6 and 7 are completely sequential, and the difference between them is expressed by the words "spontaneous" and "deliberate" in their respective titles.

What we must do here is to develop the experiences initiated in

**Fig. 7–1**
André Volten
**Construction—Galvanized Steel, 1958**
*(Stedelijk Museum, Amsterdam)*

# The deliberate creation of space

Chapter 6 by adding progressive steps to the spatial experiments. These additional steps will demand some deliberate and conscious reasoning in response to spatial design possibilities. I did not mean to imply in Chapter 6 that only intuitive responses produce art, although I believe that such natural, spontaneous, and uncontrived factors play perhaps the most important part. On the other hand, I think that most artists would agree that a completely logical approach to art tends to inhibit feeling, spontaneity, and unconscious motivations which are vital to the creative process. An intellectual perfectionism devoid of these elements is pretty sterile. We should strive, then, to keep an intuitive attitude alive, even when the objective is clearly stated and demands a logical and conscientious application by the artist. As you begin to explore space in this new work, you will be required to make mental decisions, yet at the same time preserve intuitive ideas and feelings for the spatial values your design will be developing.

Let us take Mondrian's *Composition No. 10* (Fig. 7–2) as an example of this dual, intuition-cum-logic process at work. Here is space disturbed by marks; but unlike our experiment in making free, rhythmic,

**Fig. 7–2**
Piet Mondrian
**Composition No. 10**
*(Rijksmuseum Kröller-Müller, Holland)*

**Fig. 7–3**
**Model, York Minster Chapter House roof**
*(Yorkshire Archaeological Society)*

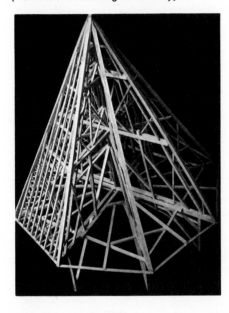

**Fig. 7–4**
**First stage in construction of model of York Minster Chapter House roof; view from below**

brush dabs over an empty ground, this is highly organized and controlled. Mondrian did not arrive at this result by chance. You should look up his series of apple tree drawings to see a possible derivation for this design. (See Fig. 1–6, but I wish it were possible to reproduce them all.) With each drawing, Mondrian eliminates more and more of the formal, physical, properties of the tree itself, until he comes ultimately to a subtly modulated design of vertical and horizontal lines. Each line signifies a surface—the original surfaces of tree limbs in space. Although Fig. 7–2 was made a year or two later than the apple tree series, let us regard it as a spatial design which springs logically from the earlier drawings. There are many ways to interpret *Composition No. 10,* but for the purposes of this chapter I want to suggest that it is a drawing in which a tree has ceased to be tree and has become instead *tree space,* by which I mean that we can see the drawing as a design of the *spatial environment* of apple trees in general. As a drawing of space, revealed through the disposition of surfaces, it illustrates the thesis we have developed. We perceive the layout of space in this drawing in much the same way as we do in our own brush point drawings (Fig. 6–3). Where does your eye finally come to rest in Mondrian's composition? Is the focal point frontal or in depth? Does the dynamic movement of the marks create spatial tensions between competing focal points? All of these questions relate to the illusion of depth in the image. Notice how the changes in space intervals create a "rushing in" of the marks to one particular region. All of these factors activate both two- and three-dimensional space perception, but, as we have said, Mondrian's drawing is a very ordered design. His analysis of the free growing, organic apple tree of nature in its space field has been regularized into a perceptual system of linear surfaces and forces [1] which reveal the general shape of "apple tree space." As such, it manages to combine organic vitality with geometric rigidity—a perfect combination for Mondrian's purpose. The drawing reveals both the artist's intuitive and his intellectual response to his involvement with the perception of linear forms in space. It is space, not tree, that he gives us, and our perception of this space is helped considerably by the geometric simplification and abstraction of the image.

---

[1] The compression of space suggesting forces in operation is the concern of Chapter 8.

THE DELIBERATE CREATION
OF SPACE

**SPACE III**

**THE DRAWINGS** The third experiment in this group is not a drawing in the conventional sense, but a linear exercise in three dimensional design. It may be performed independently of the other work described.

### Drawing 1

We are now going to take the calligraphic brush drawing to a more sophisticated level. The aim is to produce more depth than is normally created in a straightforward brush drawing of this type and to produce it through a series of deliberate steps. The collage (pasting up) technique will be used to develop the image. First, you will require a sturdy piece of gray or white mounting board to serve as the base on which to paste up the forms. This can be any size, but I recommend you work between maximum and minimum dimensions of about 14″ x 22″ and 10″ x 8″ respectively. Second, you will need several sheets of a thin, white drawing paper of roughly the same size as the board. It is essential that this paper be thin enough to be fairly transparent. If it is placed over a black brush mark, the mark should just show through as a vague tone or surface. For the adhesive use a transparent rubber cement.

Take a sheet of the thin, white drawing paper and make a calligraphic brush drawing, just as you did in Chapter 6 (Fig. 6–1). Make three or four similar drawings on the other sheets, keeping all the characteristics of rhythmic sweeps and thick and thin line surfaces as prescribed for the previous work. These drawings are the raw materials

for the new image. To use them, they have to be cut or torn up; not into small bits, but, depending upon the size of paper used, into three or four pieces, so that the sweep of a brush movement or the change in a line's surface is not lost as it would be on a small fragment.

Select several of these cut or torn pieces at random, and lay them out on the board. Move them about, allowing them to overlap or to leave portions of the board showing, until you have an arrangement possessing interesting rhythms, counterrhythms, and linear tensions. Then, glue the pieces down. You will notice that where the pieces overlap, the brush marks underneath show as vague secondary shapes. If you use gray board and have left some of it exposed, yet a third level of depth in the ground will be produced. The next step demands careful consideration. Take the remaining pieces of cut or torn paper and lay them over the design already created. Allow parts of the existing image to remain uncovered, and relate them to the new design

which is being superimposed. You will now have a complex, fragmented, black, primary image at the top level, and a vague secondary image running beneath it. This secondary image is simply the covered black marks of the first collage operation showing through. Glue these pieces down when you have achieved an interesting relationship between primary and secondary images. When it has dried, put the board in a strong oblique light and observe the result closely. You have created a collage made up of two obvious levels of depth. But there are more to be developed.

Study the image you have made and decide how you might work over it with a brush to connect broken rhythms and give a homogeneous appearance to the design. See where you could take your brush, and, turning it through its range, continue some lines *over the edges* of the various glued pieces to effect a continuity of inked surfaces. This will strengthen the primary, frontal image. But avoid the temptation to do too much of this, or the effect will

**Fig. 7–5**
(Courtesy, Professor J. Reardon, State University of New York, Buffalo)

become much too obvious. A certain fragmentation must remain in the frontal design if space is to come and go. Tightening up the design would lose this, as well as destroy the characteristic ''scrappiness'' of the collage treatment, which aids our aim in this experiment. At this point, consider whether the depth of the drawing would be heightened by taking some pure white fragments of paper and sticking them down in positions where they would blot out altogether parts of the lower design or diminish parts of the dominant design. Opaque white water paint could be used for this purpose with equal effectiveness. Strong white areas of the ground will tend to come forward in the drawing. (See Chapter 5.)

The final step is concerned with the spatial implications of certain types of line—a factor which was discussed in Chapters 1 and 2. Take a pen instead of the brush and, remembering that the weight of a line as well as its quality—incisive or dull—may determine its position in space, decide where pen lines might be added to the drawing to define differing levels of depth. Add freehand or ruled pen lines which will stand in a specific depth relationship to the levels you already perceive. These new lines can also function in providing further dynamic and visual links between badly related spatial areas. They can do this by their two-dimensional movement as well as by their three-dimensional implication. They may run along torn or cut edges to exploit a paper shape as a spatial field per se, thereby heightening its directional movement; or they may connect calligraphic marks more

**Fig. 7-6**
*(Courtesy, Professor J. Reardon, State University of New York, Buffalo)*

THE DELIBERATE CREATION
OF SPACE

**SPACE III**

delicately than the brush could do; or, more significantly, they may provide a subtle connection between a primary and frontal brush mark and a secondary "underneath" mark, by continuing the line of the former to the edge of the masking collage piece before seeming to disappear under it into the vague shape beneath.

Figure 7–5 incorporates all the steps we have described. Every stage contributes to the several layers of depth. The contrast between the barely visible brushed surfaces underneath and the strong black surfaces on top invites the first perception of depth. Then, the cut or torn edges of the paper pieces give a suggestion of low relief to the drawing, providing a physical three-dimensional aspect. The pure white areas of the ground become more frontal in contrast with the shadowy tones beneath. And the contrast between brush surface and differing pen lines makes for more pronounced three-dimensional qualities. Last, but not least, the fragmentary appearance of the image suggests an "over and under" movement of broad and thin linear surfaces appearing and disappearing in a sea of space. Notice how the edges of the total design area have been used as recommended in Chapter 6. There is no limiting border; space flows in and out on all four sides.

Figure 7–6 shows a slight modification in the method of working, for some of the dark, underground forms were brushed in *en masse,* intended as large areas of underneath tone. They are not calligraphic brush markings. In Fig. 7–11 much use is made of white paint to mask out parts of the first collage

**Fig. 7–7**

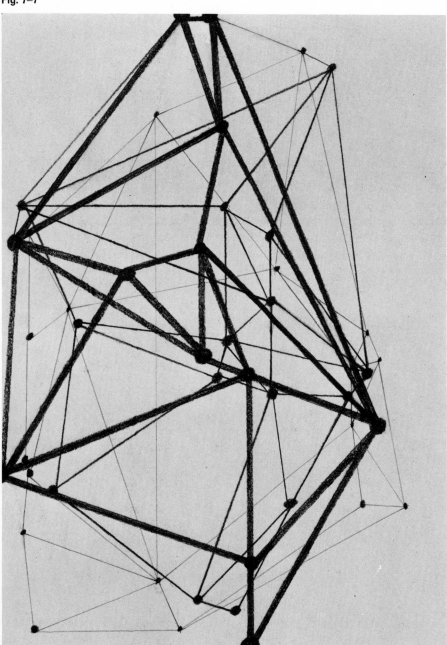

ground. The complex, grass-like, calligraphic surfaces of the dominant image have been very deliberately cut out and assembled, and stand strongly over the broken surfaces beneath.

### Drawing 2

This is to be a drawing of a completely different nature. It should produce two results: it should reinforce a belief in our natural or intuitive ability to create spatial images, and it should also indicate how we "read" a scattered and random arrangement of marks on a ground—how we imaginatively project lines between the marks that seem significant. These lines connect the marks most obviously in a two-dimensional field, but I hope this experiment will show that the connection can be made three-dimensionally also, by a deliberate and controlled use of drawing.

First, take a handful of variously sized pebbles and lay them out ready for easy selection. You will need another sheet of large white drawing paper, a sharp pencil, and a ruler. Selecting random pebbles from your collection, place them quite unself-consciously anywhere on the white paper. There is no conscious aim behind this, no particular end in view—just an instinctive putting down of the stones in the area at your disposal. Stop when it seems right to stop. Now indicate with a pencil the position of each pebble, using large, medium, and small dots to correspond to the size of the pebbles used. Remove each pebble as its position is marked.

Figure 7–8 reveals the balanced yet dynamic arrangement of dots over the ground. As you continue to look, you will find that your eye tends to start at the bottom right-hand corner of the paper and move up through each dominant pebble mark, creating an imaginary line as it does so. Your first perception of this sheet is of a collection of black marks agreeably dispersed; but then a line is suggested moving through the marks and pulling them, rather like the beads on a string, into a two-dimensional linear organization. This effect is similar to the fascination of joining dots with lines that one experienced at a younger age with children's puzzles. The eye is always ready to be led onward, particularly when new and interesting changes of direction are suggested by the next jump. A distribution of marks thus leads the eye and the imagination a merry dance—perhaps from a starting point to a finishing point, or perhaps to no definite end at all, but just in a perpetual movement. The fact remains, however, that our eye is led over surfaces through points of emphasis and points of directional change. This is as true for the surface of a canvas as for the wall of a building. Notice both the horizontal and vertical divisions which are suggested over the wall surface of the Palazzo Farnese (Fig. 7–10). One's eye jumps along the top of the window pediments, bridging the gaps between them, and seeing horizontal "lines" which make proportionate divisions of the total wall surface. Vertically, the eye moves up the pilaster-like columns which frame the windows, again "filling in" the spaces between, until it is halted by the deep projecting cornice of the roof. Thus, the surface of a wall becomes a vertical and horizontal grid from which one might construct a Mondrian-like frame.

Now regard your own pebble-placing diagram. Find the starting point for your eye, and follow where it leads, connecting the marks with a pencil line wherever it goes. When the eye stops, you stop. Consider this the compelling and primary linear dynamic of the marks. If, afterward, you notice secondary connections between marks here and there, indicate them with a dotted line. Figure 7–8 illustrates this phase. We have a design which is basically two-dimensional, the line moving over the length and breadth of the ground. However, as our real aim in this chapter is to produce a strongly three-dimensional image, we will make a second drawing in which we can accomplish this. Take a tracing from the first drawing of the pebble position and transfer it to a new piece of paper. Take care to make the pebble marks exactly the same size as those in the

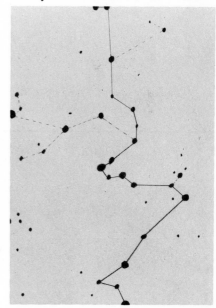

**Fig. 7–8**

original. Three different weights of line must now be used to develop the ground in depth: a frontal, heavy line; a middle distance line of intermediate weight; and a distant, delicate line. Regard the traced pebble markings and perceive which dominate by virtue of their size. Join *all* these large marks with a ruled heavy line, irrespective of their position on the paper. Now distinguish the medium sized marks which stand between the largest and the smallest. Join these with a line of intermediate weight, moving all over the ground and disregarding the lines already made. Finally, using a delicate line, connect all the smallest marks. Figure 7–7 illustrates the result which might be called a free-form space structure. Certainly, the physical form of the structure is not very significant—in fact, it is not an object which has emerged here, but a linear layout of space in depth. Planes of space have been defined in depth by allowing the difference in pebble sizes to correspond to three abitrary positions in depth—front, middle, and rear. Using the appropriate weight of line to tie together marks in common depth positions, a series of superimposed spatial planes is produced. It now takes a firm act of perception to sort these planes out, in terms both of their apparent position one above the other in depth, and of their various angular changes of direction. Originally, the uncontrived placing of pebbles produced a basically two-dimensional diagram. This has been deliberately developed into an image which is virtually a space model.

Many variations are possible on this theme. There is no need to rule the lines, and there is no need to use straight lines exclusively; a curvilinear space model of freehand lines may be more perceptually intriguing. After making a drawing following these instructions, why not do another that is somewhat freer? In this drawing, knowing what is coming, you might change pebble positions consciously, according to size (and therefore depth position), in order to achieve a greater spatial clarification in the final drawing by thinking it out in advance.

**Drawing 3**

This is probably the time to move from two-dimensional practice—from drawing on a ground in order to make a space model, to drawing in the air three-dimensionally. We shall take a line of wood strip into the air and construct a physical space model.

The most suitable wood strip to use for this work is a balsa strip of the sort normally used in making model aircraft. About four to five feet in length is required and this should be ⅜″ or ¼″ in section. Any of the appropriate cement fixatives will be satisfactory. However, before taking this line off the ground, one important stipulation has to be made: the line must move only at right angles to itself; every time it changes direction, the angle must be 90 degrees. There are two principal reasons for this stipulation. First, it simplifies the actual making of the construction, since the wood strip, being square in section, glues together easily at a right-angle joint. Second,

it will make you concentrate on proportionate lengths and three-dimensional direction. This experiment will help you see that a line moving in space creates volume or compartments of space, and that these volumes also have proportional relationships to each other and to the total construction. In addition, you should find a particular fascination in "drawing in depth" in the three-dimensional freedom of the air.

Before the line of strip wood can ascend into the air and start its wanderings, there should first be a base to support the construction, although the ingenious construction illustrated in Fig. 7–12 balances perfectly on the single point of the first vertical length of strip. Leaving the base open (unconnected to its other members) at the point from which the vertical line takes off into the air will help the viewer establish the starting point. On leaving the base at the appropriate point, the strip should ascend vertically into the air at right angles to the base. After this stage, you are very much on your own. It is your job now to move the strip constantly in changing directions, once it is safely airborne. Obviously, the strip will require constant support while the cement of the angle joints is hardening. But while this is happening at one part of the construction, the next few moves of the line may be seen in advance and can be prefabricated, ready to attach to the part that is drying. With every length of strip attached to the growing object, you will be forced

into making decisions which involve both physical and visual balance, the compartmentalization of space, and the working out of directional and angular forces. In this experiment these forces are both actual and implied. There is a thrust and counterthrust of mechanical forces as strut supports strut and unit supports unit, and there is also a more subjective, psychological awareness of the tensions formed in the structure, as lines suddenly change direction in a three-dimensional environment, creating a diversity and confusion which is nevertheless resolved by the next directional change. The fact that you can now perceive *actual* depth, as opposed to the illusionary depth of two dimensional design, should help you when drawing normally to imaginatively "grasp" physical space in the ground on which you are working.

At some point along the way, you should both think and feel that any further change of direction or prolongation of the strip would merely confuse rather than clarify the form of the construction. Stop at this point. When completing the construction, make sure the strip line emerges into the open, so it can be seen clearly in relation to the starting point on the ground.

In conclusion, Fig. 7–12 provides a good example of a conscious working out of the problem where a feeling for proportionate and related areas of three-dimensional space has been rationally developed through the

**Fig. 7–9**
Alberto Giacometti
**The Palace at 4 a.m.**
*(Collection, The Museum of Modern Art, New York)*

**Fig. 7–10**
**Façade, Palazzo Farnese, Rome** (1530–1548)
Sangallo and Michelangelo, architects
*(Photograph by Alinari)*

wood-strip line. The starting point and the end point can be clearly seen, and the continuation of the line through its many right-angled phases can be followed out in either direction to both ends. The construction has a nice asymmetrical balance, both in terms of line and volume. At the same time, as we pointed out earlier, it is also perfectly balanced physically. The thrust of line against line creates tensions in the structure of which the viewer is aware, as he is also aware of the resolution of these tensions through the equilibrium achieved by the construction. Space is obviously a crucial element here. The space compartments contained within this strip drawing are organically part of the design, and they grow out of the construction; the outside space becomes a part of the drawing by entering into the construction. This interchangeability of *contained* space with *surrounding* space is an important factor in three-dimensional design, affecting our appreciation of structural tensions in the object as well as our perception of the relativity of space to the layout of strip form and its surfaces. The illustrations of three-dimensional design (Figs. 7–3, 7–4, 7–9, 7–12) all possess an architectural quality—a physical handling of three-dimensional space. The models of York Minster Chapter House roof (Figs. 7–3, 7–4) are a contemporary architect's models of the thirteenth-century timber roof still in position at York. On one side, the common rafters are omitted for clarity; the view from below helps to show the basic structure of the model and the spatial regions it defines. Compare this view (Fig. 7–4) with the free space drawing illustrated in Fig. 7–7, and you will notice affinities in the way lines cross lines and create defined areas of space in depth. The Giacometti construction (Fig. 7–9), made of wood, glass, wire, and string, is architectural inasmuch as it alludes to rooms scaled to human dimensions. It is a constructivist theater stage set in which the wood strip says no more than is absolutely essential in defining space. The imagination fills in the rest, insofar as the idea of "palace" is concerned. The symbolic forms cunningly placed in their compartmentalized spatial environment are something else: the construction exists for them, but they themselves are more than space defining motifs. Their meaning is not clear. They intrigue one's thoughts and feelings about life in the palace, and, like all symbols, touch on deep, human experiences. André Volten's *construction* (Fig. 7–1) in galvanized steel is a highly professional example of the spatial definition which we have tried to achieve using strips of wood.

**Fig. 7–12**

**Fig. 7–11**
*(Courtesy, Professor J. Reardon, State University of New York, Buffalo)*

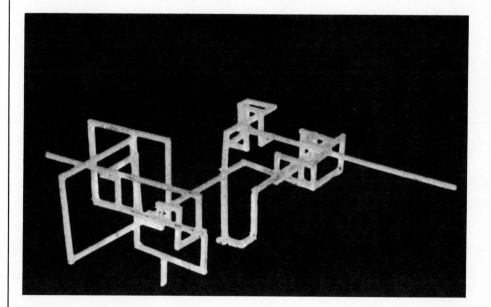

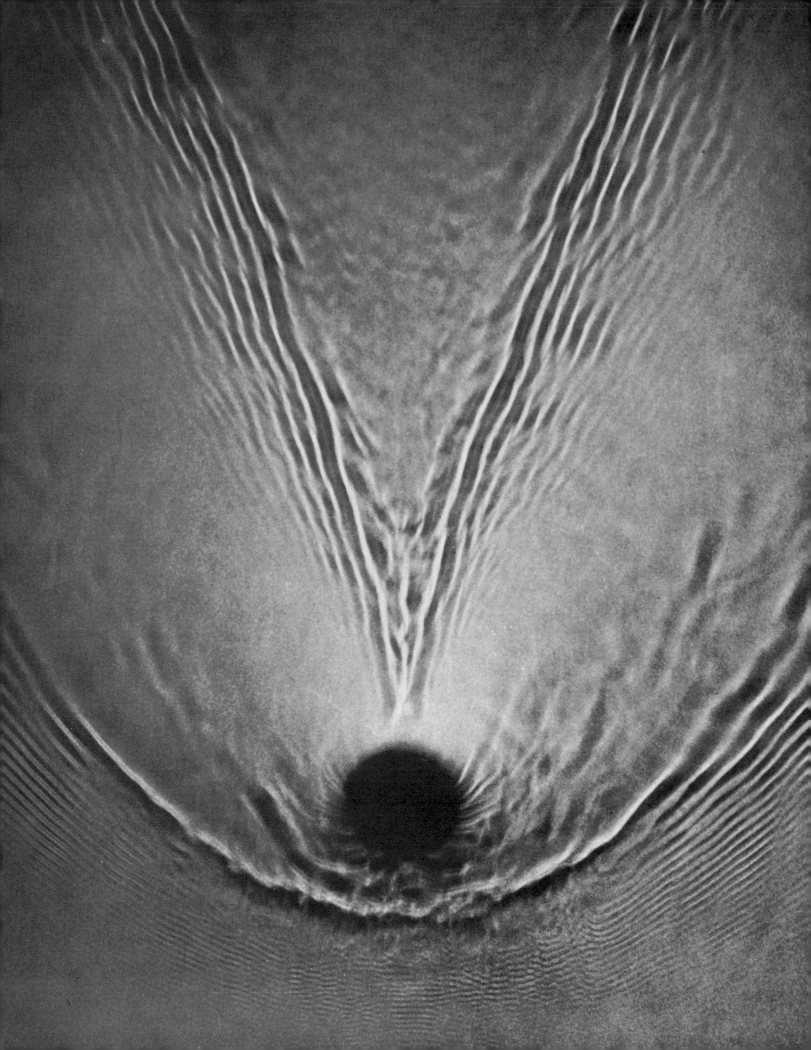

# 8

**FORM AND SPACE II**

We must now attempt to come to grips with a difficult issue—the dynamic implications of a work of art. What is it that makes a work of art alive, active, operative? In attempting to explain this phenomenon and in supporting the practical work of this chapter, I must borrow heavily from Kurt Badt's cogent exposition of Eugene Delacroix's philosophy of drawing. His interpretation of Delacroix's statements on drawing is full of insight. Badt takes Delacroix's "great law," extends its application, and widens its terms of reference. In doing so, he describes the dynamic aspect of drawing in terms which move beyond the mechanical implications of words like "forces" and "tensions." Mr. Badt writes:

Delacroix did not believe in the power of a single line, or indeed of any particular type of line, to create Beauty. He went further and denied the power of the single line in art. "One single line," he noted towards the end of his life, "is of no significance; a second one is needed to give it expression. Great law." These two latter words are surprising, and unexpected when related to such a simple remark; they are not to be found in the Journal a second time. So it is necessary to deal somewhat more explicitly with this assertion. Delacroix has indeed discovered a "great law" the value of which, even today, needs to be fully recognized.[1]

[1] Kurt Badt, *Eugène Delacroix Drawings* (Oxford: Bruno Cassirer, 1946), p. 47.

**Fig. 8–1**
**Fluid passing an obstacle**
*(Courtesy, General Electric Company)*

# Dynamic relationships: tension, equilibrium, and stasis

Mr. Badt then goes on to discuss two different types of line found in drawing. The reader will recognize some of the characteristics and functions of line which we described initially in Chapter 1, and subsequently in Chapter 5 when discussing space and mass volume.

...One can draw a line in such a way that the eye is induced to follow its direction, the rhythm of its curves, and the elegance and beauty of its movements. Such a line has the character and value of a *pattern*, but, in itself, has "no significance." ... On the other hand one can draw lines—not just a single one; two are almost necessarily required for this purpose— related to one another, in such a way that the eye has to interpret them as the bounds of a corporeal, a plastic form situated within them. To put this another way; these coupled strokes are drawn in such a manner that the eye is prevented from following them lengthwise, but must apprehend them in a direction independent of their own. It must proceed beyond the flat sheet of paper on which they lie, and to which they are tied down, in three dimensional space. In this case, the lines have a "significance" beyond the charm of their own lead and their descriptive capacity; they signify a spatial extension, and are at the same time expressive, demonstrating by means of their forms the inner tension, the lively vigour of the body which they make apparent.[2]

The significant phrases here are "spatial extension," "inner tension," and "lively vigour." The first of these is the most specific and we shall see later some of the various ways in which spatial extension occurs. We can take it to refer to drawing which captures the mass of an object three-dimensionally, rather than just its length and breadth. On the other hand, the terms inner tension and lively vigor go together, for they connote the potential capacity for movement or life which is present in art forms by virtue of their plastic nature. In other words, they refer to the *plastic life of form*, which is realized through the artist's capacity to bring form into being; to shape it, modify it, endow it with vitality, or give it order and repose. We must suggest, therefore, that by virtue of this plasticity, art forms possess their own dynamic life *within the plastic characteristics of the medium used*. Hence, in drawing, the lines themselves are potentially "alive" because their graphic plasticity enables them to realize three-dimensional form and space. But let us go on with Kurt Badt for a moment:

Delacroix's "great law," however, covers only half the facts. It leaves out of account the capability of ornamental lines which—singly—have their

---

2 *Ibid*, p. 48.

**Fig. 8–2**
**Choir Vault, Amiens, Cathedral,**
**France** (1247)
*(Photograph by Clarence Ward)*

**Fig. 8–3**
Victor Pasmore
**Linear Motif** (1961)
*(Courtesy of the artist)*

Fig. 8–4
Eugène Delacroix
**Lion and Tiger Fighting**
*(Albertina Sammlung, Vienna)*

Fig. 8–5
**Chart of furniture forms**
*Designer, George Nelson; Irving Harper
Associates, New York, 1949
(Photograph, The Museum of Modern Art,
New York)*

DYNAMIC RELATIONSHIPS: TENSION,
EQUILIBRIUM, AND STASIS

**FORM AND SPACE II**

own power of expression. Delacroix was unable to do justice to the value of these lines because they play no part in expressing *active* life. On the contrary, they are opposed to it, tending to *restrict* the richness, vigour and abundance of living forms. Ornamental line has no "significance" for him, because it achieves exactly what his own art never aspired to: it stills life, reduces its fullness and curbs its vigour. But an impartial observer is forced to admit that ornamental drawing also has highly significant possibilities.[3]

Badt then modifies Delacroix's "great law" into a statement that includes the single, passive line. He also makes another very important point. The plastic nature of art, in its many varieties, is used by the artist to make an image that "commands the *life* of the objects which drawings represent." Hence drawing does not imitate nature but imposes its own life upon her as directed by the attitude of the artist. He proceeds as follows:

In art drawing—which has been called a wizardry—two types of magic wand are used, both of which command the *life* of the objects which drawings represent. By means of the first—the ornamental line—an artist dominates life, by soothing and purifying it and setting it in an emphasized order.... By means of the second—and plastic line—an artist dominates life by extolling its power, expressing its vigour, and implying its volume and richness.... Between these two alternatives the art of drawing swings. There is no third, unless, indeed, one be arrived at by the synthesis of the former two. Such synthesis, uniting calm and purity with power, vigour and the richness and volume of Life has been rarely achieved, and by very few masters.[4]

Let me sum up this discussion as it now stands. Drawing is essentially plastic. Several expressive lines acting in concert produce vitality, tension, movement, and three-dimensional power in the image. The single ornamental line (of beauty) produces a more two-dimensional, passive, ordered calm in the image. The use of one means or the other is dependent upon the artist's own attitude—how he experiences life for himself and how he sees the life of the world around him. So when we talk about the dynamic aspects of a work of art—particularly a drawing—we are referring to the way in which the artist commands the life of the forms he creates. These forms may represent objects found in the world, or they may be the personal creations of the artist. From this thought one is automatically brought to wonder at the pre-

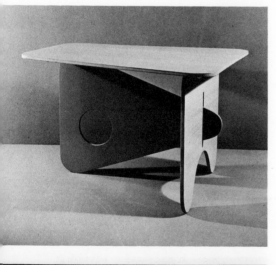

**Fig. 8–6**
**Butterfly table**
Designer, Dan Cooper;
Drexel Furniture Company, 1942
*(Photograph, The Museum of Modern Art, New York)*

---

[3] *Ibid.*          [4] *Ibid*, p. 51.

sumptuousness of man, who would "command life," even if only in a drawing; and this leads one to the question—what is the spiritual significance of an art which is based on man's subjective attitude to material phenomena. For peace and order constitute one reality; tension, vigor, and dynamic action, another. Both types of image signify an act of the human apprehending intelligence, and both reveal a possible truth concerning the forces underlying life. But this is not a question I should try to answer here, although I feel it should be mentioned in any discussion of the dynamic aspects of art. Delacroix was very concerned with *how* the artist's lines are related to the objects they represent. To quote Kurt Badt:

> He [Delacroix] knew, from his inner experience, that these were linked together in the mind of the creative artist because, and in as much as, both participate in the ultimate fact of Life.[5]

The contrast between the single passive or ornamental line and the dynamic activity of several expressive related lines is shown in Figs. 8–3, 8–4, 8–8, and 8–9. It is interesting to compare the abstract drawing by Victor Pasmore (Fig. 8–3) with Delacroix's *Lion and Tiger Fighting* (Fig. 8–4), for both men use short, broken lines in the same dynamic way. The subject matter appears but incidental for Delacroix—one is hard put to find the tiger. The lines express volume and movement; they act in concert, thrusting against each other, enlivening space; the power of the drawing lies in its physical and emotional tensions. The case is similar with the Pasmore, but there are no lions or tigers here—yet the dynamic aspects of the drawing echo the Delacroix for space is disturbed by the movement of energized hair lines, moving, twisting, turning against each other. The forms created by Pasmore's lines are dynamic in themselves as they expand and contract and push against one other. Surely, in five minute's time the whole layout will have completely changed.

The stillness of the drawing in Ben Nicholson's painting *Still Life, 1947, Odyssey* (Fig. 8–9), is in direct contrast. Nicholson uses a pure line. (I'm not sure that "ornamental" is the right word to use.) Each line, continuous and unbroken, plays its part singly. It shapes both space and form into specific, clearly delineated elements which are stilled and almost frozen. The line gives a sharp contour to form and

---

[5] *Ibid*, p. 52.

**Fig. 8–7**

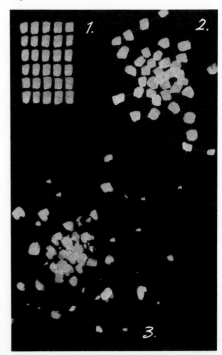

space, an edge, which denies the power of volume—this is an impossible statement to make for either the Delacroix or the Pasmore. Nicholson soothes space and motion, and controls, if not eliminates, tensions. Similarly, Matisse, in his etching *Loulou in a Flowered Hat* (Fig. 8–8), shows an equal purity as well as a great economy of line. Each line flows easily over the ground, creating still, shallow pools of space. The nervous vitality which is present in the line provides a ripple across the surface which cannot be dynamically compared to the short, stabbing marks of Delacroix. Matisse's drawing is relaxed and misleadingly simple in its placing of a few beautiful lines which are so sure, so right. The line of the chin completes the oval movement started by the brim line of the hat; the neck line, a reinforcing ripple of a line, echos this counter movement of the chin. The line for the top of the hat makes an arc which completes the whole circular movement. The flowers alone break the rhythm, and in doing so emphasize the oval form of the whole design. Matisse commands an ordered tranquility in the plastic life of his forms and space. His drawing is not hard-edged and frozen like the Nicholson;

**Fig. 8–8**
Henri Matisse
**Loulou in a Flowered Hat** (Etching)
*(Collection, The Museum of Modern Art, New York)*

**Fig. 8–9**
Ben Nicholson, **Still Life, 1947. Odyssey** *(Collection, The British Council, London)*

it is not static but gently vibrant, a drawing of equilibrium rather than of stasis, but hardly an image of tension.

Before going on, we had better define our terms. I use the term *dynamic relationships* to suggest:

**1.**
That the spatial extension of a single form creates a stress between form and space (greater or lesser), and that this stress involves a time factor as a surface travels from here to there.

**2.**
That when several forms are present in a region this stress is aggravated. In addition, the forms develop stress relationships between themselves as they impinge on each other and thus crowd the space field (Fig. 8–12).

When these various stress relationships are forceful, multi-directioned, in restless opposition, and unresolved, the word *tension* will apply. (See Figs. 8–4 and 8–3.) Such a situation represents impermanence and instability. I use the word *equilibrium* to apply to a forceful and active situation in which a balance of power is achieved, when such a resolution represents permanence and stability. Architecture obviously supplies fine examples of equilibrium, physically realized. Look at Fig. 8–2, the Gothic choir vault of Amiens Cathedral. The mass of the vault is supported by the stone ribs which make a downward thrust to fixed points. These fixed points are met by the counterthrust of the vertical, up-pushing piers; and to complete the stability (although it cannot be seen in this photograph), a flying arch is thrusting in to the same point from an exterior free-standing buttress. This "linear" thrust and counterthrust through space effectively stabilize the forms of mass and volume, creating an equilibrium as visible as it is actual. The equilibrium achieved in Matisse's drawing (Fig. 8–8) is less tangible. The fluid nature of this drawing, which renders it less permanent, also

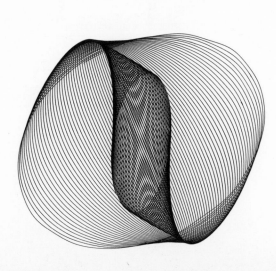

Fig. 8–10
**Mechanical figure expressing the dynamic, plastic extension of the surface of form in space using the continuously moving line.**
*(Sheldon Zola)*

Fig. 8–11
Jecabs Zvilna
**Time and Motion Study**
*(Courtesy, George Braziller, New York)*

DYNAMIC RELATIONSHIPS: TENSION, EQUILIBRIUM, AND STASIS

**FORM AND SPACE II**

ensures its vitality because one is aware that the balanced spaces and lines may not cancel each other out indefinitely. Finally, the word *stasis* implies complete stillness, the absolutely static, in which the dynamic potential for spatial extension and for positional change is completely removed. Form and space become fused into a crystallized homogeneity that can never be broken. Figure 8–9 is, in my opinion, such an image. Compare it with the balanced yet vibrant equilibrium of Matisse (Fig. 8–8). In Matisse, line counters line and space balances space in a living encounter. Everything is stilled forever in the Nicholson.

We can now see that the life of form in drawing is revealed in two ways. First, in the way the artist uses a long, pure line to shape his forms —to contain them within a strong contour or edge and so "flatten" and pacify them; or to use several vigorous lines, grasping the forms by their centers and working outward, leaving their apparent edges broken, thereby suggesting a volumetric vigor. Second, in the way he allows lines or marks to pacify or activate space. In this chapter, therefore, we are developing another aspect of our previous work in form-space perception—namely, an introduction to the basic types of dynamic relationships which we perceive in nature and in art. We have already had some experience with linear dynamics in the first graphic exercises with passive and active lines; we have also had experience with the dynamics of form with skeletal and mass structures, and with spatial dynamics by using spatial intervals in the brush-point drawings and pebble connecting experiments.

**Fig. 8–12**
Jean (Hans) Arp
**Objects Arranged According to the Law of Chance or Navels,** Varnished wood relief (1930)
*(Collection, The Museum of Modern Art, New York)*

DYNAMIC RELATIONSHIPS: TENSION, EQUILIBRIUM, AND STASIS

**FORM AND SPACE II**

**THE DRAWINGS** This is a long chapter and calls for many drawings. I suggest that you first make the drawings which interest you most, returning later to complete the work when you reach the end of Part I.

**Drawing Group 1**

In these first drawings we shall concentrate on the *spatial* aspects of dynamic relationships. Figure 8–7 is a diagram illustrating how three differing spatial arrangements produce varying dynamic implications in the image. In the first arrangement, the regular and tight grouping of marks and the even distribution of space allow for little suggestion of movement. But the marks are grouped irregularly in the second arrangement, and the space is unevenly distributed. You will notice that a tension is developed where the marks cluster and that the dynamic relationship between all the marks is strong and unresolved. It is a fluid situation. This tension is even more apparent in the third arrangement. Here, there is considerable spatial contrast between the central, clustering nucleus marks, and the outer dispersed marks. As a result, the movement suggests a powerful and disintegrating force at work. Three conclusions emerge:

1.

When space is evenly distributed in a regular arrangement of marks (forms), the dynamic relationships tend toward equilibrium or stasis: there is little movement.

2.

When space is unevenly distributed and marks cluster, causing space in one region to become compressed, the

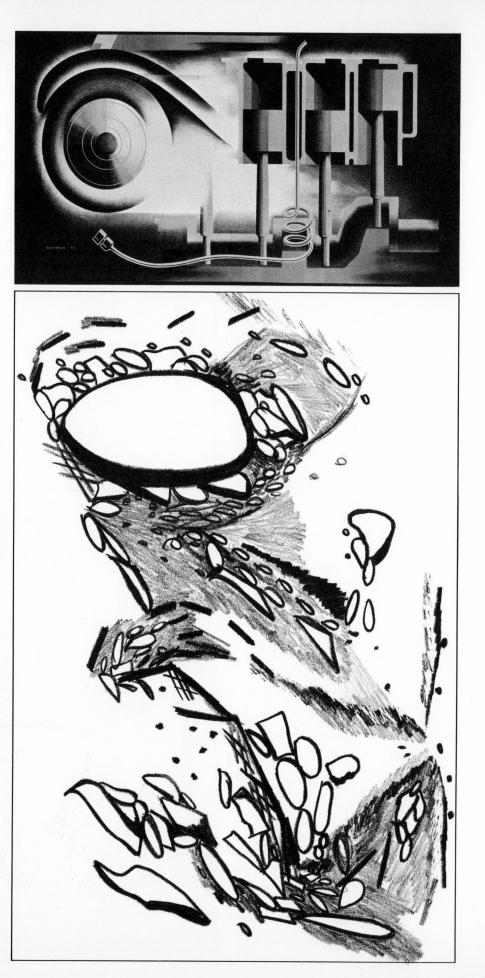

Fig. 8–15
( *top* )
**Detail from a poster for Shell Oil Company,**
England, 1935
*Designer, J. S. Anderson*
*(Collection, The Museum of Modern Art,*
*New York; courtesy Shell International*
*Petroleum Ltd.)*

100                        Fig. 8–16

dynamic relationships move toward tension: there are strong suggestions of movement.

3.

The more generally diffuse the space between marks becomes, the weaker become any dynamic relationships; each mark exists independently. Using large dots, make a number of experimental arrangements trying for specific dynamic relationships—for strong tensions, for a rigid stasis, or for a vital equilibrium. Achieve this entirely by spatial distribution. It may help to consider that you are making diagrams of movement and flux; think of people moving into a football stadium or into a subway via one narrow entrance; or of a rioting crowd struggling with police attempting to contain them. Let each dot represent one person's position.

**Drawing Group 2**

These drawings are to deal with two specific aspects of the life of forms in space. First, we shall find certain basic shapes which give suggestions of the spatial extension of form. Second, we shall see how lines possessing different characteristics of movement travel differently through space from point to point. To see some basic form-extending shapes, look at Fig. 8–14, Ben Nicholson's *Still Life*. Here you will see forms which thrust like growing points and swelling, curvilinear forms which bulge into space. The point-to-point movement of line through space is shown in Victor Pasmore's *Linear Motif* (Fig. 8–13). Here it is the path of a movement which is traced; the artist is not making forms, although these are created indirectly.

Vertical movement meets horizontal movement while curved movement counters both. Notice how the heavy black line produces a frontal horizontal movement, thus creating a depth field in which the actions of the drawing happen. The curvilinear lines suggest spiral movements or stylized ripples, activated from some central point.

Figure 8–5 shows a chart of furniture forms. The designer is concerned with the spatial extension of form through the thrusting points at the extremities, through extruding or intruding angles, and through swelling, curved surfaces. The forms possess a great deal of movement. Consequently, the dynamic implications are strong. When forms of this nature are placed together, as in the table illustrated in Fig. 8–6, the dynamic-extension characteristics of each shape are used to produce both a visual and a practical equilibrium. It is thrust and counterthrust all over again, as vertical, horizontal, and diagonal movements are integrated into a dynamic unity. Figure 8–17 shows a few diagrammatic examples of characteristic extensions of form into space, together with some dynamic types of line. The basic linear movements which are illustrated here are those of direct vertical and horizontal lines which produce a stability when operating together. (This stability results from the fact that the strong gravitational pull in the vertical line is canceled out by the sustaining flatness of the horizontal line.) Then we have converging lines which ultimately come together to form an arrowhead thrust through space. These are followed by lines of coiled movement, by lines of swell, and by lines of vibration. Simple linear statements of this sort reveal the energy contained within the line, for, as was shown by the pebble connecting experiment of Chapter 7 (Fig. 7–8), a line may be seen as a number of dots which thread themselves together. Thus, from starting point to finishing point, the energy moves along the line, and at any point a dot possesses position and direction relative to any other dot. We have already suggested that the movement of a line activates the space around it (Figs. 8–3 and 8–4), and that speed is implied by the time-space factor—that is, the time it takes for the eye to traverse its length. We are also familiar with the expressive qualities of line as they relate to the emotions, and with their ability to mark differing regions of depth depending upon their weight, quality, and tone value. All these factors must be borne in mind when drawing.

Fig. 8–17

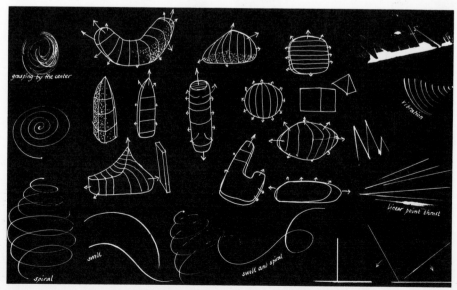

Observe the lines of movement in Figs. 8–11 and 8–1. The first of these is a Time and Motion study, in which the vortex-like spiraling lines indicate the movement of oil in motion affected by gravity. The second photograph shows the directional movement lines created by fluid passing an obstacle. A study of these two images will help you considerably in the work that follows.

Now observe Figs. 8–19 and 8–20. Ernest Mundt's *Dance 1* is a stationary wire which one reads as a line moving between two points in space; one also perceives the volume defined by the wire. But, when this form is revolving, as in *Dance 2*, we perceive line and volume simultaneously, not separately. Because this effect is a characteristic of rapidly moving objects, in a drawing any loss of the firm outline of a form will suggest movement. And of all dynamic movements, a line which revolves around a fixed center is most volumetric, for it defines space multi-dimensionally. The problem is, how would you draw *Dance 2* to best reveal the speed and nature of

its movement? A careful analysis of both images will relate the stationary form to the moving one, and could result in a careful diagrammatic presentation of the movement. Or, you may "feel" the movement and spontaneously transfer it by means of a line (or lines) to the paper. In either case you have the choice of all kinds of line. There is the single line, long and evenly flowing; or the shorter, more expressive, space disturbing lines which act in concert to reveal volume and power. There is no reason why they should not be used together. Figure 8–11 shows such a combination. Make as many drawings as you like of *Dance 2* until you think all the possibilities have been exhausted.

Because it involves the dynamic aspects of form's extension into space, as well as the point-to-point movement of a line through space, the next problem demands a more comprehensive treatment than did any of the foregoing. I hesitate to make abstract propositions concerning which a student may have had no personal experience, and so would

suggest that a visit to a river or a beach would be worthwhile before making a final drawing here. Nature provides the most obvious and tangible visual experiences of dynamic relationships, for there things grow, and the elements are powerful forces which erode and move objects. Figure 8–21 is a photograph of a beach in which the spatial disposition of objects bears witness to the force of the tide. The objects themselves extend three-dimensionally into space, angled or curvilinear, thin of surface or massive. Lines of tidal force can be determined over the beach by studying the stones, the logs, the density of the sand and the slope of the surface. A drawing of this beach should take these dynamic relationships into account, in which case it might ultimately be as abstract as Fig. 8–13. Consider a bird's-eye view of a rock-strewn river bed when only a shallow and comparatively weak flow of water is running. Large pebbles, small pebbles, big rocks, all either sharp, angled and pointed, or swelling and smooth, lie on the river bed. The way they lie has been determined by

**Fig. 8–18**

Fig. 8–19
(right)
Ernest Mundt
**Dance 2**
(Courtesy of
the artist)

Fig. 8–20
(far right)
Ernest Mundt
**Dance 1**
(Courtesy of
the artist.
Associated
Press News
Photograph)

the water flowing over them; their spatial distribution is indicative of their mass and of the water's force. For example, a large and heavy stone will resist the water, but the lighter pebbles will be moved until they come up against a large rock where they will then cluster. Look back to Fig. 8–7 where marks cluster together and compress space, thus suggesting a lively force and movement. The spatial intervals between stones will tend to correspond to their respective weights—the larger the interval, the heavier the rock and vice versa. Also, when the water flow is strong, the smaller pebbles will be swept together until they come up against a large rock where they will conglomerate and form a barrier. This barrier will occasion a new direction of water flow, which in turn will create a new movement of pebbles. The result is a constantly changing pattern, with each barrier producing a change in movement and each change in movement creating new barriers.

You have two things to consider:

the plastic form of the rocks—that is, how they extend into space as mass, through pointed extremities or swelling surface; and their spatial distribution, which will signify both their weight and the strength of the force affecting them. Lines of force may well intrude to heighten the indication of water movement. A study of Fig. 8–1 will show some of the tensions and thrust lines in such a situation. Make a drawing of a river bed or of a rocky tidal beach using any drawing medium you like. Figures 8–16 and 8–22 are river bed drawings which only partly succeed because all the emphasis is given to spatial distribution—to the movement factor—and not enough concern is shown for the three-dimensional extension of the rocks themselves. They appear flat, and their volumetric occupation of space is indicated by neither point thrust nor angled or swelling surface. Refer back to Fig. 8–17 for guidance on this point. In a comparison of the two river bed drawings, Fig. 8–16 suggests a sudden and violent movement of the water which produces an unstable

Fig. 8–21

**Fig. 8–25**

**Fig. 8–26**

**Fig. 8–27**
John Piper, **Bullslaughter Bay** *(Courtesy of the artist)*

DYNAMIC RELATIONSHIPS: TENSION,
EQUILIBRIUM, AND STASIS

**FORM AND SPACE II**

bombard the form. By definition, this will be a drawing of stasis, for neither force nor object can win. See Fig. 8–18 in which vertical linear forms strike at a solid horizontal mass. No types of linear force movement per se (spiraling, etc.) are introduced, but the drawing might have been more effective if they had been. A similar sense of stasis is given by Ernest Mundt's sculpture (Fig. 8–24). The two interlocking forms are interchangeable as either force or object, linear thrust or immovable mass.

3. In this purely linear experiment; take a series of fixed points in space and align an intensive series of point thrusts to each. The result suggests concentrations of energy and forceful point-to-point movements through space. It also introduces time as a dynamic factor, for a line moving to a point in space becomes minutes or days long. Figure 8–23 is a drawing of this sort which would be improved by greater variation in line weight and quality.

4. Finally, experiment generally with thrusting lines and points, and spiraling, rippling, and swelling lines; invent some dynamic situations of tension, equilibrium, or stasis. Could you show in a drawing the mechanical forces at work in the internal combustion engine as ignited gas pushes the piston down? (See Fig. 8–15.) Think of the movement involved—cylinder, piston, connecting rod, crankshaft, and all. What are the lines of movement? The crankshaft is revolving, the piston is going up and down, and the gas explosion is thrusting vertically downward. This is only one suggestion, and Figs. 8–28

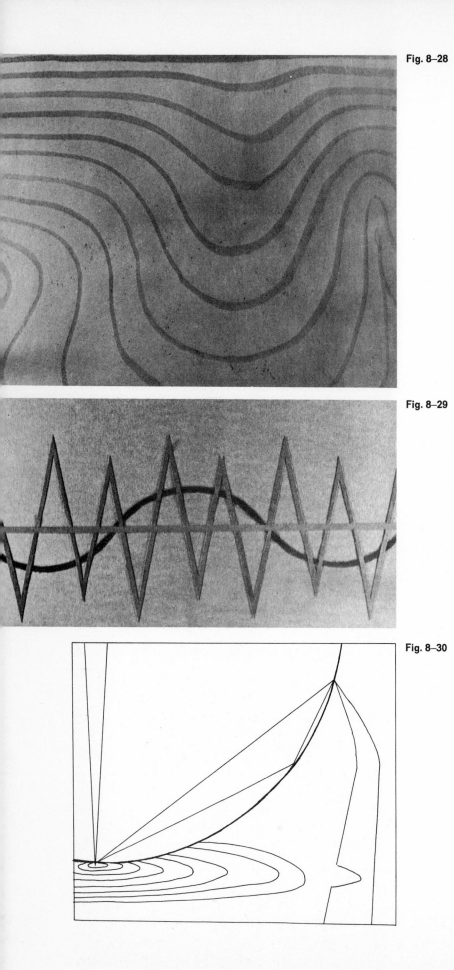

**Fig. 8–28**

**Fig. 8–29**

**Fig. 8–30**

to 8–30 show other ideas. In Fig. 8–30 three point thrusts are balanced; but the vertical thrust creates a ripple movement which is eating through the stabilizing point thrust on the right. How long will this situation last? Again the time factor enters into a drawing of this sort. In Fig. 8–28, the ripple thrusts of water advancing over the sand as the tide comes in show the final disintegration of the wave as the horizontal line bends to give that last shallow ebb and flow. Figure 8–29 shows the contrast in energy and movement between straight, swelling, and point thrust lines, when they are juxtaposed in this way.

5. If you do not find your powers of invention very satisfactory, then turn back to Figs. 8–21 and 8–31 for a visual point of departure. Take the beach scene or the piled rocks and translate these photographs into drawings which intensify the dynamic relationships between space and object as well as between objects themselves. In doing this you can concentrate on realizing the dynamic nature of the objects—the swelling, angular, or pointed surfaces of their mass, and how they impinge on each other; or you can make a drawing of movement by using lines of direction and force only, in order to signify the potential movement of the objects in space. Figure 8–27, *Bullslaughter Bay* by John Piper, is a strong drawing of the dynamic relationships between rock forms. As the forms extend through point and swell, and as lines of movement thrust through space, tensions are created between form and

DYNAMIC RELATIONSHIPS: TENSION, EQUILIBRIUM, AND STASIS

**FORM AND SPACE II**

space and between impinging forms. Try to find a quarry or an outcrop of rocks on a hillside which will inspire you to make a powerful drawing.

It should be pointed out that in making these drawings, one can use all kinds of line and combinations of line, from short expressive lines acting in concert to realize mass, to the single pure line of directional momentum.

**CONCLUSIONS** Rather than write a lengthy summary, I think it would be more valuable to recapitulate the ideas expressed in this chapter visually by a series of reinforcing illustrations. We need to confirm:

1.

That the dynamic life of forms is plastically realized through their spatial extension.

2.

That different types of point to point line indicate the movement tendencies of objects and the nature of the forces which affect their position.

3.

That spatial intervals between forms (marks or surfaces) are related to both 1 and 2 above and also to the action of forces on forms in space.

These three factors comprise the essence of composition in art and design. Study the illustrations which follow, together with their captions. They are chosen specifically to help you understand these three conclusions.

**Fig. 8–31**

In this great design, the speeding movement
of God in the void is, for a fraction of
time, held suspended, as the point thrust of
his outstretched arm and extended
forefinger meets the limper movement of
Adam. An intense electrical energy seems
to jump the gap between their fingers.
The slow spiraling movement of Adam
contrasts strongly with the thrusting
extension of the figure of God, but for a
moment an intense yet delicate equilibrium
is achieved between heaven and earth.

Fig. 8–32
Laszlo Moholy-Nagy
Nickel Construction (1921)
(Collection, The Museum of Modern Art,
New York. Gift of Mrs. Sibyl Moholy-Nagy)
The lightweight spiraling strip is in strong
contrast to the ponderous base and the
vertical piece of heavy angle iron. Quite
suddenly, one becomes aware of the
incredible distance between the front of
the base and the top of the vertical piece.
The strip could spiral its way for miles
or weeks before reaching its destination,
had the artist so desired. Also, catch
the sense of speed involved. The thin
flatness of the ceiling strip seems to move
quickly through space, like an electric
charge or a sound vibration. The spiraling
motion and the delicacy of the strip
make a vital contrast to the static resolution
of the heavy vertical and horizontal forms.

DYNAMIC RELATIONSHIPS: TENSION,
EQUILIBRIUM, AND STASIS

FORM AND SPACE II

**Fig. 8–34**
Victor Pasmore
**Abstract in Black, White, Brown, and Olive**
(1960)
(Victor Pasmore)
*The breakaway of the central form from the mass on the right has caused its tilting movement to the left, where it is exerting considerable force. This tension is produced by the contrast between the spatial intervals on left and right and the swelling spatial extension of the pushing end of the central form. The right-hand space is obviously going to widen while those on the left diminish.*

**Fig. 8–35**
Leonardo da Vinci
**A Deluge** (Pen and ink wash over
black chalk)
*(Royal Collection, Windsor Castle)*
*Observe how the spatial interval between
swirling water and whirling trees heightens
the sense of time in this drawing. Spiral
lines denote the wind coming from the
clouds and pushing the heaving, swelling
water before it. The trees are set in motion
by drawing them with small vibratory lines.
Leonardo does not make much use of the
angular thrusting line—the point thrust. He
was fascinated by spirals and radial
swelling forms.*

DYNAMIC RELATIONSHIPS: TENSION,
EQUILIBRIUM, AND STASIS

**FORM AND SPACE II**

**Fig. 8–36**
Leonardo da Vinci
**A Storm of Water and Rocks**
(Bistre over black chalk)
*(Royal Collection, Windsor Castle)*
*Leonardo's preoccupation with the force and movement of water is well known. Here, the force of its spiraling movement and thrust overcomes the static inertia of the rocks, bends them outward, and sends them crashing to the ground. Surely few drawings have ever shown tensions leading to complete disintegration more forcefully.*

**Fig. 8–37**
Victor Pasmore
**Abstract in Black and White** (1960)
*(Victor Pasmore)*
*All three of our conclusions are illustrated by this drawing. Lines of movement stand in a precarious relationship to the swelling forms—vertical and horizontal movements stabilize each other—and spatial interval plays an important part in determining where the main confrontations of force and mass are soon to take place. This drawing should be compared with the Michelangelo (Fig. 8–33), for it is almost an abstract rendering of the dynamic relationships in Michelangelo's design.*

**Fig. 8–38**
John Piper
**Cuckmere Haven and Seven Sisters**
(John Piper)
Notice how compulsively the cliff line
directs your eye through space, and how
it connects a series of dots (which remind
one of bass notes in a line of music).
The movements of the sea against the
beach and the wind against the cliff are
indicated by spiraling lines. The heavy
diagonal line at the cliff base acts as a
barrier to the waves and as a direction
pointer to the distant cliff line. Points and
lines create many changes of direction and a
powerful sense of movement through space.

**Fig. 8–39**
**Stairway, Offices in London** (1958)
Erno Goldfinger, architect
(The Architectural Review, London)
An example of the spiral movement through
space in architecture. The supporting
forces originate at the center and radiate
through 360°.

**Fig. 8–40**
Reg Butler
**Brush Drawings Series 1 and 2** (1963)
*(Hanover Gallery, London;
Photographs, Brompton Studios)
These drawings show stages in the spatial
extension of form. From the first point
thrust extension of a circular shape (top
left) through the developing variations,
the artist is constantly extruding and
intruding his form. You can see how
important both directional lines and basic
thrusting or swelling shapes are
for his purpose.*

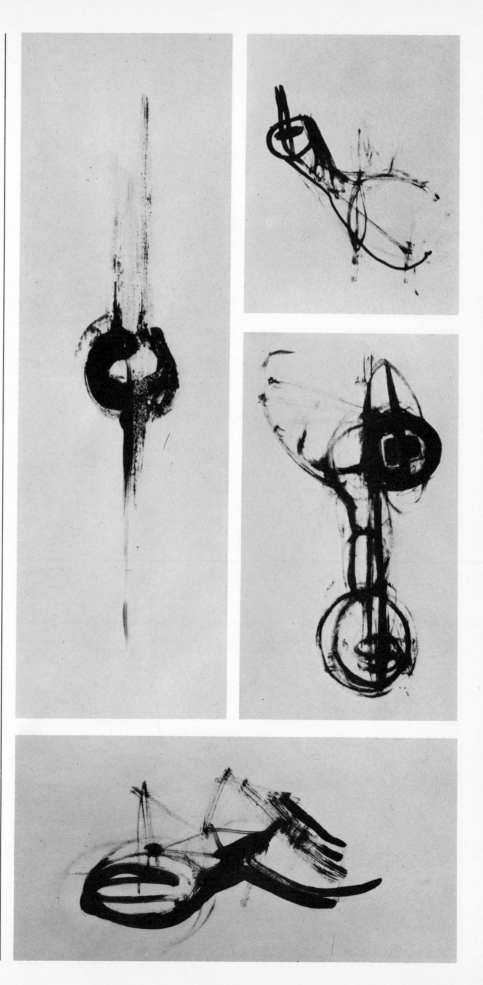

DYNAMIC RELATIONSHIPS: TENSION,
EQUILIBRIUM, AND STASIS

**FORM AND SPACE II**

**Fig. 8–41**
Reg Butler
**Brush Drawing Series 1** (1963)
*(Hanover Gallery, London;
Photograph, Brompton Studios)
This powerful line of movement, suggesting
speed and velocity, may be seen either as
a movement into a target or as a movement
projected out from the form. The dynamic
nature of the lines is self-evident.*

DYNAMIC RELATIONSHIPS: TENSION,
EQUILIBRIUM, AND STASIS

**FORM AND SPACE II**

**Fig. 8–42**
**Geometric figure showing
spatial exploration**
*The heavy black line follows a
two-dimensional path from left to right,
and its serpentine movement shows a
regular oscillation between high and low
points of the curve. Note that when the
second oscillating line is constructed it
appears behind the first, primarily because
of its lighter weight. But as the various
constructional lines project between the two
oscillations, producing hyperbolic and
parabolic arcings through space, a deep
three-dimensional field is created. The lines
converging on the confluence of the
oscillations describe a space-time situation
in which great distances appear to be
involved, for there is no point in space
where the line stops. It flows into a new
oscillating movement and is flung out again
into a multi-dimensional space field. There
is a suggestion of perpetual motion in the
diagram, but I have chosen to use it here
principally to illustrate how a mathematical
construction of this nature creates a spatial
figure from a line moving originally
in only two dimensions.*

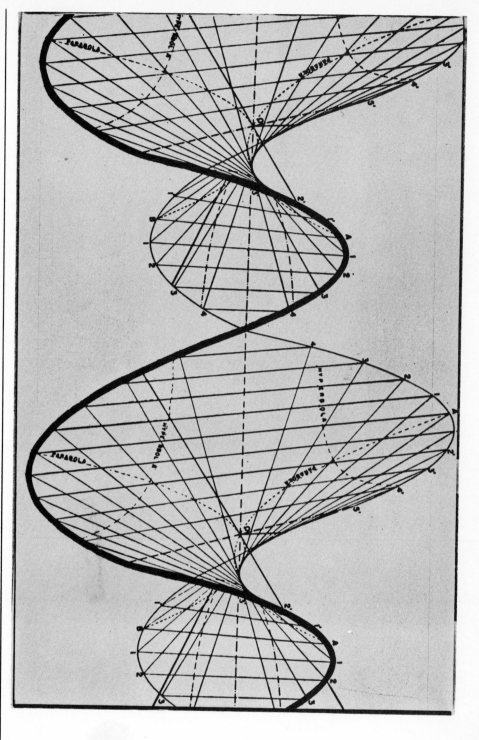

117

**Fig. 8–43**
Joan Miro
**Person Throwing a Stone at a Bird** (1926)
*(Collection, The Museum of Modern Art, New York. Purchase)*
*There is no need to say much about this delightful painting, save to draw your attention to the use Miro makes of lines of direction and force. The stone is flung at the bird and assumes a certain trajectory. The bird takes evasive action as indicated. A prolonged study will perhaps reveal the symbolic implications of man, bird, and moon in this dream-like contest.*

**Fig. 8–44**
Giacomo Balla
**Speeding Automobile** (1912)
(Collection, The Museum of Modern Art,
New York. Purchase)
Speed and movement are essential
elements in Futurist painting. With the aid
of light projection from the speeding car,
the concrete world of form and space loses
its solidarity, and the spatial intervals
between forms become inextricably mixed
with the fragmented pieces of forms
themselves. Perception diminishes as speed
increases. All this is accomplished by the
speeding lines of movement which
disappear into an infinity of space. When
the lines are thin and sharp they seem to
accelerate; when they become black and
heavy or ill-defined, their pace slows. The
arc formed by the headlights creates a
vortex which pulls one into the painting
before expelling one into distant space.

119

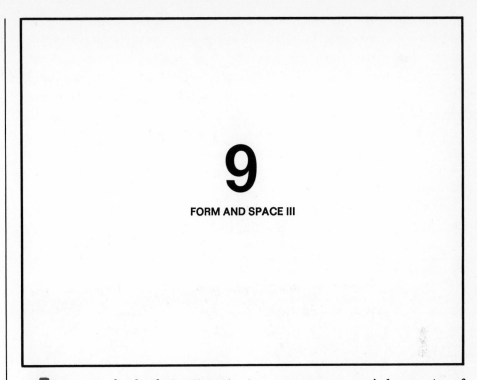

**9**

**FORM AND SPACE III**

Any one book that attempts to cover many varied aspects of drawing and design can avoid neither unfortunate generalization nor the superficial treatment of some complex issues. This, I feel, is particularly true of the preceding chapter, for if there is one particular experience of the world which has caught man's imagination and inspired vital drawings and paintings, it is that of landscape. We touched on this subject in Chapter 8, but inadequately, considering the subject's importance. Therefore, this chapter is an attempt to compensate; it is a follow-up to Chapter 8, a consolidation of the dynamic issues there expounded.

The life of nature is exposed on a grand scale in the spacious world of landscape. There is continual change, and nowhere else is the immensity of space so completely experienced.[1] The dynamic relationships between space and form are more positively and inescapably asserted in landscape than elsewhere. The growing point of a tree thrusts against the sky; the bud slowly opens and the leaves spread

[1] See Space I (Chapter 2) and Bernard Berenson's remarks about the space composition of Perugino.

Fig. 9–1

# Dynamic relationships in landscape

themselves in the air; the wind blows, the clouds scud along, the sea advances and retreats, the rivers flow; gravity attracts objects to the earth; sun, wind, frost, and rain erode and weather the forms of both nature and man. Yet nature's dynamic forces maintain a basic equilibrium among themselves. The tree may bend to the gale, but the roots will hold fast. The boulder will run down the hillside but it will stop in the valley. And as one tree dies, a sapling is pushing out its growing points in branches and roots. When the forces are not balanced, as in drought, earthquake, or tempest, then the equilibrium is lost and the result is disintegration.

Man reacts in differing ways to this pulse of nature. Some see a universe of space in which objects, including man, are delicately dis-

Fig. 9–2
Samuel Palmer
**Valley with a Bright Cloud**
*(By courtesy of the Ashmolean Museum, Oxford)*

Fig. 9–3
Gherardo Starnina
**The Thebaid**
*(Uffizi Gallery, Florence)*

persed like some tiny points in the Newtonian web of the cosmos. In these images, space dominates form, as you see in Francesco Guardi's wash drawing, Fig. 9–4. Some artists develop massive, burgeoning forms that dominate and press against space, thus reducing it to a secondary role as in Samuel Palmer's ink drawing, Fig. 9–2. Others treat space as the battlefield for the elements, and bring it into sharp collision with swaying forms, producing a strong tension in the drawing—see Constable's brush drawing, Fig. 9–5. Yet another way is to see space and form in a more balanced relationship, in which space is almost solidly stated as space-volume. In the painting *The Thebaid* (Fig. 9–3) by the fourteenth-century Florentine painter Starnina, the spatial extension and thrust of the earth's surface is strongly realized. The massive clarity of the forms also serves to give a sharp definition to space, allowing it to be positively experienced as volume. A further definition is given to space by the backdrop-like character of the sky, signifying the end of space. These characteristics work together to produce a stillness in the image, a balance between form and space.

Such equilibric relationships in landscape were eventually to be completely realized by Paul Cézanne. In the painting *Mont St. Victoire* (Fig. 9–7) one is not aware of any opposition between form and space. Space is not treated as mere emptiness; it neither dominates form nor is dominated by it. It is, in fact, difficult to distinguish form from space, for Cézanne treats the space as a perceived area which is positively defined by the layout of the surfaces of form. The result is stability and a feeling of permanence. This unity is heightened by Cézanne's simplification of natural form to shapes which re-

**Fig. 9–4**
Francesco Guardi
**The Piazzetta in Venice**
*(Cà d'Oro, Venice)*

veal the characteristic spatial extension of each object. They thrust in certain ways—planes or curves moving in certain directions—yet even these movements are in harmony with each other. For although every movement leads independently away from the surface nearest the eye, they come ultimately to a focal point determined by Cézanne's manipulation of the cone of vision. He makes a unified over-all design of forms while allowing them their individual spatial extension. Cézanne then turns his attention to space, which becomes a shape—a shape counteracting the spatial extension of the form, moving against it, and neutralizing its pressure. In this way, Cézanne produces a pictorial image which banishes impressionistic confusion from visual sensations, for it crystallizes all the dynamic aspects of nature in one ultimate act of heightened perception. His objective eye, analyzing mind, intuitive intellect, and passion for the mountain have all worked to this end.

**THE DRAWINGS** Although this work may call for several preliminary drawings, we are primarily concerned with two final drawings of landscape which will result from the first sketches. The first of these will be concerned with the dynamic aspects of landscape objects, and the second with force and movement in nature. That is, we shall concentrate on:

1.
The spatial extension of objects in nature as characteristic of their dynamic plastic life.

2.
The potential movement of objects in landscape and the action of natural forces.

Select some small and intimate corner of a landscape which has positive character and distinct features with which one can come to grips, rather than a widespreading vista. First, make a straightforward lively sketch of the view using any medium; if this does not satisfy you, make several drawings until you have one which does. Drawing in this way will provide you with an intimate knowledge of the forms and their arrangement as nothing else can. And even though you may work directly from the landscape for the two principal drawings, keep the best of the first sketches by you. Reference to it will help in solving problems arising from the abstract quality of the new drawings. You may find that it is best to work entirely from the first sketch.

**Fig. 9–5**
John Constable
**Trees and water on the Stour**
*(Victoria and Albert Museum, London)*

DYNAMIC RELATIONSHIPS
IN LANDSCAPE

**FORM AND SPACE III**

As I have indicated, both principal drawings are to be based on the same landscape, but in neither case are we to be concerned with the purely "pictorial" aspects of the scene. The preliminary sketches have taken care of this. The first new drawing will

**Fig. 9–6**
Sketch extracts from the paintings of Paul Cézanne indicating the spatial extension of surface given to forms in landscape

Fig. 9–7
Paul Cézanne
**Mont Sainte-Victoire Seen from Bibemus Quarry** (c. 1898–1900)
*(The Cone Collection, The Baltimore Museum of Art)*

attempt to show the dynamic vigor of shape possessed by the principal objects. Observe closely the nature of their spatial extension—how they swell or thrust and in what direction their planes and curved surfaces move. In the drawing, attempt to simplify the objects (rocks, trees, etc.) to a shape which clarifies and reveals the dynamic movements of their mass in three-dimensional space. You will remember that in Chapter 8 it was suggested that this movement of form varied between the extremes of a point thrust, the thrust of angled planes, and the swell of a curved surface (see Fig. 8–17). In Fig. 9–6 I have attempted to give a sketchy indication of Cézanne's treatment of some basic surface extensions into space. If you study Fig. 9–7 you will notice that Cézanne gives a reciprocal shape-movement to space, and does not restrict his dynamic drawing to objects alone. (We will not attempt to treat space in this drawing, but it is something you could try for yourself in a later drawing.)

Try, therefore, to produce a drawing which intensifies the manner in which the object presses against space—that

is, show its characteristic spatial extension.

Observe the thrusting, burgeoning vitality of Wen Cheng-Ming's ink drawing *Cypress and Rock* (Fig. 9–8). The point thrusts of the tree pierce the space in strong contrast to the heavy swelling pressure of the rocks; and notice the contrast between the completely flat rock planes at the center and the heavily ridged protuberance of the left-hand rock pile. The forms push and thrust against each other, against the ground, and against space with great vigor. Many short active lines and longer broken lines act together to produce this liveliness; the objects are not pacified or calmed, but live their life in the drawing as dynamically as they do in nature. For an example of a student drawing, regard Fig. 9–1. Although more abstract and geometrically stylized, the drawing does manage to convey the pressure of rock against rock, to suggest the thrust of tree roots between the rocks and the point extensions of tree limbs into space. But the heavy line of contour tends to flatten the forms and render them over-smoothly, despite the strong

stippled modeling. You should try for more three-dimensional extension than this—more contrast between plane and curve, thrust and swell.

Our second major drawing in this exercise is one in which the objects will disappear to be replaced by linear signs signifying the natural forces at work in the landscape. These forces may themselves be capable of moving through space (wind, running water), or able to cause the movement of an object through space (gravity, growth forces). (See Leonardo da Vinci's drawings, Figs. 8–35 and 8–36.) The three types of linear movement which are signs of such activity, and which we have described in Chapter 8 are:

1.
The thrust moving in a straight line; think of the vertical growth of a tree or plant, or the downward pull of gravity— the vertical line opposed by the horizontal line.

2.
The coiled line moving around a central impetus like a spring; think of currents in air or water.

**Fig. 9–9**
*(Courtesy, Professor K. Forman)*

**Fig. 9–8**
Wen Cheng-Ming
**Cypress and Rock**
*(Courtesy of the Nelson Gallery—*
*Atkins Museum, Kansas City, Missouri*
*[Nelson Fund])*

**3.**

The curving, swelling line of expansion, distributed over a large area; think of the wind, of tide water, of the scooping

force of glacier movement, or the radial vibrations of heat energy that may crack a rock.

Using these linear signs where appropriate, translate your first sketch into a drawing which corresponds to these forces at work in nature. Your approach must obviously be intuitive, for you cannot empirically observe these forces at work. You may deduce how wind has moved a tree, how a boulder would roll were it not for the opposition of a hillock, how a valley has been scooped out by a glacier, or how wind and rain together have eroded a surface; but in the last resort it will be an intuitive feeling for this dynamic activity in nature that will govern your choice of lines and their arrangement. Figure 9–9 shows two drawings made by a student. On the left is the first pictorial sketch, and on the right is the linear abstraction of nature's forces and the potential movement of her forms, one against the other.

**CONCLUSIONS** There are many ways by which total abstraction is attained, and the following conclusions are only concerned with that suggested by Cézanne in his realization of the landscape motif.

**1. The derivation of the abstract form** As the artist probes beyond the first visual sensation of things, other aspects of reality impinge on his awareness. In our study of space and form, we have moved finally to nonvisible phenomena. In so doing, we have used signs which attempt to correspond to the forces that lie behind the world of appearances, and the result is an abstract or nonrepresentational design. It is important to realize that these abstract images now constitute visual experiences in their own right; they can even be used and developed without further recourse to the object. The artist today realizes that he is free to design from his own intuitive and imaginative resources. A visible object need no longer be the first stimulus. Unfortunately, too many people consider themselves to be working in "the abstract" when all they are doing is producing jazzy patterns or derivative clichés. That is why I believe these experiments are important. They provide a clue to how art works, how it is rooted in a tradition of inquiry, and they show that "modern art" has not just dropped from the sky. Cézanne blazed a trail to a new visual revelation and illustrated once again how necessary it is for the artist to have an inquiring eye and an analytical mind, as well as an intuitive sensitivity to the life of both nature and man, if he is to conceive experience in visual terms.

**2. Possibilities of development** The drawings you made should open the door to the dynamic world of landscape forms, and to an invisible world of natural forces. The drawings themselves should help you to feel free to shape and manipulate form for your own ends, and to develop schemes of linear activity which may be used generally in future work, without any specific landscape context. They provide one introduction to the art of total abstraction. But it should also be remembered that the plastic life of forms, and the linear movement of a point in space (which is a line and a force), may relate to our own psychological experiences as well as to physical phenomena. A passive form soothes and relaxes. A vigorous three-dimensional form made up of active lines, or spatial turbulence, can quicken the mental life and arouse deep and powerful feelings. And we are free to use form and line to serve these ends. The interested student should go and look at the landscape drawings of Vincent Van Gogh to see line working in this way.

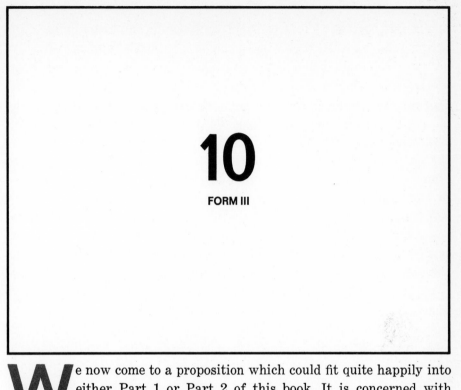

**10**

**FORM III**

We now come to a proposition which could fit quite happily into either Part 1 or Part 2 of this book. It is concerned with form and structure as well as with vision and imagination. But since the basic aims underlying the experiment concern form, we rightfully should take it up here. We have already examined the two structural families of form. Now we come to the stage of analyzing a particular kind of form, where search and discovery should be second nature to the inquiring eye confronted by a structure of some complexity.

It is all too often obvious, however, that not every person possesses an inquiring eye. In too many of us, curiosity, the capacity for wonder, and any sense of a personal response to the complexity of other forms of life in the world (Fig. 10–8), have given way to the perceptive lethargy of an automatic and mechanized civilization. Even the machines, often things of rare beauty and structure, are taken for granted by a great many people, for whom the analytical and inquiring faculty of eye fused with the imagination has become stunted. Few people are aware of the "style" of a thing.

The practice of drawing (and all the design activities that spring

**Fig. 10–1**
**Lily seed pod—cross section**

# Basic structural units

from drawing) first makes this demand of the eye: that it should search out objects of interest, and concentrate on them, fixing them in the mind so that they may be more completely understood; thus will the imagination become active and the emotions quickened. Some of the most complex forms readily available to us, on which we can sharpen the failing powers of an inquiring eye, lie all around us in nature. Everyday things—such as the dandelion seed-head, the thistle seed-head, the various types of fir cones, the wide range of weed flowers turned to seed, and the spinal vertebrae of fish, etc.—are specimens from which to choose in order to study how the form is made up. Nature is a most efficient designer, in whose complex world of form the superfluous and the wasteful have little place. Nature is very much concerned with the *unit* of structure, with the basic part which, constantly repeated, makes up the total form. It is with this unit of structure, with the small elemental part cunningly used in a built-up system to create the whole, that this section on form is concerned. If you will study the page of illustrations, Figs. 10–2 to 10–6, you will observe that in every case one specific unit (which may vary slightly in size and shape) is repeated many times to build up the total form. The units may be predominantly skeletal or mass, ranging from the hair-like thread of the clematis seed to the cylindrical mass of the shark's vertebra unit (Fig. 10–8). It is cheating a little to give the starfish (Fig. 10–6) as an example of an object compounded from one particular unit. Nevertheless, one's eye is fascinated by the hundreds of tentacle-like tubes which make up much of its form, and the imagination begins to conceive of new strains of starfish possessing odd organizations of tubular tentacles. For this exercise, the student is required to find a natural object—one in which he can find a dominant unit that repeats itself in a certain way and thus determines the characteristic form of the object. It may be that an object will not reveal this unitary aspect of itself from the outside. It may be necessary to cut into it and examine it internally, as the cross section often reveals modular structural characteristics. Figure 10–1 shows the cross section of the lily seed pod, and it can be seen how the seeds fit together within the six-sided pod case. The shape of each seed and its position relative to the others determines the six-sided structure of the case. It is interesting to compare this structure with open architectural forms as seen in Fig. 10–13. Here each sun screen of clay tiles is a complex

**Fig. 10–5**
**Clematis seed structure**

honeycomb made from a small, standard unit. The smaller picture shows the honeycomb units in process of construction, set up without mortar. The pod case of the lily is almost identical in shape. Compare it with the architect's drawing of the sun screen unit.

Find some natural object for yourself which fits the general description of compound form; that is, one which is composed of many units possessing common characteristics. You must then look hard at the object you have found, be it a seed-head or a fish's backbone, and select the smallest basic unit from which the complete object is built. You are then to use this unit in a *new structural system* to produce a new natural form which might be called a variant or a mutation. For the artist, this looking for a unit of structure becomes a habit, whether he is regarding a dandelion seed (see Fig. 10–7, the salsify seed-head reduced in drawing to its basic units), a contemporary architectural structure, or the honeycomb of the bee. When he is faced with a compound form, his eye searches to discover the structural unit. In making the final drawing demanded by this chapter, the "designing" of the new natural form, one important factor about the multi-unit characteristic of form becomes apparent. For the mutation or new form to be convincing, it must appear to be the result of organic structural growth, rather than a "clever" attempt to create an artificial novelty. It is, of course, necessary to imaginatively project from what is to what might be, but equally important is a realization of what is meant by an "organic structure,"[1] by the growing, living, purposive organization of the parts of a form.

---

[1] A full explanation of organic structure is provided in the *Conclusion* of this section.

**Fig. 10–2**
**The unripe pine cone**

**Fig. 10–3**
**Center of magnolia flower**

**Fig. 10–6**
**Starfish, viewed from below with a small scallop in its stomach**
*(Shell International Petroleum Company, Ltd.)*

**Fig. 10–4**
**Willow staminate catkin**

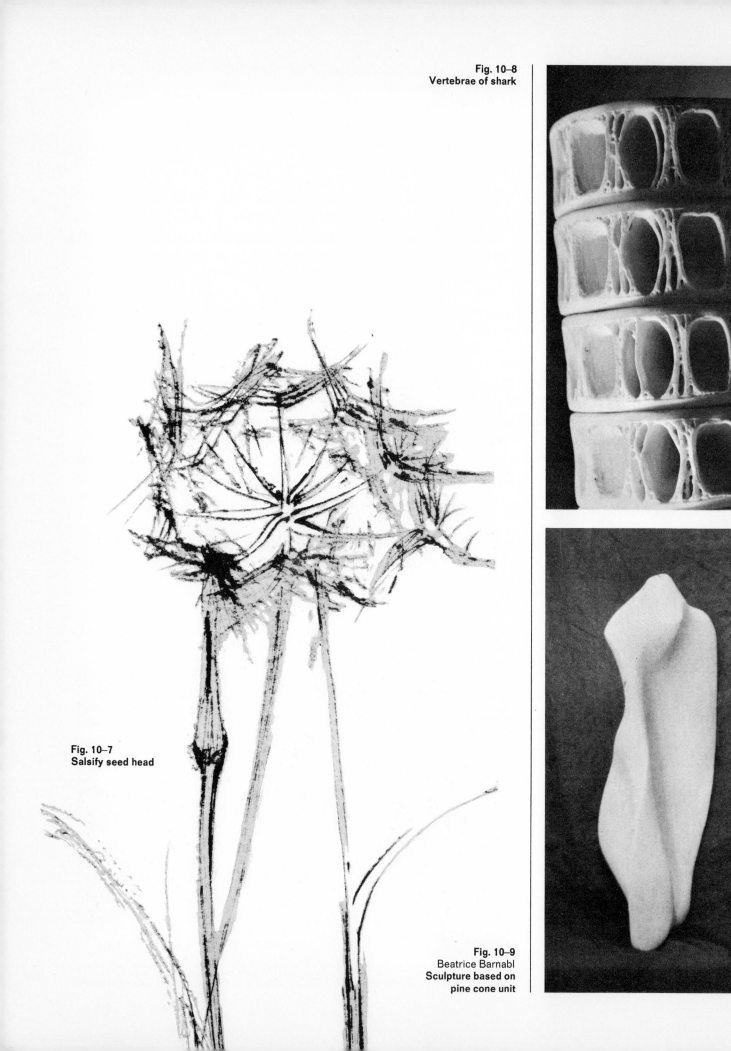

Fig. 10–8
Vertebrae of shark

Fig. 10–7
Salsify seed head

Fig. 10–9
Beatrice Barnabl
Sculpture based on
pine cone unit

**THE DRAWINGS** Seed-head formations of plants probably provide the most complex natural objects for study, and it is possible you will find some so complex that a magnifying glass will be necessary for finding the unit of structure. Depending on the season, some flower formations—as well as all kinds of pond weeds and seaweeds—composed of repeated units can be found. When the chosen plant is before you, examine it closely to determine the smallest unit of structure to which it can be reduced and then extract this part and study it individually. Now make lots of little drawings of this unit part, with pen or pencil or wood in ink on a clean sheet of drawing paper. Make drawings from many angles until you know this part pretty thoroughly, for this is the structural unit of the plant. Drawing an object is one of the best ways to know it. By the time you have sorted out proportions and parts from many different viewing positions, in order to describe them by drawing, you will know a great deal more than you did when you were just observing the objects.

At this stage, return to the principal object itself and examine it again. Notice particularly how the small unit attaches to the head or stem or core of the object, or even to itself. Notice the regularity of the pattern of attachment, the point of attachment, the angle of attachment, and so on. When you are fairly confident that you understand how the complete object works, both structurally and organically, make a drawing of the complete seed head or plant. In Fig. 10–12 you see the milkweed systematically analyzed to a

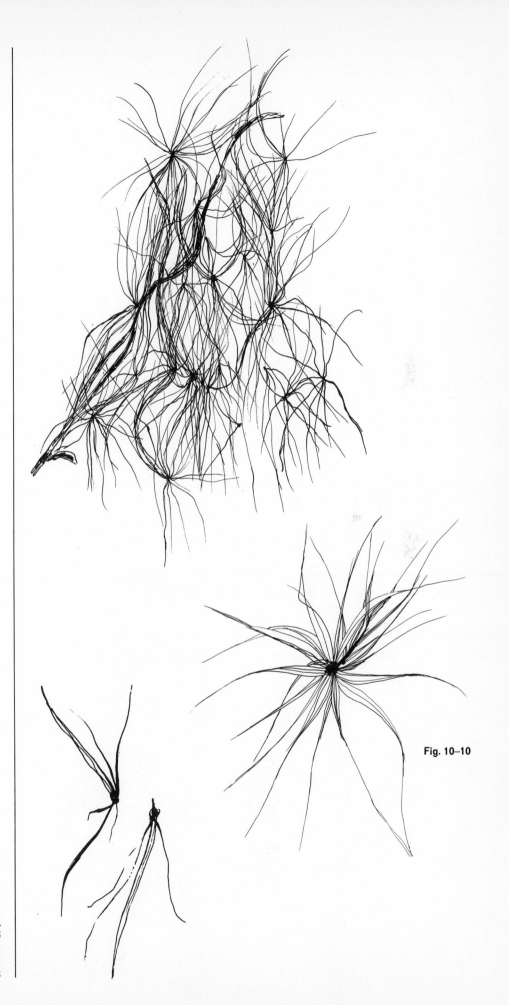

Fig. 10–10

BASIC STRUCTURAL
UNITS

**FORM III**

geometric plan and elevation. There are five units to every part, and in the plan they are superimposed in a counterpoint structural rhythm of three, two, three. This produces an asymmetrical organization of the units which is totally balanced visually. This kind of analysis is very rewarding and one really gains an awareness of nature's structured rhythms after making such a drawing. Your drawing may verge on the impressionistic, or it may be more analytical; this is up to you.

You now have made drawings of the unit of structure and of the major object itself. To produce them, you had, in fact, to be a surgeon—to take to pieces and then build up again. Now with this knowledge of the *parts* and of the *whole,* you are asked to use your imaginative ability to design a new plant form. You must take the small unit of structure and by inventing a *new grouping system* of the parts, a *new*

*organization of structural pattern* having its own principles of attachment and directional movement, produce a new total object. This new object will be a variant from the original, the kind of object not yet seen in nature, but which could be produced by some interference with the biological laws governing heredity and growth—in other words, a mutation or new development.

The drawings in Fig. 10–11 illustrate this procedure using a large pine cone as the object. The drawing at far right was made first to gain a general impression of the object, to find its rhythms and gain a sense of its over-all form. The drawing next to this, showing the cone with some of the units removed from the central stem, was made after studying how these units attach themselves around the stem. Third from right is the drawing of the extracted unit and at far left is

the mutation. This new object has been produced by fitting the units together like vertebrae, and, in fact, they do fit physically very well together to make a model from which to draw. The pine cone unit is common to both the original object and the new form, yet these have little in common. It is the grouping organization of the units which determines the ultimate shape of the object, and this has been radically changed from a radial system of attachment to a linear interlocking of piece to piece. In Fig. 10–10 the wild cottonseed has been treated. The top drawing left shows the natural irregular complex of nuclei and trailing threads. At bottom is the extracted unit of one nucleus with its threads, and at middle is the new plant form. This has been accomplished by grouping the nuclei together to form a large central compound nucleus from which the threads flow, thus making a comparatively regular, radial structure.

Fig. 10–11
Beatrice Barnabl
**Pine cone drawings**

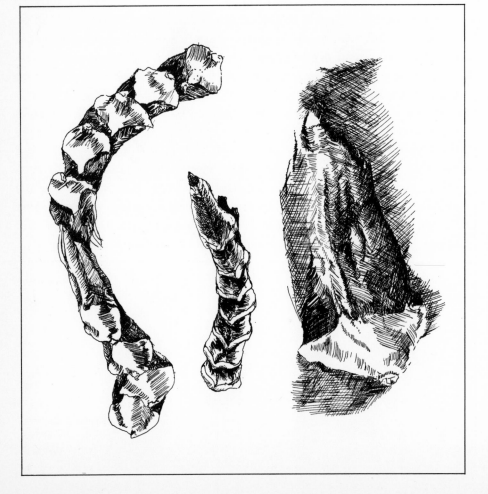

**CONCLUSIONS** Many of the obvious conclusions to be drawn from this work have already been stated, both in the introduction to this chapter and in the description of the project itself. But when a task of this kind is completed, one or two factors always loom up large and clear as the most important aspects of it to remember. In this case a clue is provided by the three words used earlier in the final paragraph of the Introduction, the phrase "organic structural growth." The implication of the word "organic" is one of a living condition or of a systematic, nonaccidental organization of parts. The dandelion and the fir cone are living objects, and their parts consequently are structured in an organic way. Our perception of these objects as "living" and "growing" is assisted by this organic structural organization. On the other hand, an object like a steel desk, which has not arrived at its final shape through the living, growing process of the repetition of a structural unit or cell, is perceived as an inanimate object, artificially made.

By far the greatest problem you had in creating your mutation lay in the organization of the new structural pattern, using the old structural unit, because—at the end of it all—your new plant form would either appear artificial and incapable of life or it would be as believable an organic structure as the original object. The deduction to be made from this fact is that your early analysis of the plant should contain an appreciation of its organic element, for such an appreciation is part of one's aesthetic response to this kind of object and would be sensitive to the rhythmic structural relationship of part to part and of all the parts to the complete form. Such a relationship of parts does not necessarily imply a mathematical or geometric regularity of structural organization. The structure can be completely irregular—curvilinear or angular to varying degrees—yet still possess an organic structural growth.

If you were concerned with designing a chair to be made completely from wood, you probably would try, consciously or otherwise, to make the legs belong structurally to the seat, to make the back grow from the seat, and to give both back and legs some relationship to each other, some kinship which is imparted to them through an organic rhythm or sense of living structure. A chair design which is just "thrown together," the parts at sixes and sevens with each other, will appear ludicrous and quite unconvincing in comparison.

# 11

## FORM IV

Fig. 11–1
Pablo Picasso
**Woman's Head** (1909)
Bronze, 16¼" high
*(Collection, The Museum of Modern Art,
New York. Purchase)*

**B**efore proceeding through this chapter let us briefly recapitulate the aspects of form previously touched upon. We started by defining two structural families of form, and then, in the last chapter, we examined compound form to see how the repetition of a unit makes up a complete object. In each of these studies we have been concerned with a relatively small, single, free-standing object whose characteristic surface movement could be readily appreciated from one viewing position. In contrast to this situation, we ourselves *have to move in space* in order to apprehend the full implications of surface movement when we are faced with the expansive forms of architecture and landscape. Our visual involvement with surface on this scale introduces a time-space experience into the act of perception. It is not that there is any fundamental difference between large and small forms in terms of their surface organization and movement, but rather that the power of surface to affect us visually and psychologically is heightened when the time-space factor is introduced. I think we are more deeply affected by plane and curve at the macro level, and consequently are less able to analyze the surface dynamics involved. Because we remain detached with the small object, we can analyze it

# Structural forces
# and
# surface tension

more easily and make drawings which reveal its surface organization, but this is not the case when we are enveloped physically by the surfaces of macro form. Therefore, we shall work first with a small object of some surface complexity, and then apply the knowledge gained to larger forms, in order that we may be able to handle and appreciate the surface movement of architecture and landscape which spreads expansively in space. As we stand within the gracious space sculpture of contemporary architecture, such as the T.W.A. building at John F. Kennedy International Airport (Fig. 11–2), we are led visually through organizations of undulating wall movement and sweeps of ceiling, where surface movement on a grand scale takes us through large areas of space. We have a similar experience in landscape, in the sweeping movement of the earth from mountain to valley, except that nature does not complete the shaping of space with a finite vault or dome.

The principles involved are those of forces and pressures affecting the surface organization of form. This aspect of form is concerned with planes and curved surfaces, with the external shape of form as surface movement reflects structural pressures and forces. If you will look for a moment at Dürer's drawing of drapery, you will see that surface movement can be of two kinds. It can be gentle and curvaceous or sharp and angular—gentle *folds* or crevice-like *angles*. And the surface movement you see in the drapery is similar to that in landscape—the rolling countryside or the sharp-angled mountain. In architecture, too, these same kinds of surface movement occur (see Figs. 11–2, 11–3, and 11–8). It is therefore possible to make two general statements about surface movement: that it is (1) a series of multi-directional planes producing through their juxtaposition an *angular* surface quality where plane meets plane; or (2) an undulation of curved surfaces producing a

**Fig. 11–2**
**Interior view of Trans World Flight Center, John F. Kennedy International Airport** (1961)
Eero Saarinen, architect
*(T.W.A. photograph by Ezra Stoller Associates)*

*folded* surface quality. It is, of course, possible to find both types of surface side by side in the same form, the sharp angle and its plane giving way to the fold with its curve. Architects, particularly, make use of this sudden transition of surface movement.

The work which this section is now going to propose makes a definite statement. It suggests that the folds and angles of a crumpled piece of paper have a direct relationship to the planes and curves of the earth in landscape and to the planes and curves of surfaces in architecture. The fact that the scale of a crumpled piece of paper is so much smaller than that of a mountainside or the dome of a cathedral is no objection to this proposition. Scale is not relevant because the common characteristics of surface plane and surface curvature shared by all forms, irrespective of their relative sizes, are in other ways so pronounced. For example, if part of a photograph of a crumpled paper were to be greatly magnified, it would appear perfectly credible as an aerial view of a mountain range. The planes, angles, and valleys of the paper are only a smaller version of the surface characteristics of mountain terrain. This is a rather important point: the realization that all surface formations are made up of planes in juxtaposition or curved surfaces in series, either separately or together, and that it is only in scale that differences occur. No other formations of surface exist. So once again, for the artist the minutiae of form are as important as the monumental aspects, and a study of the surface organization of the one yields information about the other. Hence, the crumpled piece of paper can become Mount Everest or the folds in the lay of the land. *The surface of the form*—that is our concern in the drawing experiment of this section.

**Fig. 11–3**
**Ingalls Hockey Rink, Yale University,**
New Haven, (1958)
Eero Saarinen, architect
*(Photograph, Ezra Stoller Associates)*

THE DRAWINGS First, select two pieces of paper, each one about 2' square, one a crisp, strong paper and the other a soft, absorbent paper. Using both hands, deliberately crumple up each piece separately, not so strongly that you reduce it to a small and formless ball, but with just enough strength to produce a complex of planes, angles, and folds. With this accomplished, you now have some personal experience of force being responsible for surface organization. At the same time, you will notice a difference between the crumpled papers. The strong paper will have formed sharply defined planes and clean angles, while the soft paper will be altogether more "blurred," less angular, and with a suggestion of curved surfaces rather than planes. This difference is due to the varying resistance that the paper offers the pressure. After seeing this, we are now in a position to make a further generalization about the formation of surface planes and curves: the stronger and more rigid the material, the sharper will be its angles and the more distinct its planes when forces operate to shape the form. Hence, soft fabric under such conditions develops a surface that is curved and folded rather than planed and angular.

As your eye wanders over the planes and curves of the crumpled paper, you will appreciate the impact of the force of your hand on the once flat paper sheet. Each plane and curve, angle and fold is the surface result of the force to which the material was subjected. This, then, is what I mean by the words "structural organization" as applied to surface. The surface of form takes the

Fig. 11–4
Albrecht Dürer
Study, knee drapery of God the Father, for the **Ascension** of 1508
(*Albertina, Vienna*)

shape it does because of the forces exerted on it, either from within or without. As you crumpled the paper, your thumb may have pushed down into the form or a finger may have pushed up from underneath. Each of these forces would produce a specific result in terms of the structured organization of surface in the crumpled paper object. Or think of it in another way: if one drapes a piece of material over the top of a vertical pole, the resulting folds are organized around the point thrust of the supporting pole; but if one drapes the same material over the seat of a chair, then a different organization of surface fold will result because the flat area force of the chair seat exerts a totally different kind of pressure to check the pull of gravity. It is easy to see the position of the supports in Dürer's drawing of fabric (Fig. 11–4), for they thrust into the material and the organization of folds results from their position and pressure.

Now you should make two drawings of each crumpled paper form. Choose your own drawing medium for this exercise. The first drawing of each piece of paper is to be entirely a line drawing which will attempt to define, strictly as seen, the organization of the angles and planes of the crisp paper object, followed by the folds and curved surfaces of the soft paper object. Figure 11–5 shows two line drawings made from a crumpled piece of stiff paper in which planes, angles, and sharp edges predominate. The second drawing of each piece of paper is to dispense with sharply delineated edges. Close your eyes halfway and see the object as a "solid" form,

Fig. 11–5

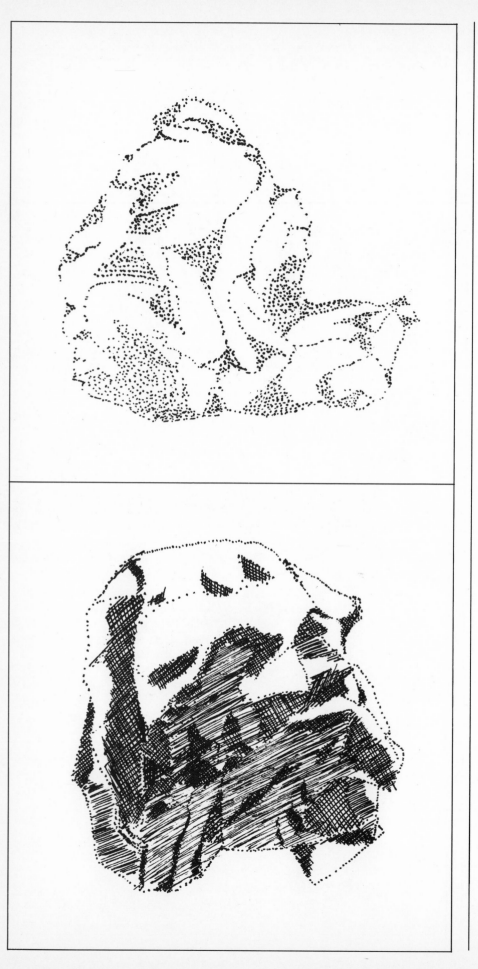

built up from a series of planes and curved surfaces. *Do not concentrate on the edges of these surfaces*, but use tone (shading) to block in each plane and each curved surface as an area, in the manner of building with bricks piece by piece. Any lines or edges that are formed will occur automatically where tone stops or changes in value. The value of the tone, its light or dark quality, should be taken directly from the objects. In Fig. 11–6 we see a soft paper object treated in this way. The artist avoided drawing positive line-edges, but "felt" her way along by first blocking in with dots and then developing tone value through varying intensities of crosshatching. The result is a more solid, architectonic paper form.

Fig. 11–6

STRUCTURAL FORCES AND
SURFACE TENSION

**FORM IV**

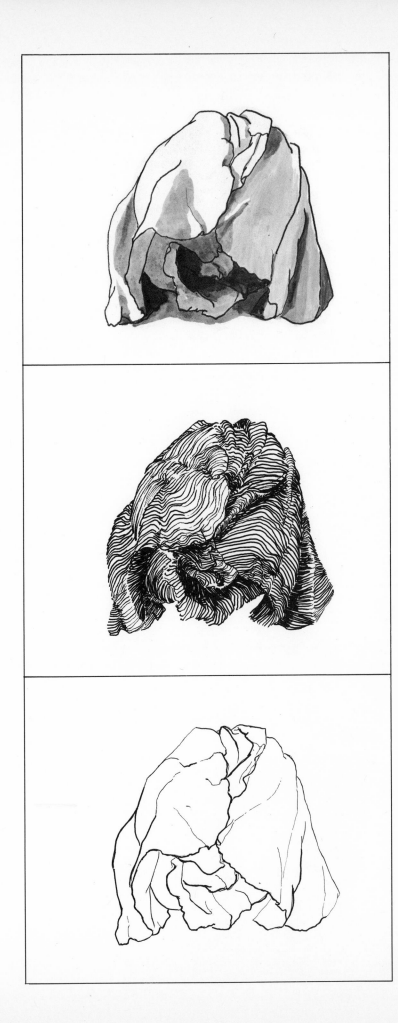

**Fig. 11–7**
Barbara Raney
**Studies of a Cabbage**
*(Courtesy Professor Kenneth Forman)*

A variation on the crumpled paper theme is provided by the three drawings in Fig. 11–7. Here are three drawings of a cabbage which concentrate on the folded shape of the leaves as they cluster to form the heart of the cabbage. If the drawing is turned upside-down, the general formation of folds and curved surfaces is not unlike that of the cloth in the Dürer drawing. This is partly because the cabbage leaves grow from a single and common point of attachment to the stalk, which governs their surface movement much as the points supporting Dürer's cloth affect the movement of the folds. The drawings illustrate three approaches to the problem—outline alone, line and wash tone combined, and the use of the continuous surface line to heighten the movement of every crease and fold. The cabbage is essentially a "soft material" object in which planes and angles are almost unknown. With these drawings complete, some conclusions should now be made, conclusions which suggest the importance for the artist of an awareness of forces and *surface tensions* when he is faced by surface movement of plane and curve.

**CONCLUSIONS** The carefully crumpled piece of paper is no simple form; and when one has the task of drawing it, deciding where and how to start is a difficult decision. As the eye searches the surface, moving over planes and curves, the intellect is also working along with the eye, trying to relate these surface tensions to the forces which determine the object's structure. This aspect of the structural organization of surface has already been briefly discussed in the preamble to the drawings. But we have not as yet suggested what is implied by the phrase surface tension. An awareness of strain is involved here, and it is likely that the eye will stop its wandering when it reaches the area where the surface appears strained to the breaking point. As an example, take a flat sheet of aluminum, which is a plane surface when held in any position. But if mechanical force is exerted to pull the two sides round together, then the aluminum sheet becomes a curved rather than a plane surface. We sense a strain or tension over the curved surface which was not apparent when the aluminum sheet was flat. And the stronger the force applied, the more apparent is the tension over the surface of the curve.[1] Surface tension

---

[1] In this particular example surface tension is the result of forces in opposition—the molecular forces of the substance versus the mechanical forces exerted on it.

Fig. 11–8
**Philips Pavilion, Brussels International Exhibition** (1958)
Le Corbusier, architect
(Architectural Review, *London*)

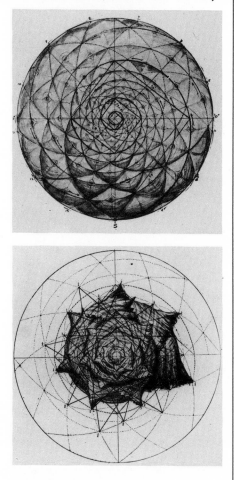

is thus greater over any curved surface than over any plane surface, and the more pronounced the curve, the more surface tension is induced. From this it will be seen that when a sharp angle is eventually produced (as it would ultimately be with the aluminum sheet, prior to breaking, if great force continues to be exerted at the sides), then the surface tension over the *angle* is very considerable. Hence sharp angular changes of surface direction produce strong sensations of tautness. Skin stretched tight over projecting bones, for example, produces a considerable surface tension. Consequently, skeletal-form surfaces are more dramatic than gently curving volumetric surfaces. This can be observed in architecture (see Figs. 11-2, 11-3, and 11-8) and is particularly apparent in Buckminster Fuller's angled aluminum dome where the attachment points of the skin to the exoskeletal structure can be clearly seen (Fig. 11-11). It is seen in still life (Fig. 11-4), sculpture (Figs. 11-1 and 11-12), and in nature (Figs. 11-9, 11-10, and 11-13). The "plan" drawings of the Oregon Pine and the Murex shell provide a fascinating analysis of the dynamic characteristics of surface movement. The spiraling movement of the pine is centrifugally contained, while the surface of the Murex throws itself out into various point thrusts. These lines of movement relate directly to the work discussed in Chapter 8. The surface tension of the Murex spiral is more strongly felt than that of the Oregon Pine spiral because of the point thrust extensions. In both examples, however, the breakdown of surface movement through major points of directional change produces a plan which is virtually a skeletal structure supporting the "skin" of the surface. This skeletal structure is not unlike Buckminster Fuller's dome framework. In Le Corbusier's structure (Fig. 11-8), the gradual transition from plane to curve reminds one of a huge piece of tent cloth. The organization of these sweeping surfaces is governed by the supporting points of force provided by the great "tent poles." Their relative heights and angles determine the characteristics of the wall's surface movements. Picasso's cubist form (Fig. 11-1) gives a pronounced emphasis to the planes and curved surfaces of the head, and the sharply formed angles produce a surface tension which heightens the dramatic quality of the form. But notice how these surfaces are organized around the force thrust of the major subcutaneous bones of chin, cheek, eyebrow, and nose. It is the operation of these forces pushing beneath the surface that affects the shape of the surface. The effect is the same when this exoskeletal treatment becomes purely abstract, as in Fig. 11–12. Again we see this tent-like quality of poles and stretched skin, heightened in this case by the extremely plastic, membranous surface of the planes. The result is dramatic and the surface tension is considerable. It is interesting to note that the three architectural illustrations (Figs. 11–2, 11–3, and 11–8) favor the swaying *brio* of the curved surface. Although Fig. 11–13 is a photograph of a yard or so of beach, it could be passed off as an aerial view of mountain ridges. Both mountain and ridged beach are the result of forces operating in and on material substance. In this case, it is the action of the incoming tide on soft sand which forms these corrugations of surface.

We can summarize these findings as follows (and in reading through the summary, check the statements against the illustration):

1. Surface planes and curves tend to be organized in groups of two, three, or more, and planes or curves in the same group all tend to emanate from a single point. The arrangement can be seen by following the angle lines through to the source of a group. It is fairly obvious what this point is: it is the point of force operating internally

**Fig. 11–11**
**Kaiser Aluminum Dome, Honolulu, Hawaii** (1957)
R. Buckminster Fuller, architect
*(Photograph, Lece Photo Service, New York)*

or externally on the form. Think again of the cloth over the vertical pole: all the folds will originate from the point of suspension or the pushing-up force. Thus, a plane with its angles does not exist alone on a multi-directional surface. It is organized with other planes, angles, and curved surfaces about a point of force. If this is not understood in a drawing, then this special relationship between the surface of the form and the forces that have operated to shape it will not be conveyed, and the drawing will not convince.[2]

2. The material of the form will tend to move either vertically or laterally (depending upon the type of force exerted and the nature of the material), until it meets an opposing directional movement occasioned by a second and different force. To take the example of the cloth over the vertical pole once more, the folds of this material hang vertically throughout the whole length of the material, and no horizontal folds run contrary to them. But as soon as the cloth is supported at a second point—say halfway down, by placing an arm beneath it—then a

---

[2] Students' still life drawings and drawings from the model, in which plane and curved surfaces abound, often fail to show an awareness of surface relationships that result from the forces at work—from skeletal thrusts or from the pressure of a supporting force such as a table or a hook.

**Fig. 11–12**
Lynn Chadwick
**Encounter VI** (1957)
(*Courtesy, The British Council, London. Photograph, David Farrell*)

horizontal movement develops which interrupts the sweep of the vertical. Thus a contrast between types of force is to be found in the opposing horizontal and vertical movements of the planes or curves. The vertical movement has the upper hand, since the force of gravity constantly pulls the material in a downward direction.

This scheme of vertical plane opposed and met by horizontal plane can be seen in the crumpled paper or on the mountainside. In architecture the same principle is observed where the horizontal ceiling meets the vertical wall. As long as the forces are roughly equal in strength and capable of being contained by the material (the paper did not disintegrate under the forces exerted upon it), then equilibrium results. The crumpled paper represents an organization of planes and curved surfaces in a state of vertical and lateral opposition, which is yet a state of stability rather than one of disintegration.

**Fig. 11–13**

**A FINAL EXPERIMENT** To see how you retain the foregoing theory and use it in a project which deals with the organization of surface, let us tackle an imaginative problem of surface design. Using pen or pencil, line or tone, make a drawing of a strange and fantastic rock surface. It can be a cliff or a free-standing rock; it can be composed of planes or curved surfaces; it can be stratified horizontally, vertically, or in both directions. To do this you may wish to work from the crumpled paper, using it as a stimulus for an imaginative projection involving expression or distortion; or you may just sit down and let the surfaces and their shaping forces take over and grow on the paper imaginatively. Either way, you should now have enough background knowledge to work confidently. The proof will be in the drawings, which will indicate how strongly you have felt and expressed "force" as the cause of surface structure. See Fig. 11–14 as an illustration of mountain surface design. But should you prefer to work objectively, find yourself an interesting rock to draw—one of contrasting plane and curve, angle and fold. Concentrate on showing its primary surface organization, the "big" movements of its surface. Handle the object and feel its flatness or roundness, its concave and convex characteristics. In Fig. 11–15 a dry-brush technique has been used to shape the planes and curves of the rock. Notice the thrust of the top surface, as if the stone had been squeezed around the neck, and the movement of the ripples beneath the surface, from left-hand top corner to bottom right, indicating a structural tension between these two points. This drawing allows you to "feel" the surface organization of this rock without actually handling the object.

Fig. 11–14

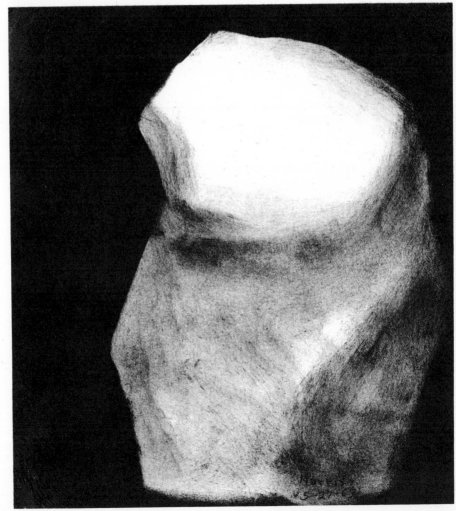

Fig. 11–15

# 12

**FORM V**

There is a tremendous interrelationship between the visual sense and the tactile sense, between *looking* and *touching*. More than once we have drawn attention to one's ability to "feel" an object imaginatively with one's fingertips, merely by looking hard at it. This interrelationship probably exists among all the five senses; for example, a particular smell will create in the mind's eye an image of the object associated with it. Wassily Kandinsky goes so far as to talk about "the scent of a triangle." But sight and touch, especially, have this power to stimulate each other.

Any study of form would be incomplete without some discussion of the "touch" quality—of its hardness or softness, dryness or dampness, smoothness or roughness, and so on. This aspect of form is most often revealed by its surface texture. In the work just completed, dealing with surface structure, little reference was made to texture, although it vitally affects our reaction to form. Strongly contrasting textures have considerable power to arouse a strong aesthetic response of either attraction or repulsion. Think of a smooth stone half covered by a soft growth of moss; or an apple smooth and shiny on top but soft, rotten, and fungus-covered on the bottom; or the skin of a woman's

**Fig. 12–1**

# Surface texture

153

face against the texture of a fur collar; or silk stockings in contrast to woolen ones; or, finally, imagine drinking cold milk from a fur-lined bottle. The list could be continued indefinitely. It would be interesting to pursue a study of various psychological types and their differing responses to surface textures, for some people are fascinated by cold, polished, and reflective surfaces, and repulsed by mold or fungus, while the reverse is true of others. I wonder, as pure speculation, if such a study might reveal that introverted personalities prefer soft and furry textures, while extroverted types are attracted by hard and polished surfaces? Of course, surface texture is usually an indication of the nature of the material itself, and so provides a palpable introduction to the physical substance of form. The architect, the sculptor, the designer in industry, and the painter all use surface textures to capitalize on the sensitive psychological relationship between sight and touch. An immediate question arises: how effective is an artificially contrived texture when compared with the natural texture of a material? I think we must answer that the artist is free to do whatever he wishes with the medium. Michelangelo treated the surface of his marble in many different ways, allowing the rough to coexist alongside the smooth and highly polished, and thereby heightens the observer's psychological response to the sculpture. The raw material metamorphoses into living form. Look at the variety of textures over the surface of his unfinished "Saint Matthew" (Fig. 12–3). Yet, when the baroque-rococo style of architecture was at its height in eighteenth-century Europe, wood and plaster were skilfully treated to resemble marble, bronze, gold, or silver. Is such falsification of surface legitimate, or must it inevitably flaw the work of art? The immediate effect on entering a late baroque church is wonderful. It is a visual *tour de force*. But as one wanders about and inevitably touches a magnificent marble column, it is not cold, crystalline, and smooth; it feels of wood, and immediately something is wrong. Is this too purist an attitude? Should one allow the tactile element to flaw the visual? These are personal issues, and I mention this particular example only to indicate the strong connection between looking and touching. I hesitate to make an aesthetic dogma out of it as I did in the first edition of this book. For perhaps the means justify the ends. The Greeks painted the features of their marble sculptures and stained the body with a hot wax —and the draped form of the archaic kore (maiden) was apparently

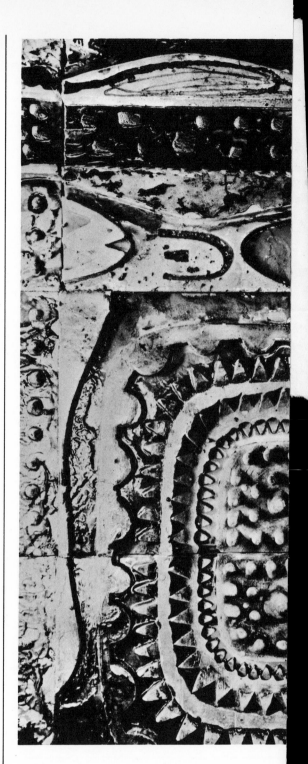

SURFACE
TEXTURE

**FORM V**

154

Fig. 12–2
**Corner repeat pattern**
Anthony Holloway and William Mitchell, designers
(The Architectural Review, *London*)

Fig. 12–3
Michelangelo
**Saint Matthew**
(*Florence, Accademia*)

colored to a polychromatic grandeur. The natural texture of the marble can be seen today, but was it perceptible in the fifth century B.C.? The Greeks invented the concept of "fineness" or beauty yet did not seem to insist upon maintaining the natural surface of the material. And then, think of the strange and powerful effects created by the Surrealists when they give a familiar material a bizarre texture. Surely the means justify the ends here? Look at Meret Oppenheim's *Fur-covered cup, saucer, and spoon* (Fig. 12–4). How do you respond to this? It plays havoc with one's perceptions and produces a strong psychological reaction. Fur itself can unnerve some people, but when a furry surface is given to metallic or ceramic substances, then reason is offended, emotional reactions are stirred, and the imagination is activated. The irrational part of ourselves is intrigued, and the rational intellect loses its firm hold on our consciousness. This is one of the aims of Surrealism. Its images make concrete the worlds of dream and unnatural metamorphoses; imaginative changes in surface texture play a large part in Surrealist art.

Some materials which are extremely useful in themselves possess an unattractive surface quality. Plaster is one of these, and there are things one can and should do to plaster to enhance its textural quality. The baroque craftsmen used it for its easy moldability, and then proceeded to gild and paint it. The texture of concrete can be enriched in the molding process, as we see in Fig. 12–2. The rich, decorative texture of surface on these concrete cladding panels brings to mind the sculptured stonework of twelfth-century Norman stonemasons. And many architects make use of wood grain textures which are imparted to the wet concrete from the planks forming the mold (Fig. 12–6).

The aim of this chapter is to bring the student into firsthand contact with surfaces—to involve him in looking and selecting, in the actual touching of surface, then in the representation of texture through drawing, and finally in using texture imaginatively to create surrealist images.

**THE DRAWINGS** For the first part of this work you will need a large, soft drawing pencil or a large, black grease crayon, together with some small sheets of tracing paper. (Any reasonably strong semi-transparent paper will do.) For the next hour or so, attune your eye toward a sensitivity for surfaces, both indoors and out: wood, metal, plastic, concrete, textiles, bricks, rocks, leaves, skins—any surface that excites the eye and imaginatively activates the touch sense. From each surface take a rubbing of a small area (about 3" x 3"); use the tracing paper and the soft lead or grease pencil, so that you produce a graphic simulation of the surface quality of the material. When you have some thirty of these, gather them all together, trim down the edges of each piece, and mount them all together on a large sheet of paper. The result will be something like Fig. 12–1, which incorporates rubbings ranging from an auto tire and an iron-stranded cable to a loaf of bread. If, when making these rubbings, you find one particular surface exciting, go to the trouble of making a special print from it. Ink it carefully with a brayer, choose a paper with a texture which you feel will respond well to the inked surface, and take a hand print. In Fig. 12–7 you see the result of making such a print from the end of a cut log. It makes a strong tactile design.

The second part of this experiment is to produce a free yet controlled arrangement of selected textures. From your page of mounted rubbings select seven or eight which span a range from the most black and vital of surface, through less active grays, to the weakest and most unobtrusive

Fig. 12–4
Meret Oppenheim
**Fur-covered cup, saucer, and spoon**
*(Collection, The Museum of Modern Art, New York)*

SURFACE
TEXTURE

**FORM V**

textures. Try and repreduce these textures using any medium and instrument that you think will suit. Most artists choose a medium for its natural texture. When a painter chooses water color, he wants its transparent, limpid softness; if you select a dry tempera paint and a hog bristle brush, it will be because you desire a crumbly surface texture. Now make a textural collage using both your own texture drawings *and* the rubbings. Start by selecting one texture from either drawings or rubbings. It may be a positive, neutral, or negative texture. Using a pair of scissors, cut the selected texture area into any free shape, large or small, curvilinear or angular, and paste it down on a clean sheet of white paper. Having made this first statement, the job is now to build a textural collage around it. As you select other textures to paste in juxtaposition to the first, cut them into shapes which relate to each other, for the completed collage should possess some distinctive form. You must also visually weigh one texture against another, for the contrasts between surfaces will play an important part in determining the vitality of the completed texture design. This is where the difference in graphic quality between a rubbed texture and a drawn texture can be used to advantage. There will be a stage in the assembly of the collage when the emerging image achieves a positive character. At this point it may be completed by *drawing in* selected textures here and there over the ground instead of continuing the collage method. This would give you a finer control over the finished result, for this direct application of texture would allow you to specifically design

Fig. 12–5
Paul Zelanski, **Grass Texture**

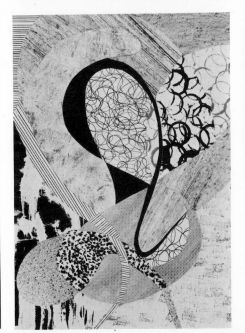

Fig. 12–7

Fig. 12–6
**Concrete surface for London County Council Tidney Street Scheme**
Anthony Holloway and William Mitchell, designers
(The Architectural Review, *London*)

Fig. 12–8
(right)
(Courtesy, Professor K. Forman)

Fig. 12–9
(far right)
**Assemblage of contrived paper textures**
(Courtesy, Professor R. Kiley)

a surface to complement the existing collage textures. Figure 12–8 shows a textural collage made in this way. Various mediums have been used in drawing the textures, including pen and ink, pencil, grease crayon, and hog bristle and sponge with tempera paint.

The third phase of this work with textures involves the handling of paper material in order to create textures physically. A look at Fig. 12–9 will give you all the information you need. It shows blocks of differing textures which have been made entirely by doing things to various types of paper. The problem calls for the production of twenty-five textures to be mounted on a board. Paper may be shredded, folded, scraped, cut, rolled, or twisted;

it may be hardened with shellac, pulped with water, or made into papier-mâché. Surfaces can be modeled and built up three-dimensionally. Your ingenuity will be tested in making so many different surfaces, and you will discover what can and what cannot be done with certain papers. As you use your hands to develop these new textures, the link between sight and touch will be strengthened and your sensitivity to textural contrast between juxtaposed surfaces will be heightened.

You should attempt to create a symphony of textures—a full orchestral range of tactile sensation, from a sharp staccato pricking to a legato of rounded, smooth swellings. The coloring of certain selected surfaces

may help to enrich these tactile relationships.

A study of Fig. 12–11 will reveal a further important aspect of textured surfaces. In this painting the varied textures impart a strong three-dimensional sensation. Notice the carefully textured background, over which surfaces are then built up, and observe the transparencies created as one texture appears behind another. Assess the role played by dense black and reflective white among the heterogeneous surfaces of grays.

Finally, as an imaginative exercise, let us see what strange and mysterious effects are produced when a familiar form is given an unfamiliar texture. Make a series of small drawings of objects with which you are reasonably well acquainted—things like the human eye, or apples, faces, fish, or eggs—and invest them with a new and alien surface quality. The results appear incongruous and, on the whole disturbing because now they possess a surrealist quality. It is the violation of normal perceptual experience that causes our repulsion, or, equally, our attraction. This phenomenon indicates how our attitude to an object is affected by its surface texture. In Fig. 12–11 the human eye is given an unfamiliar surface texture of scales, while the lids become speckled and strongly pored. The apple has lost its shiny firmness and is now rotten and moldy.

The cold clammy feel of a toad, the slimy scales of a fish, the silken sheen of a butterfly's wing, sheets, blankets, or sackcloth against the skin: eye, touch, and mood respond immediately to the texture of the form presented.

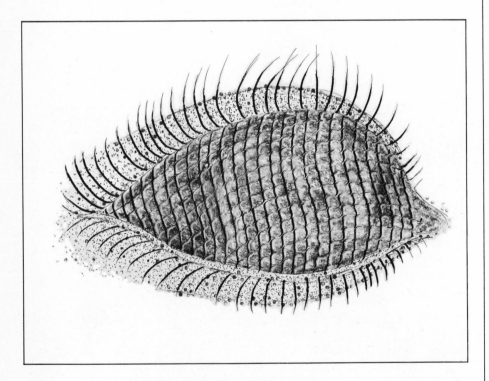

Fig. 12–10

**Fig. 12–11**
Irene Rice Pereira
**White Lines** (1942)
Oil, with various fillers, on vellum
(Collection, The Museum of Modern Art,
New York. Gift of Edgar Kaufmann, Jr.)

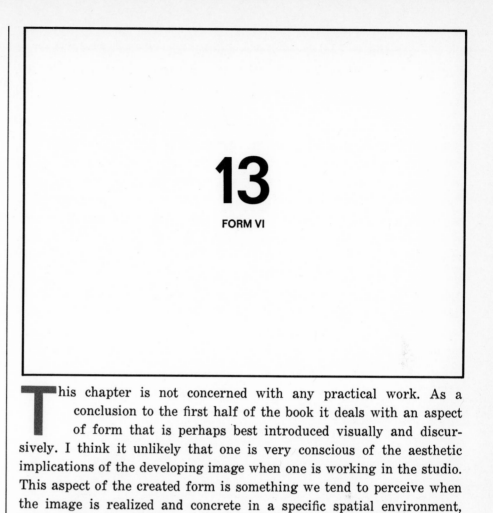

# 13

## FORM VI

**T**his chapter is not concerned with any practical work. As a conclusion to the first half of the book it deals with an aspect of form that is perhaps best introduced visually and discursively. I think it unlikely that one is very conscious of the aesthetic implications of the developing image when one is working in the studio. This aspect of the created form is something we tend to perceive when the image is realized and concrete in a specific spatial environment, for the aesthetic qualities of an image or an object determine the degree to which its formal characteristics inspire psychological (mental and emotional) reactions in the viewer. We cannot try to treat the complexities of aesthetic perception here, but I think that your attention should be drawn to the fact that different shapes affect us in different ways. It has been shown that the organization of shape is governed by skeletal or mass structural characteristics, by the dynamic nature of surface in terms of planes and curves, and by surface texture. The ability of shape to affect us is determined by all these things. It is therefore fitting to conclude a treatment of form by discussing its aesthetic implications. Webster's definition of form as "the shape and structure of anything" is concise and adequate, but it does not go

**Fig. 13–1**
**Greek amphora** (675-650 B.C.)
*(The Metropolitan Museum of Art, New York)*

# The aesthetic implications of form

far enough for the artist who wants to imply that form has an aesthetic potential in that it provokes some kind of reaction in the beholder. I would prefer to define form as "a particular organization of shape capable of arousing the emotional and ideational participation of the beholder."

In its pure meaning, the word "aesthetic" applies to qualities of fineness or beauty expressed in terms of form. An image or an object is generally described as elegant or splendid when its parts are in a harmonious, balanced relationship, and when its structural and surface characteristics are in accord with this *a priori* relationship existing between parts. We then perceive a unity to the form. But here we are using the word in a broader sense, to cover form which evokes responses other than a comprehension of beauty or fineness. For the form which is gross, whose parts are disproportionate, whose structure and surface are crude evokes a powerful emotional response which is less rational than our response to beauty. Let us take two ceramic pieces to illustrate these formal differences, and see how we respond to them. Figure 13–1 is a Greek amphora of the seventh century B.C., and facing it is Fig. 13–2, a corrugated cooking pot from New Mexico of about 1050 A.D.

**Fig. 13–2**
**Corrugated cooking pot, New Mexico** (c. A.D. 1050)
*(University Museum of Archaeology and
Ethnology, Cambridge)*

**Fig. 13–3**
Amedeo Modigliani
**Head** (1912)
*(Musées Nationaux, France)*

THE AESTHETIC IMPLICATIONS
OF FORM

**FORM VI**

162

The amphora has a symmetry, a logical regularity, and a rhythmic *contraposto* that makes a calculated appeal to the intellect. The Greeks understood structure and form through a system of harmonious linear and area relationships involving great skill and craftsmanship in the creation of the piece. The form satisfies; there is nothing we would change. And regular though the shape is, the proportions are dynamic and maintain a strange tension between the parts. By comparison with this Greek conception of fineness, the cooking pot from New Mexico appears primitive and crude, and yet it possesses its own kind of attractive quality. It is very physical and organic, tactile and immediate. It is heavy and bulbous and coarsely textured, whereas the amphora is light, smooth, and elegant. Our response to it is somewhat ambiguous, for we would hesitate to call it beautiful yet we recognize its power to stir our feelings. Its voluptuousness touches some deep instinctive response to life's physical urges, and we are unconcerned about its proportions or its regularity or its subtlety. It does not make its appeal to the abstract, logical mind.

Thus we have two extremes of ceramic form—that which is refined, clear, and conceptual, and that which is organic, imprecise, and expressive. I think it is possible to follow these two extremes through the history of art, whether the object is a ceramic piece, a human figure, a landscape, or a building. For example, can you imagine the head by Modigliani (Fig. 13–3) sitting on the shoulders of a Greek torso (Fig. 13–4)? The aesthetic implications of the two objects are completely different, like the cooking pot and the amphora. (Of course, between these extremes of man-made form—that which results from a conceptual approach and that which is the expression of inner feelings and intuitions—are to be found many intermediary forms combining aspects of both types.) To take a further example of these formal contrasts and their differing aesthetic implications, let us regard two religious paintings. The clearly delineated forms of Madonna, child, and angel in Fra Filippo Lippi's painting (Fig. 13–6) are in marked contrast to the vague materializations painted by the contemporary artist, Francis Bacon (Fig. 13–5). Most people, I think, would agree that Lippi's Madonna may be described as beautiful, for she is close to the Greek aesthetic ideal with those finely proportioned shoulders, neck, and head. The gentle curvature of line and the unblemished, translucent texture of her skin contribute also to the rational unity of

**Fig. 13–4**
**Greek torso,** III-II cent. B.C. Roman copy
*(The Metropolitan Museum of Art,
New York. Fletcher Fund, 1928)*

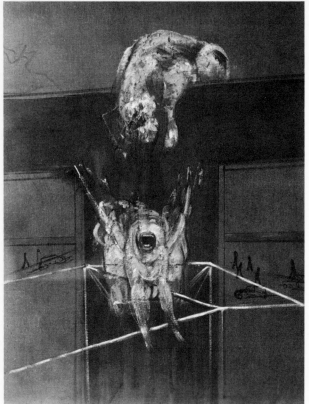

Fig. 13–7

**Fig. 13–5**
Francis Bacon
**Fragment of a Crucifixion**
*(Hanover Gallery, London)*

**Fig. 13–6**
Fra Filippo Lippi
**La Madonna con Bambino
e Angelo**
*(Uffizi Gallery, Florence)*

Fig. 13–8

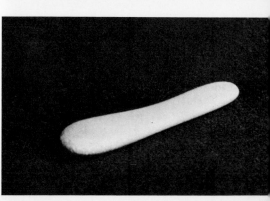

Fig. 13–9

her form—to her beauty. None of these statements apply to Bacon's crucifixion. In fact, the reverse is true. A spirit of unease, foreboding, and horror haunts these macabre, materializing or immaterializing forms. There is no beauty or serenity here. These coarsely textured, fragmentary, disproportionate shapes are echoes of deep emotional cries, stirred by the horror released through the violation of a man by crucifixion.

These few examples indicate that the various elements of form, such as structural precision or imprecision, texture, proportionate harmony or distortion, clarity or ambiguity, etc., work on our personal thoughts and feelings. We live surrounded by form in that which is nature's creation as well as in that which is made by man. We can do nothing about nature, but it is stating the obvious to suggest that architects and commercial and industrial designers should always consider the aesthetic implications of the objects and images they produce for society. We live surrounded by too much visual squalor that is man-made, and living in a visual slum is hardly likely to foster the development of a sense of beauty or a realization of man's deep emotional experiences.

Many of us who live in cities experience the need to "get away from it all" and seek some refreshment at the springs of nature; it is there that we find ourselves reacting to what might be called "pure" form, to squareness, roundness, sharpness, smoothness, roughness, and balanced or asymmetrical proportions. We can respond to these qualities in their own right, irrespective of any meaning the objects possessing them may have. Yet here again we can find forms which have something in common with the Greek amphora as well as with the Mexican cooking pot. Compare the river-bed stones in Figs. 13–8 and 13–9 with the metamorphic rock in Fig. 13–7. The latter is rough and coarse of surface and is imprecise in shape—one would call it "a powerful hunk of stone." The stones in Fig. 13–8 are in strong contrast to this. Their shape is clear and symmetrical and their surface is smooth; they are magnificent manifestations of "roundness" and our aesthetic response is quite positive. We appreciate their round perfection mentally, for they embody the idea of "the round"; we are

**Fig. 13–10**

also affected sensuously, for we feel roundness merely by looking at them. The stone in Fig. 13–9 is also a clear and positive shape, elegant in its thin, rounded flatness. It arouses different sensations and ideas, but I think our appreciation is more rational than emotional, more a positive understanding than a vague feeling. Of course there is always an emotional response to any act of perception involving the aesthetic implications of form; it is a question of degree. The purer the form, the more rational we can be about it. Whereas the more a form is complex and ambiguous, the more it seems to affect latent feelings and intuitions which are not easily rationalized. Look at Fig. 13–10, a piece of driftwood. Can one talk about its beauty or its symmetry, or the purity of its roundness or flatness? Or does it conjure up strange feelings, premonitions, and images?

The formal purity of Hans Arp's sculpture (Fig. 13–11) has a great deal in common with the round stones from the river bed. But we could look at another sculptor's work which would be less formally beautiful and would have more in common with the mysterious shapes of the driftwood in Fig. 13–10. See Eduardo Paolozzi's form illustrated in Fig. 13–13. The Cycladic head from Keros (Fig. 13–14) is

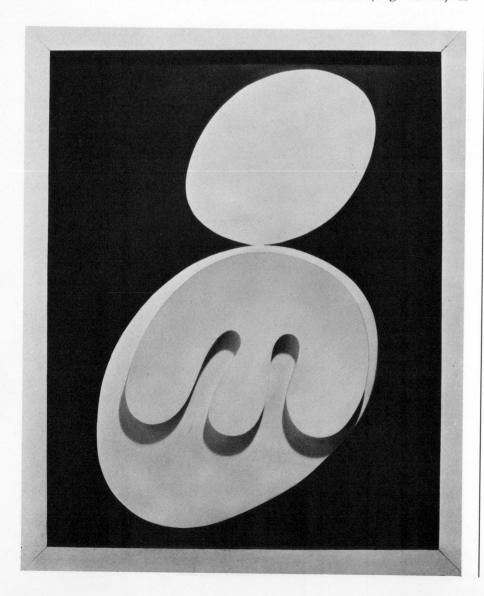

**Fig. 13–11**
Jean (Hans) Arp
**Two Heads** (1929)
Painted wood relief
(Collection, The Museum of Modern Art, New York. Purchase)

THE AESTHETIC IMPLICATIONS
OF FORM

**FORM VI**

By vision I mean the capacity of the human imagination to realize itself in the creation of a work of art. Up to this point we have been largely concerned with acts of perception—with an objective approach to visual experiences involving a tangible object in space. Now, with vision, we move away from such objectivity to the imaginative processes which spring from oneself, which result from our more private mental and emotional life, and which are sometimes referred to as "la vie intérieure."

It is impossible to generalize about the workings of the imagination, the way in which it is stimulated, and what it signifies for the human condition. But we can discern two fundamental results of its operation in a work of art —a heightening or transforming of perceptual experience and an absolute visual invention that seems to owe little to an act of perception. The first depends upon a subjective-objective balance, man *vis à vis* the physical world; the second depends upon a more completely subjective act of creation. We shall be more concerned with the first of these situations because it is effective as a training experience.

One major theme runs through these chapters. It is that the creative imagination in the visual arts feeds on images—that image begets image for the artist, as the formed phrase ideates the next phrase for the writer. The word "image" as we use it has two meanings. It may signify the *concrete image*, the world and its objects (including formed works of art), which are perceived as external to ourselves. Or it may signify the *mental image*, the picture formed in the mind's eye of anything which is generated by ideas, concepts, or feeling-attitudes while not actually present to the senses. These two kinds of image may obviously interact. Experience of a concrete image may set off a chain of mental images, while an a priori mental image may be stimulated and developed as the result of something seen. One can never be sure which comes first; and we certainly do not know how much autonomy is possessed by our interior mental and emotional processes in creating mental images. The imagination seems to work as the result of both types of image-experience, although some artists have been more internally motivated, others more inspired by external reality.

We shall assume that the stimulus most likely to trigger the imagination of the beginning artist is the experience of the thing seen, the concrete image. The degree of imaginative significance we are capable of giving to things depends on how well developed our vision is. Therefore, we use the word "vision" here to mean the ability to recognize the potential aesthetic significance of the thing seen, together with its secretive meanings and associations. As a result of this ability, ideas are generated, mood is heightened, and the artist creates a new form which embodies these personal experiences.

Not everybody possesses a capacity for the type of vision we are talking about here; yet many people, when faced with unusual objects or interesting drawings, will make some kind of imaginative jump to a new and personal mental image. This is the process we call the "developing theme" in art. Each experiment in Part 2 is concerned with these principles. They provide a concrete image of some kind to set off the reflex-like workings of the imagination. The mental image thus engendered is then produced in graphic form by drawing. This drawing is a new concrete image and inspires the imagination to a further picture in the mind, which is realized, in its turn, through drawing. And so the process goes on until the imagination has fulfilled itself. This development of a concrete or a mental image, by which the original is heightened or transformed, characterizes the creative process in the visual arts. The stages through which a work of art passes before its author lays down his tools and acknowledges its completion follow this process of the developing theme. When the image-theme is irrevocably complete, then I would suggest it satisfactorily embodies the subjective life of the man who made it.

It is a truism to state that without vision there is no art.

# Vision

# 14

## DRAWING MARKS II

Drawing, for a student, can be a very self-conscious act. While this is inevitable in the beginning, particularly when engaged in the solution of formal problems demanding controlled techniques, the ultimate aim must be to secure a release from tight drawing and composition. As I have indicated in the preamble to these remaining chapters, we are now moving into an area of imaginative freedom; therefore, in my opinion, the student should be introduced to a drawing medium which demands a spontaneous and rapid approach. The monoprint is such a medium. A monoprint is a print made from a design that is drawn into the ink lying on a flat surface, preferably a glass surface. Only one, or at the most two prints can be taken from such an inked surface. In Drawing Marks I (Chapter 1), a series of lines and marks was made by direct application of ink to paper, and each line or mark had its own quality, its own expressive character in terms of tranquility or agitation, frontality or recession. If you draw lines on the inked surface of a piece of glass, as you did previously on a sheet of paper, these lines or marks can be translated to paper by taking a print from the glass plate. But these lines and printed marks will bear a different quality from those drawn on paper,

Fig. 14–1
Black ground of inked glass before the application of drawing marks which ultimately create the white forceful lines of the monoprint

# The graphic experience: the monoprint

for they possess a special dramatic quality and make a stronger and more immediate visual impact. Assuming that the ink used is black ink, the dramatic quality is present because white lines on a black background (Fig. 14–1) are visually more forceful than black lines on white. It is this forceful quality of the monoprint drawing that we are to pursue.

We should explain what is meant by the "forceful quality" of a drawing. It appears when we recognize marks of drawing that are charged with a possibility for development, as opposed to drawings that kindle no such imaginative sparks. Such forceful drawings catch our attention immediately and continue to involve us imaginatively. The significant thing about the monoprint method is that it heightens the visual impact of the drawing, and therefore allows us greater opportunity to recognize its imaginative significance and its potential development.

To draw successfully on glass, going over and into the slippery surface of ink, now etching a line, now wiping out areas of tone, demands spontaneity and an intuitive capacity for direct expression, rather than a deliberate, calculated, and rational approach. The freedom this method gives the artist enables him to produce a greater range of marks; it allows easy experimentation and, consequently, there is a constant discovery of new line and tone possibilities. If we believe that artists and designers require a capacity for vision, then any medium should be explored which allows freedom of expression and produces vital graphic images which intrigue the eye and the imagination. Leonardo da Vinci describes how the artist's imagination will discover forms and designs of personal significance when the artist is confronted by the stains on a damp wall: for one man it will be a landscape, for another a group of figures, for another a vulture pecking at a carcass. (The "inkblot" test devised by the Swiss psychiatrist Hermann Rorschach also indicates how the shape of a blot or stain serves each individual differently as a stimulus for free association.) Leonardo wrote in his *Notebooks:*

It should not be hard for you to stop sometimes and look into the stains of walls, or ashes of a fire, or clouds, or mud or like places, in which...you may find really marvelous ideas.

The print taken from the glass possesses an "accidental" quality not unlike the images of which Leonardo speaks. What do you see in looking at Fig. 14–3? This is a print taken from a glass slab on which the drawing was made by using both ends of a hog bristle brush. The

Fig. 14–2
Graham Collier
Study for a **Baptism**

pointed wooden end drew the lines, the bristles picked out the feathery areas of tone.

In the work described in Drawing Marks I, you discovered that all kinds of "instruments" can be used to make drawing marks. On the inked glass plate an even greater variety can be used. The range in the kind of marks that can be made on the glass is almost unlimited; no other medium allows such rapid expression of a mood, an idea, or an attitude. Consequently, you should approach the monoprint freely and with a certain spirit of adventure. At the same time, you should remember the statements made about "line quality" in Drawing Marks I. But there is another important aspect of monoprint technique to be considered. This is the tone factor, the degrees of transition from light to dark; it will be described below in company with line.

As skill and confidence in using the medium grow, it is possible to exercise as fine a control in monoprint as in any other drawing method. In Fig. 14–2 all kinds of instruments have been used, from sharpened pieces of wood and bits of sponge to flexible razor blades. The drawing indicates the rapidity of execution that the method demands, but also reveals the subtlety of line and tone obtainable from the inked plate through a deliberate and controlled technique.

**THE DRAWINGS** The equipment required is as follows: a sheet of glass about 18" x 15", some tubes of black water-color printing ink, a roller for inking the glass, and an absorbent printing paper or newsprint paper.

**Drawing 1**

This is a line experiment. First squeeze out an inch or so of ink onto the center of the glass plate, and then roll it out evenly over the whole glass area. Roll it well in several counterdirections, so that the ink layer is evenly distributed and "tacky" to the roller. Now, take a piece of wood (a matchstick or small twig will do) and shape it to a flat, chisel end. This is the first instrument to use in drawing in the ink, and it should be used to produce a line of varying widths as the sharpened end is turned from the flat to the sharp edge as it moves over the glass. There

Fig. 14–3

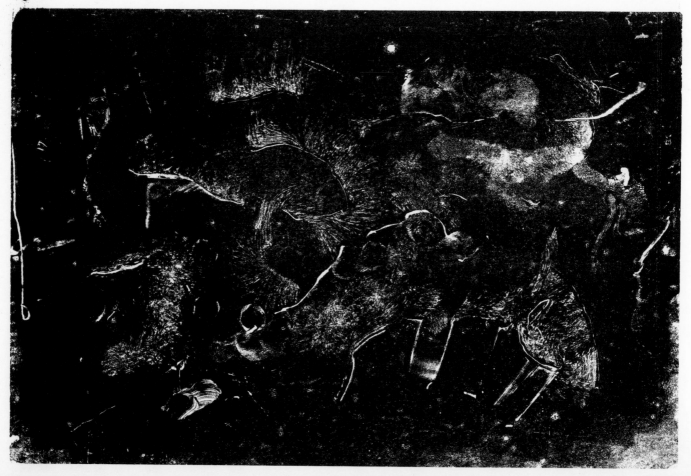

is no conscious aim to this first line. Just work freely, moving the whole arm rather than only the wrist, and produce a rhythmic movement over the whole of the glass area. Stop whenever you feel you have disturbed the ink enough. If a sheet of printing paper is now placed over the plate, then rolled over with a clean roller (or firmly impressed by hand) and peeled off, you will see an interesting reproduction of the line drawn in the ink. Close examination of this printed line will reveal that every subtle nuance of thick and thin, every break, and every variance in the pressure used to make it is faithfully reproduced. A dramatic element of intensity is added because the line is white surrounded by an area of black. But you will notice, too, that this background area is not uniformly black; some parts are grayer than others, or more grained and textured, while other areas are smooth and deep

in their blackness. This variation in background is caused by the differing pressures of the roller and the

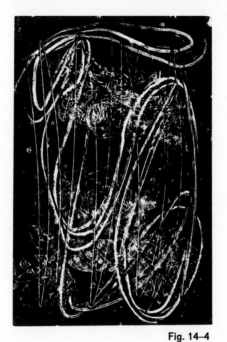

**Fig. 14—4**

directional changes made by the roller as the printing paper was impressed on the glass. This textural interest of the monoprint ground helps give the drawing its forceful intensity. It also produces the accidental arrangement of tones and shapes which intrigues the imagination, like the damp patches on the wall described by Leonardo.

Now experiment with some varied drawing instruments. Roll out the ink smoothly over the glass once more and draw in it with your finger and fingernail, then try a piece of wire, the edge of a folded piece of stiff paper, a piece of rubber, and, finally, press a length of string down into the ink. When you take the impressions from these various line markings, you will get a print of differing types of white line, forcefully presented. It is important to notice how these lines of the monoprint differ from black lines

**Fig. 14—5**

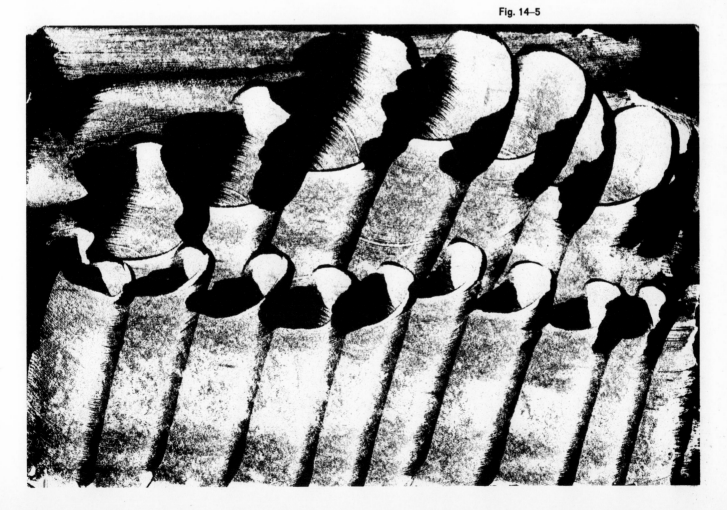

Fig. 14–6

produced on paper by pen, pencil, or charcoal. Figure 14–4 illustrates a print resulting from the use of wood and wire, together with a crumpled handkerchief which was used to dab the plate here and there.

### Drawing 2

This second drawing is concerned with areas of tone rather than line, and with values of tone in gray areas between the extremes of black and white. For this work you will need a ½" hog bristle brush, some pieces of strongly-textured rag or canvas, a sponge, wire wool—anything, in fact, possessing a textural surface that will disturb the surface of the ink; you can even use your fingers or the palm of your hand to impress the ink. Once again, prints should be taken at any interesting stage of development, or printing can be delayed until a complex superimposition of marks has been made on the glass. A good starting method is to use the brush to stroke the ink without consciously thinking in terms of a design.

Don't overcrowd the glass area with these brush markings, and take a print of them first before going on to use the other equipment you've assembled. This print will have black

Fig. 14–7

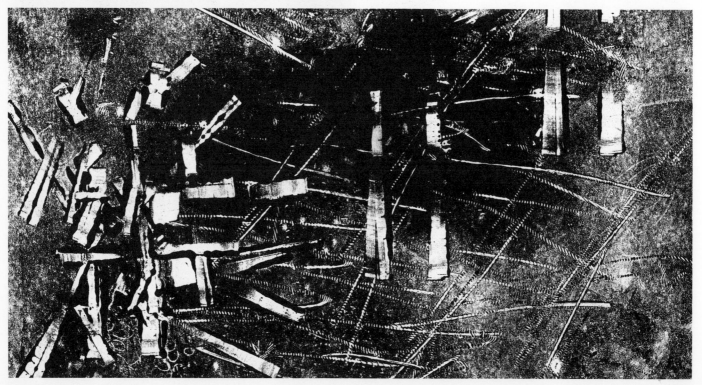

areas of background and gray areas of texture where the brush marked the ink. The surface will appear more subtly variegated than the prints obtained of lines made with the wooden stick, since it is composed of the more delicate markings of the brushes. There may be strong pictorial suggestions produced by the textured shapes these brushed areas of tone have unintentionally created (see Fig. 14–3).

Now let's take this work a little further and see what happens when we scrape off some of the ink. With the glass freshly inked and using either a corner of a rag or the edge of a folded piece of paper, or even the palm of your hand, remove large areas of ink from the glass and then work over the whole plate once more with the brush, wood, or finger, dragging the remaining inked areas into the wiped places. The result is a combination of blacks, whites, and grays, multi-textured and graphically very dynamic. The print illustrated in Fig. 14–5 is an example of this experiment in which a piece of stiff, bent cardboard was used to drag the ink back over the previously wiped areas.

**Drawing 3**

This final piece of work is even more experimental. Select one or two objects—such as bottle tops, hair curlers, interesting pices of wood, bamboo, rush matting, or simple paper clips—and impress them into the freshly inked plate one at a time. Place the object in the ink and pull it slightly to one side, or roll it round in the ink to produce a range of superimposed images. Disturb the ink as many times

Fig. 14–8

as seems necessary to produce an interesting image. The print, like its predecessors, is likely to be forceful and dramatic, and obviously this oriental-like "white" drawing can not occur in the normal way of working. Figure 14–6 shows the image obtained when a piece of crumpled linen was impressed in the ink, while in Fig. 14–9 a pine cone was rolled over the ink plate to produce the delicate markings; and the vertical lines were then drawn in with a wooden point. Bottle tops were used in Fig. 14–8, twisted slightly to produce the elliptical markings. This gives the mark a three-dimensional appearance and creates a sense of depth in the black space. Figure 14–7 results from using a short length of bamboo and a plastic hair curler to disturb the ink on the glass.

Fig. 14–9

**CONCLUSIONS** At the end of this series of experiments, you should have many prints from the glass plate, some interesting and some not so interesting, but all strong in terms of black and white. The images produced on each print owe their expressive quality to the character of the medium—to the sensitive printing surface of glass, to the fluid way water-color printing ink spreads on the glass, to the great variety of means that can be used to disturb the ink, and, finally, to the process of printing itself. But the medium itself cannot produce a work of art. To develop the artistic possibilities of the monoprint, to make prints that lead to new ideas about form and pictorial design, the artist must develop his ability to recognize the possible development of a drawing and must extend his capacity for expression in the medium.

These prints have come from a deliberate exploitation of monoprint characteristics. They involve our imagination and stimulate a capacity for vision; we can see all kinds of pictorial and painterly possibilities in them—all kinds of configurations and many regions of space. The prints can be used as visual notes from which to develop more controlled and perhaps more significant images. And if, as Paul Klee suggests, the true basis of the creative impulse lies in the unconscious, then the monoprint is a better medium than most, for it leaves little time for rational decision. The monoprint can help increase the artist's sensitivity to tone, line, and other purely graphic characteristics, and we should not rule it out as a serious drawing medium merely because there is an element of chance involved. The sensitive artist will learn to predict and exploit these factors, and will use the glass plate as a painter uses a canvas. We have employed the medium here purely to extract graphic images from the ink. But later, in Chapter 19, we will use it more objectively to discover its versatility as a serious drawing medium.

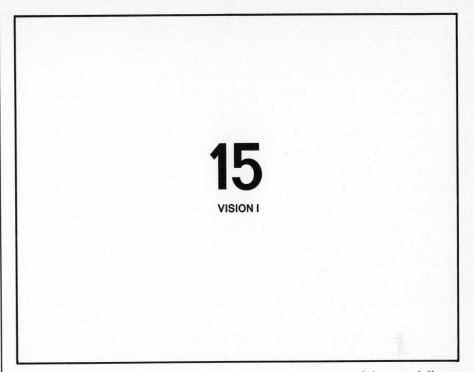

# 15
## VISION I

In the introduction to Part 2, I attempted to define vision as follows.

> . . . we use the word "vision" here to mean the ability to recognize the potential aesthetic significance of the thing seen, together with its secretive meanings and associations.

In this chapter I would like to take this proposition a stage further. Let us take the "thing seen" to be the motif, and suggest that the creative process in the visual arts is often triggered by some visual stimulus—something seen, however simple and tentative. From my own experience, and after talking to painters, architects, sculptors, and designers for many years, it becomes obvious that only rarely is a person able to visualize the whole or completed project in one flash of insight or inspiration. If most of us sit around waiting for such "inspiration" to strike, it is doubtful that we would ever produce anything. No, there is more to it than this. The theme for a work of art often grows out of a new and sudden awareness of some ordinary, perhaps familiar object, or of a few lines of an incomplete drawing. This new and vital awareness of a thing seen we call "heightened perception," and heightened perception is the herald of vision. It is at this point in the visual experience of a concrete image that the imagination begins to

Fig. 15–1
Uprooted tree

# The motif
# and its development
# through transformation

work, and mental images begin to form. It is also worth mentioning that when we distinguish an object or any external image by calling it a motif, we imply that our perception of it is heightened. A sequence of events of this sort resulted in the series of thorn paintings produced a few years ago by the British painter Graham Sutherland.

One day a common thorn bush, which the artist had passed by without notice on numerous walks, detached itself from its surroundings and demanded the painter's attention. For the first time he noticed the structural complexity of the object, the sculptural precision of its forms, and the organic vitality of its growth pattern. He experienced a thorn's sharpness without having to touch it, and wondered at nature's efficient and protective design. The imaginary pricking of the flesh stimulated a range of associated ideas and their mental images: the shrike family of birds which impales their victims on a thorn, the suffering and pain to which man is heir, a crown of thorns. The thorn bush, so long unnoticed, became a motif for a series of paintings which symbolized all of these subjective experiences. It would be useless for any other artist to try to do the same thing without the vision of the inner meaning and significance residing in the thorns, for his painting would be merely a picture of a thorn bush. When one looks at a Sutherland thorn painting (Fig. 15–2), it is obvious that the thorn bush in nature, the motif, has undergone considerable transformation. It is an "abstraction" from nature. This new image embodies the structural characteristics of thorns objectively perceived, and heightens and clarifies them through drawing. At the same time it re-forms the whole bush in a new spatial environment to a design which, through its mystery and strangeness, its clarity and ambiguity, inspires new and strange thoughts in the mind of the viewer and touches some nerve of foreboding. It is an image that stands for both artist and thorn bush. Consequently, I want to suggest that when a motif becomes transformed into the image created by the artist, two factors are involved—namely, the ingredients of addition and reduction. For the motif is reduced inasmuch as it loses some of its natural or existential reality; but it is added to inasmuch as it gains a design-form indicative of human sensitivity. This is the basis of the process we have called the "developing theme" in art.

Even if we assume that this capacity for a transforming vision exists at an intense level for only a few great artists, I think that most

people have a potential for heightened perception and imaginative response that is not always realized. Motifs are around us all the time. Is it possible that many people would walk past the great end of the uprooted tree in Fig. 15–1 without a second glance? How many individuals would find their imagination strangely affected by this object? What thoughts would race through the mind?—what mental images be born?—what emotions stirred by the fantastic structure of this powerful and evocative form?

I think the imagination can be trained and stretched by a process of gradual building, a step by step movement from a first visual stimulus, allowing each stage of development to suggest the next, until the theme can be carried no farther. The work described in this chapter is designed to illustrate the presence of a chain-reaction growth process in the transformation of a motif.

"I usually start by scratching about," a well-known industrial designer remarked in conversation one day. This is not a facetious statement. When he says "scratching about," he means that by making a series of scribbles, he will eventually see one that will suddenly leap out as an image with potential for development. But until he has something he can actually see, he has no base around which to build a theme.

There are, of course, endless ways to "scratch about." The least you need is a bit of paper—the back of an old envelope will do—and something to make a mark. The importance of this doodling process is that it produces images which in turn stimulate new associations of ideas and positive emotional responses and, thus, new images in the mind. After many sheets are covered with what is apparently nothing of significance, they can be put aside, apparently wasted. If one returns to study them some minutes later, however, it is surprising how one shape, one partial form, one twist, one angle, one proportion, or one surface texture will suddenly stand out and suggest further development. Artists' sketch books are filled with pages of such doodling activity, for this kind of *relaxed* drawing is a way of discovering things —things remembered as well as things invented. Henry Moore is a sculptor, but he often "scratches about" in order to release the embryonic forms engendered by his mental and emotional life. Figure 15–3 shows such a drawing. It is not as formally developed as many of Moore's drawings, but you can see forms beginning to grow three-dimensionally as the artist exploits an angle in the line, or moves into a space which is suddenly opened up as a line changes direction. From a motif discovered in this way, a theme and its variations may be developed until a point of complete exploitation is reached, when all further additions merely detract from the intrinsic completeness of the image. Then it is time to stop. But the ability to know when a design is complete and total requires a sensitivity which is not easily acquired.

The experiment described in this chapter attempts to follow the evolution of a motif from its beginnings as a concrete image (the thing seen) to its proper conclusion. From a simple first mark, a cut on a linoleum block which we will regard as a motif, we will move through a complex process of addition, until addition becomes subtraction (because eventually the block surface is reduced to an area beyond which additional cuts subtract from the printing surface). In the end, we return to a simple statement similar to our first mark, or rather to a negative of this first mark. We are not attempting to suggest that a random first cut on a linoleum block is a motif as profound as Sutherland's thorn bush, for one cannot simulate a live situation involving that sort of empathy. Therefore, we must substitute a more academic line- (mark) to-space, design proposition. But as a result of having experienced the stages of addition and subtraction in the development of a motif, albeit pedantically, you may respond more confidently as an artist, when confronted by an object which possesses the power to move you.

Fig. 15–3
Henry Moore
**Drawing** (1935)
*(Collection, Edward Carter)*

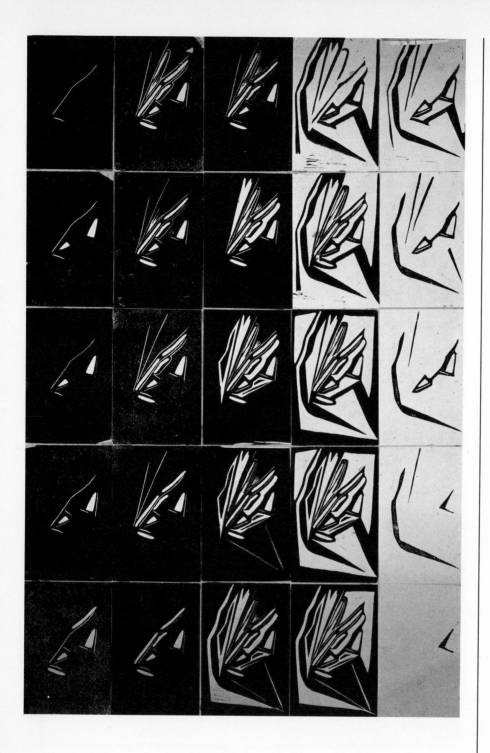

**THE EXPERIMENT** The necessary equipment includes a block of linoleum about 5" x 3", one or two linoleum cutting tools, a glass slab, a roller, and a tube or so of black, water-color printing ink. The linoleum block can be used either horizontally or vertically, and the work may involve fifteen to twenty-five operations. An operation consists of one or two cuts and the making of a print of the result.

To begin, make a cut anywhere on the virgin block of linoleum. It may be a simple, engraved line or the removal of a small area of the block; do not think long about it, just do it. Figure 15–5 illustrates the first stage.

When the first cut has been made, ink the block with the roller that has been moistened in the ink spread thinly over the glass, and take a print from the block on a sheet of newsprint. The result is not particularly significant. You will see a large rectangle of black broken only by a small white mark. It did not take a great deal of thought or cause you much worry to make the first cut because there was no "subject matter" to create a mental barrier. Now look again at this first print, for your next step is to make a second cut or series of cuts (two or three can be done together) which enlarge on, or develop, the first mark. If two or three cuts are made, make sure that you limit yourself to a comparatively simple extension of the first cut. At this point, you may find yourself weighing the possibilities quite logically. You will be aware of the dominance of the large area of black; you will notice the direction in which the first mark seems to move; you will assess the mark's angular or curvilinear character. Or

you may react quite instinctively as to where and how you should make the second cut or cuts.

After this second cutting operation, take another print from the block. Do this on the newsprint beneath the first, in order to make some visual comparisons. You will notice that this print is not so completely black as the first. The white lines or areas have moved further into the black, breaking it down, and a white pattern is emerging. This method of working should now be repeated, stage by stage. After each additional cut or small group of cuts, a print should be taken. With each cutting stage, when more and more of the surface printing area is disappearing, a white pattern will gradually emerge on the block itself. After a number of these cuttings and printing steps (which will differ

according to each person's method of working), a half-way stage will be reached when the remaining area of black approximately balances the area of white. From this point on, as you extend the white marks into the now rapidly diminishing black, you will be achieving a complete reversal of your first prints. Then you had a few white lines in a black area; now you are left with a few black marks in a white area. By the time you take your final print, this reversal is complete. One black mark will stand in a large area of white.

To study all the prints together, mount them individually, in the order of their printing, on a large sheet of paper. (Each print should be numbered as you make it.) Mount the prints in columns with number 1 in the top left-hand corner and then continue the sequence as indicated in Fig. 15–6.

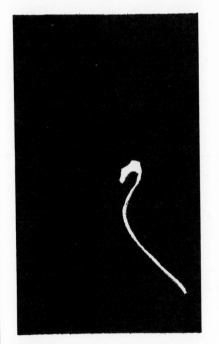

**Fig. 15–5**

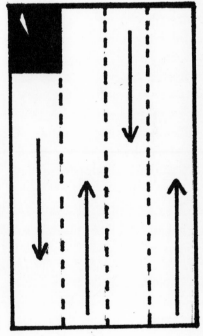

**Fig.15–6**

189

**CONCLUSIONS** With all the prints mounted, you will now see more easily how the developing process has occurred. From the first, perhaps tentative mark, the block develops an increasing complexity, progressing through the stage of balanced black with white, until it succumbs to the disintegrating cuts of the final stages. The *high point of development* exists when the pattern of lines and shapes and the black and white distribution are in a vital yet harmonious balance. Disintegration starts when this balance is disturbed by the addition of just *one more mark*. And yet it is important to remember that you were never consciously subtracting anything, but actually always adding marks, as you cut into the block.

Eight chapters of this book are devoted to the theme of "the developing idea," which, as a theory, is nowhere better illustrated than by this sheet of prints. Look at Figs. 15–4 and 15–7 for a moment and pick out the most complete print of each series. Would it be possible, do you think, to arrive at this particular print *immediately* through a flash of inspiration? It is conceivable, of course—some artists do see the whole thing in their head before starting to work—but I think it is rare. We know as we look at these two illustrations that the most interesting black-white arrangement on both sheets grew out of a logical yet intuitive response to a visual fact—the fact of the first freely cut mark which served as a motif. From making the first step, breaking down the solid weight of the block's dominant black area has been a challenge. Out of this challenge the design has grown.

Note that in both Fig. 15–6 and Fig. 15–7, the character of the design was determined at a very early stage in the cutting process. It was set on its course with the advent of the third or fourth print. It is difficult to imagine either of these designs having developed in a form other than what we see laid out here. There are no inconsistencies at any stage, yet both these students declared at the outset that they were hopeless "at art." Once the motif was well established, however, they gained in confidence and interest, for now there was a tangible image to visually develop and exploit.

This, I would suggest, is how most designing starts. A motif is perceived which engages the imagination of the artist, and which is then exploited until it reaches a stage of completeness. This process would seem to employ all an artist's creative resources—the eye senses, the mind perceives and appraises, and the feelings evaluate.

Fig. 15–7

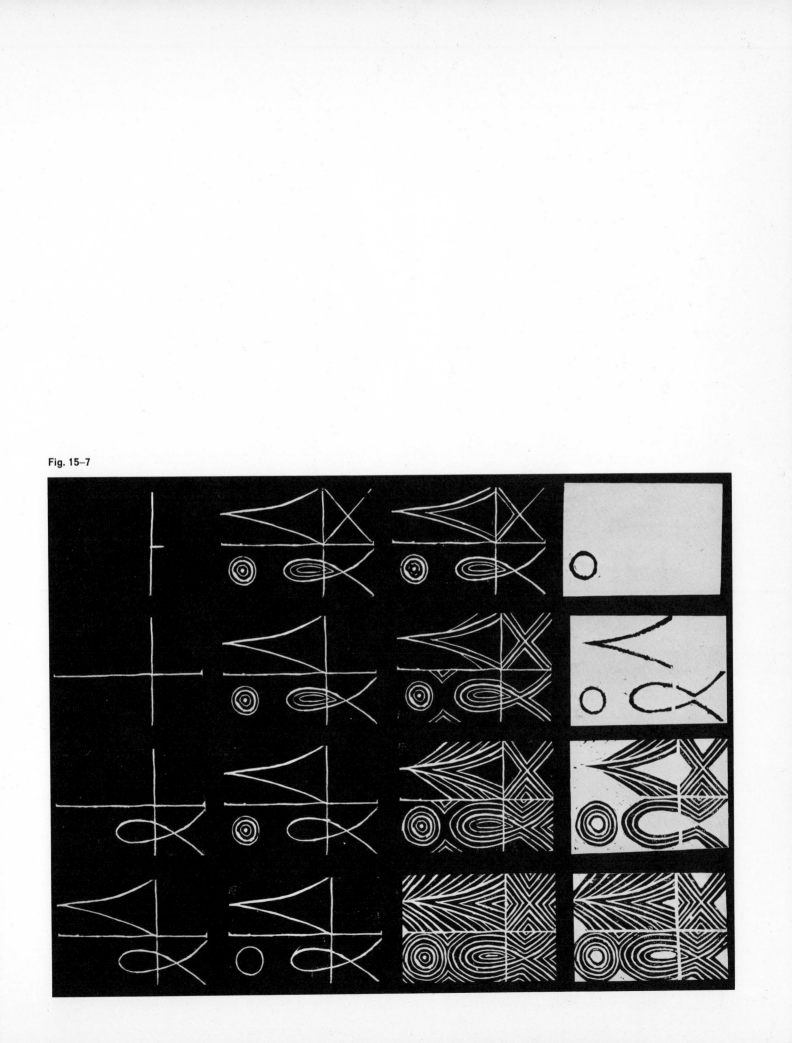

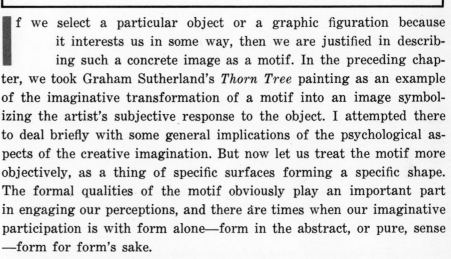

# 16
## VISION II

If we select a particular object or a graphic figuration because it interests us in some way, then we are justified in describing such a concrete image as a motif. In the preceding chapter, we took Graham Sutherland's *Thorn Tree* painting as an example of the imaginative transformation of a motif into an image symbolizing the artist's subjective response to the object. I attempted there to deal briefly with some general implications of the psychological aspects of the creative imagination. But now let us treat the motif more objectively, as a thing of specific surfaces forming a specific shape. The formal qualities of the motif obviously play an important part in engaging our perceptions, and there are times when our imaginative participation is with form alone—form in the abstract, or pure, sense —form for form's sake.

On these occasions, I have found that the imagination tends to remain preoccupied with "shapeness," and does not move into the more esoteric domains of personal thoughts or feelings about life. Instead, one's mental images are experienced as a series of associated shapes which have a significant affinity with the form of the original motif. In our discussion of the aesthetic implications of form in Chapter 13,

**Fig. 16–1**
**Roman perfume flask of glass**
*(Shell International Petroleum Company Ltd.)*

# The motif
# and its development
# through association

it was pointed out how readily the imagination would associate a mental image of "head" with a certain shape of river-bed stone—the stone being the motif in this case. I remember attending an exhibition of ceramic pieces and noticing how many people compulsively handled or stroked the large vases. It seemed obvious to me at the time that these ceramic "motifs" occasioned mental images of the nude, for there are positive similarities between the shape of a large urn and the human figure. And the responses of the viewers suggested an imaginative association between one shape and another, a sublimation of normal erotic imagery. This imaginative move from a perceived motif to an associated shape conjured up in the mind's eye can be illustrated by comparing Rodin's *Birth of the Greek Vase*, which is a study from a kneeling female figure (Fig. 16–2), with the Greek amphora shown in Fig. 16–3. The following is Antoine Bourdelle's interpretation of Rodin's drawing:

On cream-tinted paper, the pencilled outline is filled with a wash of bright terra cotta; the dark strip at right is warm gray, apparently made on damp paper with some terra cotta in the brush. Because the body of a girl first inspired the form of the classic Grecian vase, Rodin reversed the process and could see in the form of such a vase the living body of a young girl.[1]

Bourdelle's statement is self-explanatory; for the artist, one shape may suggest another of like kind.

A further example of this preoccupation with a motif which suggests new associations of form is provided in Figs. 16–1 and 16–5. The scallop shell is the original motif which suggested the glass shape of the Roman perfume flask (Fig. 16–1) and of the Chimu vase (Fig. 16–5). As you can see, all that is required to effect the change is the addition of a neck, a base, and handles. The shell itself is the basic vessel-container form used by the craftsman-designer. It seems to me that this kind of association between form perceived and form imagined is going on all the time if one is acutely tuned to the visual experiences of life. It is well known that Henry Moore spends a lot of time walking in the country, finding bones and rocks which he brings back to the studio, and then sets up in places where he can "live" with them for a time. The shape of such a piece may set him working, first by draw-

---

[1] Elisabeth Chase Geissbuhler and Antoine Bourdelle, *Rodin's Later Drawings* (Boston: Beacon Press, 1963), p. 64.

Fig. 16–2
Rodin
**Birth of the Greek Vase**
*(The Metropolitan Museum of Art, New York;
Gift of Thomas F. Ryan 1913)*

ing, then by modeling in clay, and ultimately by carving in stone or casting in bronze. But, however the final work of art comes into being, and however monumental it may be in size, its affinity in shape to the first discovered motif is undeniable. Of course, the work of art is a new thing—something other than the motif—but in the cases we are describing it is an *evolved* thing, and the form of its progenitor can still be recognized.

We shall take the urn, vase, or bottle shape as our motif for the drawings that follow. The volumetric shapeliness of containers such as these is organic and highly plastic, and is rich in associations for conjuring up other, related forms.

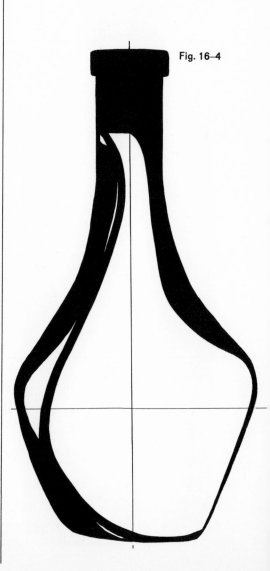

Fig. 16–3
**Greek amphora** (675-650 B.C.)
*(The Metropolitan Museum of Art, New York)*

Fig. 16–4

**THE DRAWINGS** First, make a random selection of empty bottles or find a few well-shaped vases. Ordinary glass bottles come in many varied shapes and proportions, some pleasing, some disturbingly ugly. The bottle, like the snail's shell, is essentially an object of space volume, a container whose space is enclosed, and consequently defined, by a material substance. We have already discovered (Chapter 5)

that the continuous surface directional line which moves in a continuous exploration of surface is an effective means of realizing the structure of such objects of volume. But another quality characterizes the bottle shape: it is either symmetrical or nearly so. Unlike the hole in the snail shell, a piece of wood, or a cloud, the volume is symmetrical around an imaginary axis passing through the center of the bottle. When one draws a bottle, then, it is helpful to draw this imaginary axis.

As the bottle swells and narrows around its axis, indicate on the axis, by means of horizontal lines, the widest and the narrowest portions. This produces a skeletal structure which may assist in the drawing of an object of volume, although it plays no

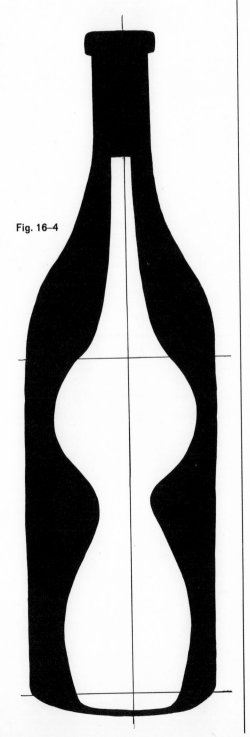

Fig. 16—4

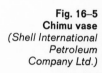

Fig. 16—5
Chimu vase
*(Shell International Petroleum Company Ltd.)*

197

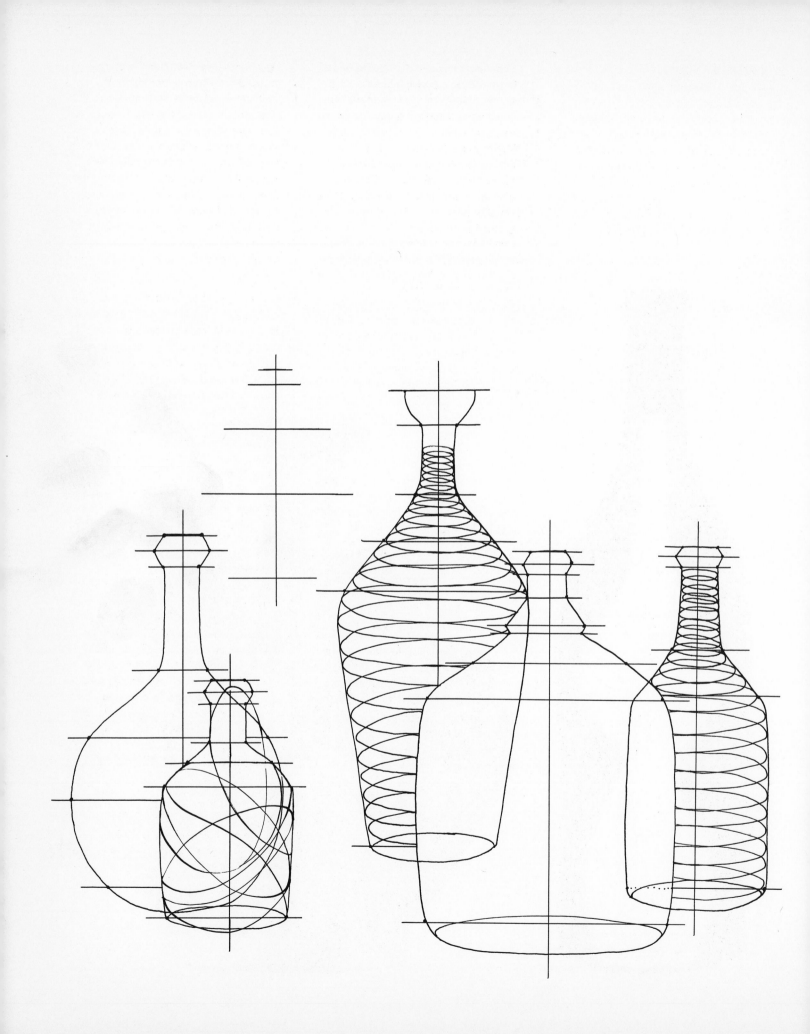

real part in the actual structure of the bottle. Make a drawing of each bottle or vase, using imaginary skeletal axes and a combination of apparent outline and surface directional line to "put the bottles or vases together." You may even explore the space inside the bottle by drawing in exploratory ellipses. Do all these drawings on one sheet of paper as in Fig. 16–6.

From this sheet of structural drawings, select one or two whose shape appeals to you most, and on a separate sheet of paper redraw the forms on a larger scale, about 9" tall. You may draw them as simply or as complicatedly as you wish. The very fact that the objects have been explored structurally and spatially in the previous drawings will help to insure that this drawing is sensitive to the volumetric form of the vase or bottle. When these larger drawings have been made, study each of them and determine what you would do to the shape to *distort* it—what changes you would make in the swelling or narrowing of the volume, in the slopes of surfaces, and so on. Whatever you do to the original drawing will produce a new shape; probably, by virtue of the distortion, it will be a more dramatic and expressive shape, but in any case it will represent a specific kind of formal development in association with the original motif.

Draw the new distorted shape *inside* the existing bottle or vase (although in places the new design may protrude beyond these limits). Complete the experiment by filling in with black ink those parts of the old bottle not occupied by the new shape, as in Fig. 16–4.

These drawings have been exploratory drawings. They are intended to familiarize you with the basic formal characteristics of the chosen motif, and to produce some elementary new associations of shape by practicing a studied distortion of the original form. The final drawing you are to make goes considerably further. For this work you can use any medium you like—pen, pencil, or brush—and you can treat it by line and/or tone. It may even become more of a painting than a drawing.

Certain plastic architectural forms, such as round, pointed, or ogee arches, and swaying wall movements based on baroque-like elliptical ground plans posses an affinity of shape with the form of amphora, vase, or bottle. If we take the amphora as a motif, it is not difficult to develop from it associated shapes possessing architectural characteristics. Of course, the motif is going to suffer distortion as did the bottle in the previous drawings, but now there is a definite mental image to put against the motif. The move from the motif to the new shape will be more controlled, for you will be trying to discover the common qualities of shape in architecture and amphora. The problem is to create a design of architectural forms which are also amphora, vase, or bottle-like forms. The design may be flat and silhouette-like, or it may be three-dimensionally modeled and volumetric. The ground may be treated as a flat surface, thus giving a decorative or pattern-like aspect to the design, or it may become an area of great depth in which the forms sit more ambiguously. (Remember the introduction to figure-

**Fig. 16–6**

**Fig. 16–7**
Amédée Ozenfant
**Les Vases Doriques**
*(Collection, The Museum of Modern Art,
New York. Acquired through the Lillie P.
Bliss Bequest)*

ground problems in Chapters 2, 4, 5, 6, and 7.) But when completed, the design, created by the juxtaposition of new forms each with its own surface-shape characteristics, should posses a duality. It should couple the formal characteristics of a vessel or container with those of architectural surfaces and volumes.

Amédée Ozenfant's *The Vases*, illustrated in Fig. 16–7, achieves this objective. The vase and the bottle become Romanesque colonnades which are open to the air in some areas and give access to a dark interior space in others. The design reveals the basic similarities in shape between architectural form and ceramic form. But we do not know which was the original motif, the vase or the building.

The purpose of this chapter is to initiate an awareness of the shape associations between forms, which is an aspect of the visual imagination. A motif may set in motion a chain of images in which a certain common shapeliness is the linking factor. Such an association provides one more example of the empirical importance of a concrete image or motif as a means of setting the artist-designer to work.

THE MOTIF AND ITS DEVELOPMENT
THROUGH ASSOCIATION

**VISION II**

artist. This brings us to consider the fact that we respond to shape and color *qua* shape and color; we react to these elements in themselves without having to consider *what* it is that has a particular shape or color. It is as if significant combinations of shape and color touch some deep but responsive chord in ourselves by which we experience a new level of self-awareness and realization. This is comparable to our experience of music, where sounds and intervals of silence combine to produce a musical form which is totally abstract, having no counterpart in the world of nature. Nevertheless, it engages our mind and our feelings, and heightens our awareness of interiorized responsive attitudes. Sometimes these sudden surges of what we can only call insight make the normal day-to-day states of consciousness seem gray and trite.

A painting may spring from many different urges. At the lowest level it may result from a desire to imitate or reproduce that which is already there—an object of some kind or another. Or there may be an urge to make an image which improves, idealizes or expressively distorts, that which is already there in the external world. Again, the created image may be the result of a need to analyze and clarify visual experience. In all of these cases an external stimulus plays a primary role in the creation of the painting. But there are times when inner necessity is so strong that the imagination and the feelings seem to be internally self-generated; it is at these times that the world of objects plays a secondary role. On occasions such as these the artist may merely make use of external forms, as vehicles to communicate his expression. He may even dispense with objects as such, and invent his own forms as, in much the same way, a powerful emotion can induce a spontaneous dance.

These statements are an oversimplification of the reasons why a person draws, designs, or paints and of the way in which a particular combination of shapes and colors has the power to affect us. But these are big questions and men have been asking them for a long time. We can only hint at some possible answers here, inasmuch as any discussion about painterly quality involves these broader issues. It is important to realize that painterly quality exists quite independently of the style or type of the painting. An abstract or non-representational painting may be totally without it; so may a representational painting. On the other hand, both types of painting may possess it. I want to suggest two major elements that make up what I describe as painterly quality. Color itself is obviously one, and the second is the particular shape given to the color and the arrangement of such color-shapes as a design. These aspects of a painting exist whether the work is abstract or non-abstract; they transcend considerations of subject matter or the lack of it and constitute basic visual elements in a painting. A color is a powerful symbol, corresponding to human states like joy or gloom, tranquility or restlessness, love or hate, spiritual or physical passion, and so on. The color blue, for example, has long symbolized spiritual states (think of the blue robes of the Byzantine Madonna), while red is associated with the physical things of earth, with human passions in the broadest sense. Color must have a shape if we are to distinguish it, otherwise everywhere would be all red, or all blue, or all yellow; how and where a color stops, or changes, determines its shape. The relationship between color and shape is a problem which has occupied an artist like Josef Albers for many years. What color is "square" color? Is red or black or yellow "right" for a circle? And what about triangles and all manner of free-form shapes...? Does every shape have its own *right* color, by which its form is made more psychologically significant? And does every color have its right shape which would enable us to experience the color more intensely?

All these questions are concerned with the issue we call painterly quality, which, stated simply, boils down to the ability to put the right color to the right shape (or vice versa), and to juxtapose the resulting color-shapes so that they heighten each other's vital nature. If this is achieved, the resulting design provides a visual experience capable of arousing and satisfying our deeper emotional and psychic needs. I would describe a color-shape design of this sort as "an expressive and significant combination of shapes and colors." I do not think there is any way one can teach a student how to produce work possessing painterly quality. The natural artist probably achieves it partly unconsciously, partly through his passionate involvement in life, and partly through his intellectual grasp of the visual problem—in short, through his imagination, which I think is all of these things. But I do believe it is possible to set up visual situations in the use of a color medium whereby some of these faculties are instinctively brought into play, and are then more consciously exercised and developed. In this way, an individual is exposed to the fascination of exploring color-shape combinations as a creative experience in its own right.

The aim of the following experiment will be to produce a non-objective painting by free-drawing means. The painting will evolve through a series of mental and concrete images, each stimulating the production of a new image which can then be incorporated in the growing design. The finished painting may have painterly quality; it may be "an expressive and significant arrangement of shape and colors"—or it may not. That will depend on how effectively you are able to capture in concrete form the new images that suggest themselves in the exercise, using the unfamiliar mediums of wax and ink. Obviously, your instinctive response to shape and color will determine how significant and expressive are your images.

**THE PAINTING** This experiment will introduce the three basic colors—red, yellow, and blue—and the range of complementary colors that can be derived from them. The following discussion treats an introduction to color in a painterly way—that is, develop a situation in which the student is involved in handling a complex color design, where, through the nature of both the experiment and the medium, he discovers empirically how colors react to each other and how secondary and tertiary colors are produced.

To exploit this exercise fully, you should be prepared to learn by experience as you go along. The work is deliberately designed to keep you one step ahead in your response to a developing color-design situation, and to encourage you to imagine the color possibilities for the next image. As in the previous work, the value here lies not so much in producing a fine piece of work as in providing a background of experience to stretch your

imagination and give you yet further means of expression.

To supply the color for this painting, waterproof inks will be used because they are both intense in color and transparent; they are also quick-drying and extremely permanent. When a red waterproof ink is placed over a yellow one. the resulting color is a pure orange. Since the inks dry very fast and do not mix together, their transparency allows them to show through each other and thus produce an orange which is purer than that gained through normal mixing of pigments. For gaining a firsthand, practical knowledge about the basic colors and their derivatives, waterproof inks offer a much more efficient and exciting method than mixing pigments on a palette and then applying the new color to paper. They also possess the advantage of allowing you to see the color change occurring before your eyes. In addition to the colored inks, we will introduce a resistant medium in this experiment—

in this case, wax. The wax will resist the ink and thus render the areas of the painting impervious to color. It will enable us to build up both shape and color in a way that could not be achieved by direct painting methods. Two sheets of paper are required, each about 14″ x 16″ in size, one a sheet of newsprint and the other a good quality, smooth-surfaced, white drawing paper. For the wax you can use an ordinary white wax candle. The best inks for this experiment are red (vermilion to crimson), blue (a pure clear blue, like Prussian, rather than ultramarine which is a more purple-blue), and yellow— the three basic colors from which, theoretically, all the others can be made. It is important to use the clearer reds and blues mentioned, because brown-reds and purple-blues do not work well when overlaying the other inks; they produce impure secondary hues that are muddy rather than clear and distinct.

To begin, cut or tear from an old newspaper a wide range of assorted shapes; just cut or tear quite freely as the inclination takes you, from long and thin shapes to fat and squat ones. When you have a good collection on hand, take the sheet of newsprint and glue a number of these cut and torn shapes onto it. Do this without too much conscious deliberation or selection, but keeping an eye on the contrasting qualities of each shape selected, and placing each where it would seem best to complement those around it. Some will overlap each other; some will be partially or completely isolated. When you feel that the sheet of newsprint is reasonably well covered, neither too crowded nor too empty, then stop. Each person will group his pieces differently, depending on his individual design-sense of the arrangement of the forms as the collage builds up.

Although you will end up with an apparently meaningless jumble of newspaper shapes, they will finally embody a combination of shapes and colors which will grow through processes of addition and reduction to an inevitable point of complete exploitation.

For the second stage, you will need the sheet of good quality drawing paper. First, make a pencil drawing of the collage of glued newspaper shapes on the new drawing paper. Do not draw merely the outline of the over-all design, but include the overlapping lines of each individual paper piece. Once this is done, the first sheet is no longer required and can be thrown away. It has served its purpose by providing the free and non-objective arrangement of shapes which you now have as a drawing. Now take the white wax candle and sharpen it down to a good drawing point (you will have to sharpen it quite frequently) so that it can do some intricate work. Approximately one-third of the total paper area has to be waxed over with the candle in this first step; and when you are considering where to wax, the apparent "spaces" as well as the shapes should be considered. Distribute the wax regions so that they are well balanced over the whole paper area, applying the wax quite firmly in order to close the grain of the paper. It is not necessary to follow the pencil outlines of the shapes or spaces

closely; and if you want to, wax only a part of a shape or space.

To obtain the best results from the overlay method, it is advisable to start with the yellow to red range of hues, and to work down to the darker (blue to green to purple) range of the color spectrum. Therefore we will start with the yellow ink.

Using a large water-color brush loaded with ink, lay a rapid wash of yellow over the whole of the paper. Do this in a few quick actions and avoid the temptation to go back with the brush to touch up areas. Notice what happens with this first lay-in of color. The waxed portions, being resistant to the color, remain white, although parts take on a certain speckled quality where the wax did not completely close up the grain of the paper. The result is a yellow sheet of paper, with some white or speckled shapes, and it already suggests some emerging concrete images. It is at this stage that the basic character of the painting can be discerned. You are now in a position to sense the latent painterly qualities in the design, as well as to visualize what could happen in the next stage of development.

The following steps become more complicated. New areas have to be protected by the wax, and some of the areas first protected have to be scraped clear of wax. The reasons for these steps are fairly obvious. The wax that must be now applied over parts of the yellow area will protect the yellow shapes from the second color to be applied—namely, red. Areas of yellow that are not waxed will become orange; areas that are protected will remain yellow or yellow

speckled with red. Scraping off some of the wax from the white or speckled parts will allow certain areas to become pure red. If all these whitish areas which were first protected were to remain waxed, then the red ink could not show up as its own pure color. Which parts of the yellow areas you protect and which areas you scrape off must be your decision. This is also true for the white areas, which can be re-protected with more wax (especially if the yellow seeped through where it was not wanted), or scraped clear to allow the pure red to settle as it is brushed on. Only when the yellow ink is thoroughly dry and these second two operations are complete should the red ink be flooded over the whole of the paper. (On no account should any attempt be made to "paint in" specific areas or shapes; each color as it is applied must cover *all* the paper.) Use a razor blade to remove the wax.

After the application of the red ink, examine the design again to see what has happened. Where the red has gone over the yellow, there will be rich and luminous orange shapes. Where the yellow was waxed, pure yellow or yellow-speckled red will remain. The areas of white that were de-waxed will be pure red or red speckled with white. Where the white was left waxed from the beginning, white will remain, although by now it may be speckled with color. A great change has come over the painting with this application of the second color. The process of waxing and de-waxing has created secondary shapes that emerge only as the new inks, brushed over the surface, produce color changes. In fact, it is becoming obvious that you are really *drawing with wax*, although the results of the drawing appear only as the ink is brushed on. A coherent design is beginning to emerge, a design that has little in common with our first page of newspaper shapes.

Before applying the blue, study the painting closely, for this potent third color has the power to eliminate all the subtle colors and textures which are now present in the work. Since this color, too, is to be applied over the whole paper, you should try to imagine what effect it will produce. The orange will become brown, the red will become a rich violet, the yellow will become green, and the white will become blue. Blue is a potent

colorizer; of the three basic colors, it should be handled with the greatest care. If applied hastily, the blue can destroy much of the quality that has already been achieved. Therefore, the final layers of wax which are to repel the blue must be carefully applied; and any wax that is to be removed should be thoughtfully considered, so that when the blue is finally brushed over the whole painting, the colors change only where change is desired. Try to work in all the possible color changes somewhere on the painting, but remember that to leave too many white areas is not desirable because they tend to break up the design.

After the blue ink is applied, a complete series of colors should appear: yellow, orange, red, brown, violet, green, and blue. Some of the areas will be speckled, and a few hybrid hues will probably show up. Note that only brown is a tertiary color, that is, a color produced from three sources—a secondary color and a primary.

But we are not quite at the end of the experiment. To see the true value of the colors (particularly any white regions), the subtlety of their gradations, and the more distinct outlines of the shapes, scrape the picture clean of wax with a razor blade. With the removal of the opaque film of wax, the whole painting should begin to glow. If you want to continue working on it, you can repeat the procedure with each color, or use other colored inks to produce a considerable range of new hues. Or you might want to repeat only one color, to enrich the picture here and there.

☐ **CONCLUSIONS** Figure 17–1 provides an illustration of this method of color handling. Only the combination of wax and transparent inks produces such textures and distinctive primary and secondary color values. In other words, some of the painterly quality results from the natural properties of the materials used—a fact that is always true in painting, and one that makes it important to know your medium thoroughly. The painting reproduced in Fig. 17–1 is, from the point of view of color values, a harmonious composition. The colors stand in a positive relationship to each other, testifying to their common origins. There is an over-all modulation of color which prevents any bizarre hue from striking a discordant note. But it must be remembered that this harmonious quality results entirely from the medium and the method of using it we have employed. It is possible to see where and how the wax has acted as a drawing medium to determine a particular color-shape. Notice that there is no white paper left (evidently it was not waxed to preserve it from ultimate coloration), and you might think this is a deficiency in the work. On the other hand, the appearance of white in the wrong place in this painting would be a discordant note which could effectively destroy the color homogeneity. In making this painting, the student had little conception of the finished result. There was no clear mental image toward which he was working and there was no worldly motif to engage the imagination. Instead, the work results from the process itself. Each stage conditioned the next development. The design of color-shapes was provided almost accidentally by the very relaxed action of making a collage, and this left the student free to become really involved with the excitement of handling color freely and loosely. There was no painting-in of specific areas, no fiddling about with color mixing—just a series of bold sweeps of color over the whole design from which, almost miraculously, new hues appeared. The non-objective nature of the design allows the student to intuitively indulge his natural sensitivity to color, while the method forces him to mentally conceive the results of his actions in terms of color change and emerging color-shape.

Figure 17–1 can be considered an effective painting (1) because all the colors in the painting were derived from the three primary colors and therefore possess a natural yet intriguing relationship to each other; (2) because the shapes originated freely and sequentially without being forced or contrived as a self-conscious "design"—that is, they resulted from the gradual, deliberate build-up of color and the intuitive response of the artist to the emerging abstract images; and (3) because they have the power to affect us as shape and color in their own right, devoid of any representational associations. The painting thus fulfills the criteria we previously established for painterly quality.

Not all of your results will be this satisfactory, but in a second and a third painting, when you know more about the medium, you should be able to get an instinctive feeling for the process and have more control over the final outcome. Many variations on this wax and ink method are possible: other colors in addition to the three primaries may be used, and more stages of waxing and de-waxing may be employed, all of which increase the possible number of shape and color combinations. The method can even be adapted to serve a strictly objective painting.

This experiment involving the three basic colors is a good visual introduction to secondary and tertiary hues, which emerge in the painting. It should also complement traditional study of the color wheel in giving you a practical introduction as to how color works, the nature of related families of color, and of opposite or complementary colors.

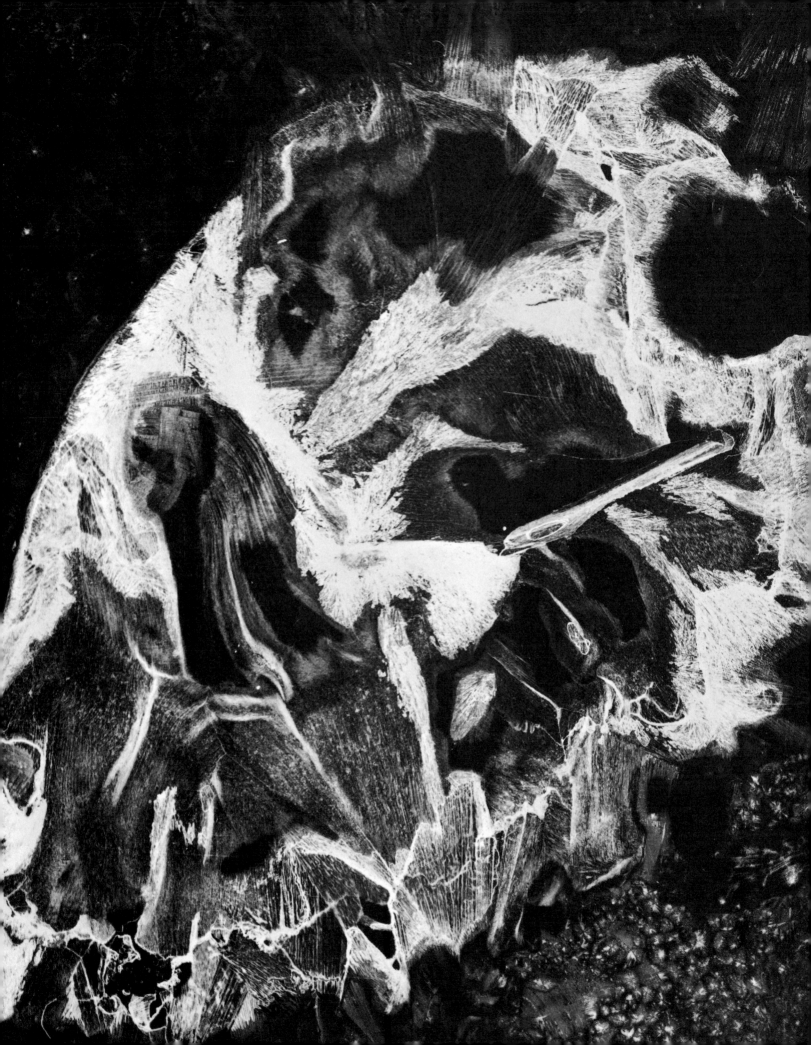

Fig. 18–1
**Photographic-photogram producing a range of forms and spatial intervals to intrigue the imagination**
*(Herbert M. Rosenthal)*

We have seen that painterly quality is an element that grows into a painting as the areas of color-shape arrange themselves, or are arranged, over the whole surface. We did not extend the discussion to suggest that a drawing may also possess painterly quality, for Chapter 17 was concerned only with an experiment in painting. But it will be realized that once a drawing begins to make use of "color" in terms of black, white, and the half-tones between, then it too begins to take on certain painterly qualities. It is necessary that we state this here, for our images in this chapter are not restricted to *color-shapes;* painterly quality is found in monochromatic images and is an important general ingredient of what we are to describe as the visual imagination.

The previous experiment attempted to reveal the authority of significant arrangements of form and color, and the strange way in which they can take over the artist by corresponding to his thoughts and feelings, and even dictating to him what he should do next. "Painterly quality" suggests the independent authority of color-shape design over the artist, irrespective of the objective or non-objective nature of the work; it is discovered and experienced by the artist while he is ac-

# The visual imagination

tually creating the image. This is why I felt it necessary for you to actually make a painting while we attempt to discuss color and its implications.

Now we move into a more general area—one with which we have really been concerned throughout the whole book. What is it that impels the artist to work in the first place? We have discussed the formal importance of all kinds of motifs for the inquiring eye, and suggested the nature of some basic psychological responses on man's part. I have taken the fundamental position that art is the result of man's visual confrontation with the world. Man responds subjectively as an image-maker—that is to say, he responds *"image*-inatively" to the external fact of his environment. At one extreme, this response may be characterized by an analytical attitude to the formal, physical, "how" of the object, which we might regard as visually scientific. At the other extreme, the artist may respond to experiences of the world by creating images from his own resources which embody no objective reality. And in the middle position, an artist may respond through a desire for a synthesis in which the separate elements of man and object become united in an image of some complexity.

In this chapter I want to be as specific as possible in describing an experiment in which a visual experience can challenge the imagination to create a new mental image which can then be physically realized in drawing. Let us take Fig. 18–2 as an example. Henri Rousseau had probably seen a lion, an Arab, a gypsy, and a guitar or mandolin. These are factual objects and may be studied for their own sake, as is evident in George Stubb's *Anatomical Exposition of a Tiger* (see Fig. 3–4). But, for Rousseau, the free-ranging visual imagination, rather than just the inquiring mind-eye, is at work, and the result is an image in which these disparate objects are brought together as strange bed-fellows. We have a vision of a landscape that suggests an infinite desert, a lunar light that transforms the material into the ethereal, and a juxtaposition of animal with man and his possessions that might be benign or otherwise. If we regard the original lion or gypsy as Rousseau's first motif, then we must admit that their present pictorial context has given them new poetic significance and meaning. They are, in fact, no longer just lion and gypsy. Like the characters in *Alice in Wonderland,* they might disappear, or change places, or converse philosophically, or go off together to some bizarre rendezvous . . . or the lion

**Fig. 18–2**
Henri Rousseau, **The Sleeping Gypsy** (1897)
(Collection, The Museum of Modern Art, New York. Gift of Mrs. Simon Guggenheim)

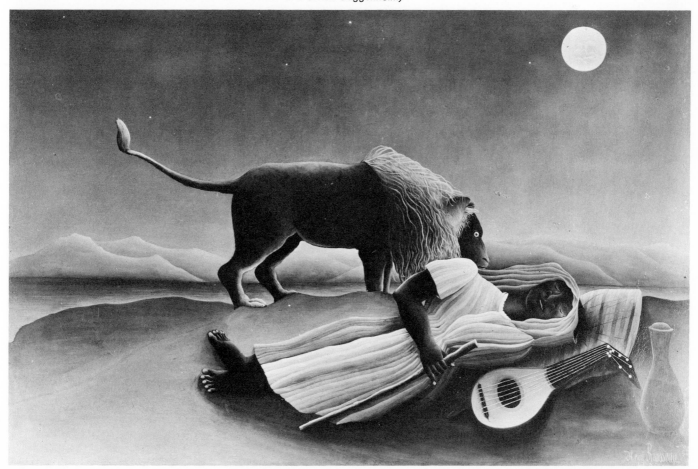

might eat the gypsy. And thereby hangs the tension; we are not sure if the unreal is real or the real is unreal. The imagination can move us into strange and foreign lands. But the question remains, what starts it off? In the case of the painter, as for the designer, I would suggest that something seen or visually remembered acts as a release for a chain of associated thoughts, feelings, and mental images. In the case of *The Sleeping Gypsy* perhaps it was the sudden appearance of a lion, either at the zoo or in a picture book, that triggered the artist's imagination and resulted in the painting. But it may have been just a sleeping Arab. In any case, the painting represents the last stage in a specific sequence of events—namely, the action by which the imaginative processes are given external form. This capacity to move from the motif or thing seen, to a new mental image and its accompaniment of ideas and feelings, and then to create a new concrete image which incorporates both motif and imaginative experience, is what we have called an act of "vision." Not all artists possess a visual imagination. Many are illustrators or recorders of events, the counterparts of journalists in the literary arts.

We have seen how the English painter Graham Sutherland experienced a moment of heightened perception and subsequent vision when a bush of familiar thorns suddenly became terribly significant for him. The thorn painting (Fig. 15–2) is the result of a visual imagination, generous in its amount and brilliant in its ability to project new images into a pictorial context. There may sometimes be a long delay between the experience of heightened perception, the subsequent vision which projects images in the mind, and the physical act of creation. The nineteenth-century French painter Eugène Delacroix commented in his *Journal* that sometimes the memory of an object is sharper than the thing seen originally, for the image in the memory is an essential image, freed from irrelevant detail and distracting associations. Consequently, years later, the memory of a thing or an event may still motivate a work of art.

The questions arise as to whether a "pure" art exists—an art generated entirely from the non-sensory resources of the artist, and as to whether such an artist need ever refer to visual objects for his inspiration. In other words, is the artist dependent on perception for the creative act? The answer must be left open. It is likely that even when an artist is working in a state of complete detachment and lucidity, divorced entirely from a sensory awareness of the world, the memory of some earlier perception is still the basic influence behind his design. But certainly in any introductory work in drawing and design, one must first attempt to increase one's powers of perception; at this stage, an act of perception is the best spur to visual imagination, and is the surest way to accumulate significant, enduring images in the visual memory. I have gathered together a few photographs of the kind of visual experience which I find spurs the imagination to create all kinds of new images. These are shown in Figs. 18–3 to 18–7. Figure 18–3 is a photograph of thin ice formed on a swamp. Turn it around and look at it from every angle to discover what new and strange images it can bring to mind. Then take some pieces of white paper and mask off parts of the photograph. This will concentrate your attention on specific areas where you may suddenly see something new which intrigues the visual imagination. Whatever you find inter-

**Fig. 18–3**

esting in this photograph need not depend upon representational associations—you may see faces or figures, or you may see textures and movements and abstract forms. But a visual experience of this sort could provide you with a motif or a series of motifs by which a chain reaction to a new image may be initiated. Figures 18–5 and 18–6 are both photographs of wooden forms, but it is stating the obvious to suggest that the first of these releases thoughts, feelings, and mental images concerning the body, while the second is seen as an architectural fantasy. The solitary pebble and wood block, isolated on the perspective-grained plain of a log-end, invoke a sense of loneliness and of nature's impersonality that is ripe for visual development (Fig. 18–7). Finally, you should look at Fig. 18–4 from every angle, for this pattern of light movement, caught on a reflective gelatin sheet, is capable of becoming all things to all men who have the eyes to see.

The following experiment attempts to stimulate your visual imagination by testing your ability to see things in non-objective graphic images (formed through the random droppings of an ink loaded piece of string), and to develop the things seen into a drawing of imaginative expression.

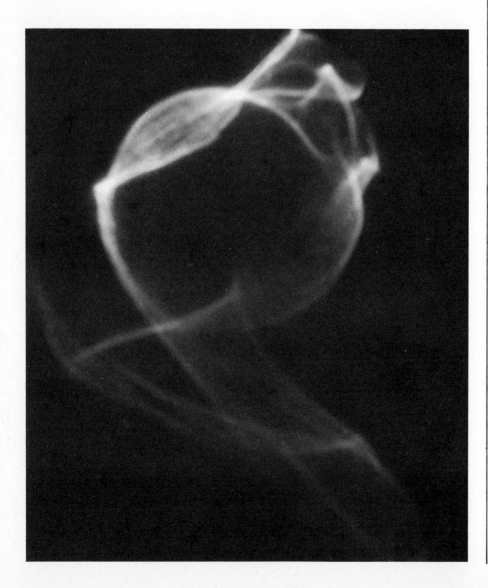

**Fig. 18–4**

THE VISUAL
IMAGINATION

**VISION IV**

**THE DRAWING** You will need a piece of string about 18″ long, which will be used to make the first strange images. A sheet of white drawing paper not smaller than 22″ x 15″ is also needed. Now make a solution of black drawing ink or black water-color paint in a fairly shallow bowl; but do not dilute the strength of the black too much, or it will produce too pale and watery a mark. Spread some newspapers on the floor for protection and place the white drawing paper in the center. Immerse the string thoroughly in the black solution. On removing it from the bowl, squeeze it lightly to remove surplus liquid and then throw it down on the sheet of drawing paper.

When the string strikes the paper, it will recoil and twist and make a distinctive line or mark. Different types of string will make different kinds of lines and the manner in which the string is used will affect the mark produced. If the string is dropped rather than thrown, or if it is held at one end rather than rolled up in the palm, a different marking of the paper will result.

Once the first marks are on the paper, you may feel that the second throwing should be made with some deliberation, in such a way that it will create a certain relationship with the first mark. If so, this is all to the good. But for the purposes of this experiment, a series of random throwings of the string can be just as effective. When it is apparent that there are sufficient black lines and marks on the paper, so that to add any more would confuse the "string drawing" already made, it is time to stop.

**Fig. 18–5**

217

Now devote some time to scrutiny and contemplation of this complex pattern. Leave the "drawing" and then return to it, for too intense a scrutiny at one time will deaden rather than enliven your imaginative faculties. The word "contemplation" suggests a relaxed and passive communion with the object or image, an attitude that is necessary here. After a while, definite shapes will emerge from the jumble of lines, shapes which start off ideas in the mind, stir the feelings, and suggest a new and more eloquent mental image. As you turn the paper around and upside down, you will see a variety of emerging forms, already partially set in a design or composition. The visual imagination must now take over. The goal is to realize these new images. Using a drawing pen and black ink, draw over and into the significant shapes that emerged from their background as you contemplated the string markings. Consciously exploit and pull out, through drawing, the new image your imagination has projected into them. But take pains to give some interrelationship to the forms in the drawing and to give the design an over-all spatial organization. The drawing, when complete, should be a homogeneous figure, since all the forms are developed from a common ancestor—the tracery of string marks. Figure 18–8 shows a string drawing developed in this way.

Art operates on two levels: the genuinely creative and the merely derivative. The first tends to explore areas of imaginative experience, and the second is a matter of reproducing that which is all ready given. The transforming miracle of art lies in the

**Fig. 18–6**

Fig. 18—7

Fig. 18—8

artist's capacity for imaginative reaches of vision, and the hope is that the rest of us can keep up with him. William Blake, the nineteenth-century English visionary, once wrote: "He who does not imagine in stronger and better lineaments and in stronger and better light, than his perishing mortal eye can see, does not imagine at all."

**Fig. 18–9**
**Detail of Fig. 18–10.**

When you are faced with a drawing such as Philip Van Aver's *My Dream* (Fig. 18–10), the fantastically complex, microcosmic structure of the image almost succeeds in swallowing up the forms of the dramatis personae. Yet, gradually, they emerge and take on their own illusionary reality. Everything is transformed through the artist's poetic vision; all is in a state of organic flux. Figures grow from leaves and bushes and are made up of berries and clusters of fruit; nothing is as it seems, for an imaginative reality has superseded the concrete. Even if you do not possess Van Aver's vision, there is a possibility that you may be allowed to see such things through the medium of a very delicate string drawing.

Imagination is our most creative faculty. We all possess it to some degree, and we use it all the time. But we can all work to increase its effectiveness. Without it, we would have no sense of curiosity about the wonder of life, no speculative daydreams, no creation in any of the arts, and no private worlds to call our own.

**Fig. 18–10**
Philip Van Aver, **My Dream**
*(Courtesy, San Francisco Museum of Art)*

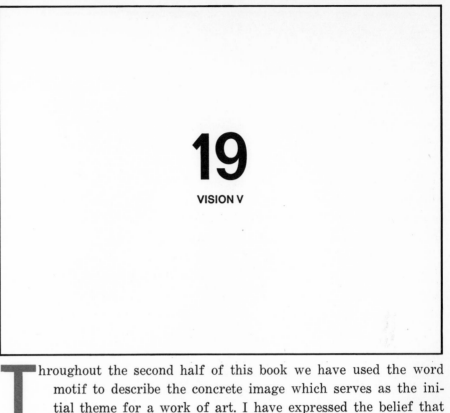

# 19
## VISION V

Throughout the second half of this book we have used the word motif to describe the concrete image which serves as the initial theme for a work of art. I have expressed the belief that the creative process in the visual arts is composed of three stages: perception (selective recognition of the motif), vision (an imaginative development of the motif), and expression (giving concrete form to the new images through some art medium). Up to now, the only *object* we have used as a motif has been an impersonal vase or bottle (Chapter 16). The motif for the other drawings concerned with the imaginative development of a theme has been a non-objective graphic image, and this has usually been the chance result of some ideation-less activity.

Therefore, at this point, it will be a new experience if we develop a situation where the motif is an object rich in human associations, and where the *aims* of an imaginative transformation are stated in advance. Theoretically, such a program limits imaginative freedom, but, in practice, I have found the opposite to be true. Through channeling the ideas and feelings inspired by the motif in a specific direction, the imaginative vision seems to be intensified and concentrated, and

**Fig. 19–1**
**Photograph on a portrait theme showing the**
**vague materialization of the head**
*(Herbert M. Rosenthal)*

# Perception
# with
# vision

to become a more vivid experience. Accordingly, I will brief you on the end result I have in mind before you start this drawing.

Our motif is to be the human head. Structurally, this is a complex object of volume and mass, possessing an intricate surface organization of planes and curved surfaces which result from the thrusting subcutaneous bones of the skull. Therefore, it is an object of considerable surface tension. (The dramatic nature of surface movement over angle and curve gives this motif some of its vital power and fascination.) As a result, using the head as a motif requires the sort of acute observation which we have described in Part One as initiating an act of perception. At the same time, the head is more than just an object—it is another human being like ourselves, and so involves us in the most fascinating imaginative experience of all: namely, a curiosity and concern about human values and human life.

It is my contention that when the motif or model possesses these dual characteristics—physical complexity of form, plus the power to excite our most personal human responses and attitudes—then it is possible for the artist to use his faculties of perception and vision almost simultaneously. So far as I can see, one major factor stands in the way of this experience for the beginning student. Any preoccupation with the technical difficulties of drawing can break the flow of expressive action which, I feel, is vital to the symbiotic relationship of perception and vision. Consequently, the student should use a medium over which he cannot fuss and linger, a medium like the monoprint. Earlier we used the inked surface of a glass plate, from which a print can be pulled, as a sensitive medium for both line drawing and tone "painting." Since the monoprint allows graphic expression to be achieved rapidly and with ease, we will use it to help overcome the technical difficulties that act as barriers to the integration of perception and vision. Our aim in using the head as a motif, and the monoprint medium as the means of expression, is to force you to study the motif, to be imaginatively stirred by it, to consciously develop new images along certain suggested lines, and to realize this perceptual and imaginative activity as spontaneously as possible.

Now for the briefing to help direct your imagination. Late medieval writers often referred to the seven deadly sins of mankind: pride, avarice, lust, anger, gluttony, envy, and sloth. In the religious mystery plays of the Middle Ages, the actor portraying a particular sin would

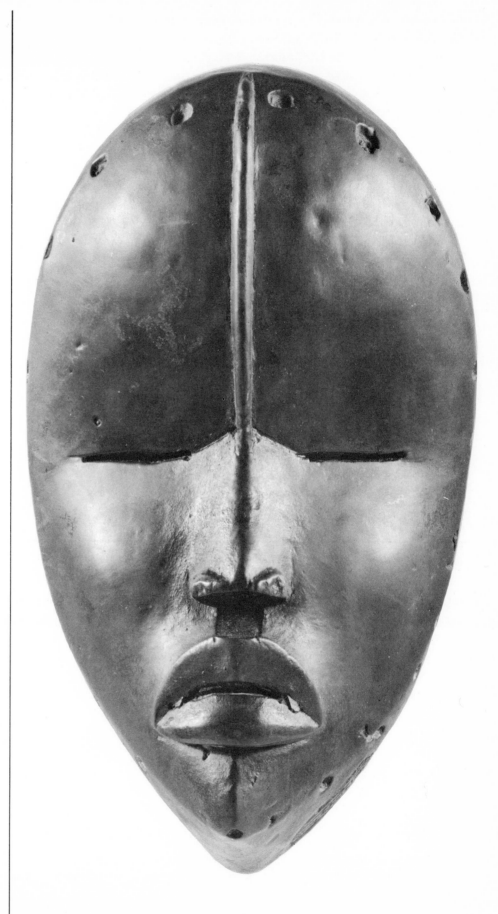

**Fig. 19–2**
**African dance mask, Ivory Coast**
*(The American Museum of Natural History)*

wear a mask that was shaped and painted to correspond to the sin. However, the aim of this work is not to design a mask, but to perceive and draw the head with all its volume, holes, and bony projections, and at the same time to imaginatively transform the head you see into an image of one of the seven deadly sins. Select one of them—what kind of head is a proud head, or an envious head, or a gluttonous head? As you draw from the model try to adapt the natural form of the motif to realize an image of one of the seven sins. Your drawing should be meaningful as head-form (the perceptual factor), and yet expressive of the sin (the imaginative transformation).

**THE DRAWING** A formally posed model is not necessary. Ask someone near you to keep still for a few moments while you observe him or her. Do this before you prepare the glass plate and assemble your drawing and wiping-off equipment. Take a good look at the profile, full-face, or three-quarter face and decide which will suit you best. Look intently at the head and explore with your eye the movement of the planes and curved surfaces as they move over high points into valleys and along the ridges. More than likely you will find your eyes returning to one point, through which all the rhythms of movement seem to pass: the cheekbone, the high point where the bone of the skull pushes hard against the skin of the face. It reflects light and is a point of strong thrust that creates a surface tension on the skin stretched tightly over it.

There are two other main thrust points on the profile: the chin and the out-jutting frontal bone of the forehead above the eyebrow. The structure of the profile is organized around these three points of the skull. If you will recall the analogy we used in Chapter 11 to illustrate the proposition that surface planes and curves tend to be organized around a thrust force—the analogy of the cloth over the vertical pole—you will realize that the same thing is happening here over the surface of the face. If we carry this analogy further, we can compare the profile to a tent where the canvas is pulled tight around poles stuck in the ground. Where the canvas pulls against a pole, it changes its plane or direction. The form of the tent is determined by the positions of the poles; although they are not visible, you perceive they are there because of the surface tension of the canvas at the places where its surface changes direction. Our perception of the face and head works in very much the same way. From the surface tension of the skin and the change in surface direction, we learn something about the bony skull we cannot see. The eyes are in sockets or holes (we have done some drawing of holes earlier), while the rest of the profile is high ground or valley.

When you feel that this study has given you a significant perception of the structural characteristics of the motif, then prepare the monoprint medium. When this is done, ask the model to pose again while you settle yourself down to make the drawing. You may then use him as you wish—a glance now and again might suffice, or you may need to observe more constantly. There are many ways in which you can change the character of the motif as your imagination is at work. Eyes may come closer together or be spread further apart; they may be deeply sunk or they may protrude. The mouth may turn up or down, be long and thin, or full and fleshy. The nose may be a beak, it may be retroussé, or it may disappear into two nostril holes. The volumes or masses may be distorted for expressive effect; the forehead may bulge and the chin may disappear, for example. But all of these possibilities will probably come to you in the act of drawing on the glass. The African dance mask that is shown in Fig. 19–2 stylizes the head-motif to reveal the basic skull structure that lies beneath the surface of the skin. The forehead,

**Fig. 19–3**
Victor Hugo, **Satanic Head**
*(Photograph by courtesy of The Museum of Modern Art, New York)*

227

cheekbones, and chin become high points through which all the rhythms of the head move. This simplification of head structure to essentials produces a formal design which possesses a great unity within itself. This is achieved because an over-all harmony exists between the several parts of the form. Yet its formal qualities do not detract from its mystery as a head—as an evocative image of man. The closed eyes, aquiline nose, and full, relaxed mouth, help to realize the artist's conscious or unconscious intentions in transforming the motif into an art object of imaginative expression and power. I have always thought that this mask is an ideal example of perception and vision coming together to make a work of art.

Now the inked surface of the glass plate does not allow too great a preoccupation with the detail of individual features. Only the basic structural characteristics which I have tried to describe, and which are so well revealed in Fig. 19–2, should be your concern. The ink dries fairly rapidly, and one cannot see too much of what is happening on the plate, so there can be no stopping to make constant comparisons with the model, and no worrying because the drawing does not "look right."

I would suggest that you work in pairs for this experiment, with one person acting as the motif while the other draws. Use all the tools previously found effective in performing the monoprint work described in Chapter 14, not forgetting a piece of rag for wiping off ink in order to make strong white parts in the drawing. The plate is ready and the head is before you. You have about half an hour to work on the glass before the ink becomes too dry. Keeping in mind the structural, perceptual implications of the motif, try to visualize the head of sloth, anger, pride, etc., vaguely materializing as you peer into the dark ink on the plate. Victor Hugo, the nineteenth-century French Romantic writer used to paint and draw a great deal. He would frequently flood the paper with a dark and blot-like wash,

**Fig. 19–4**

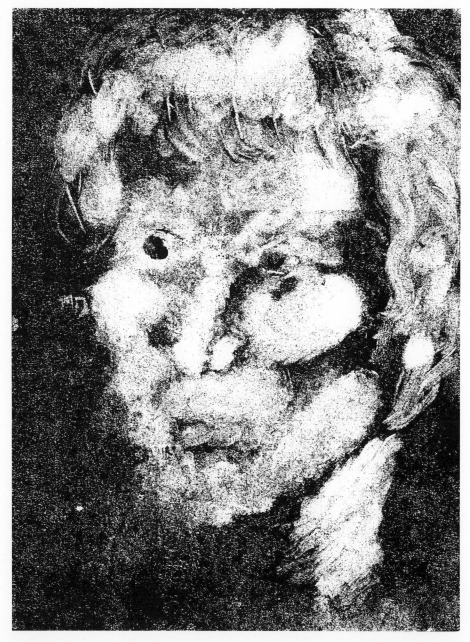

and then, using brush and sponge, he would begin to shape and clarify the image that he had partly perceived, partly imagined. Figure 19–3 shows one of his drawings, which is a perfect illustration for our experiment. This satanic head lurks darkly in the fluid paint, materializing or immaterializing. I would suggest that if you start with the rag by wiping off the ink very gently to give the high point of the cheekbone, and then do the same for the chin and the forehead, allowing the fluid quality of the medium its own freedom of movement, you may then see a vague ghost, as did Victor Hugo. Then work rapidly, moving directly into the ink: scrape, brush, scratch, and wipe.

In conclusion, we will let the illustrations speak for themselves. Two heads drawn under the conditions described above are reproduced in Figs. 19–4 and 19–5. They show a minimum of detail and emphasize the broad masses of light and dark as the structural nature of the head is realized. At the same time, each drawing reveals the human characteristics represented by one of the seven deadly sins which constitute the imaginative transformation of the motif.

When the print is finally taken from the glass it is quite a shock, for the glass itself does not reveal all of its graphic secrets before printing. The head that emerges is bold in form and full of drama. I think that any reasonably good image resulting from this experiment testifies to the synchronistic operation of perception and vision, even though teaching conditions of this sort are not ideal to demonstrate the thesis.

**Fig. 19–5**

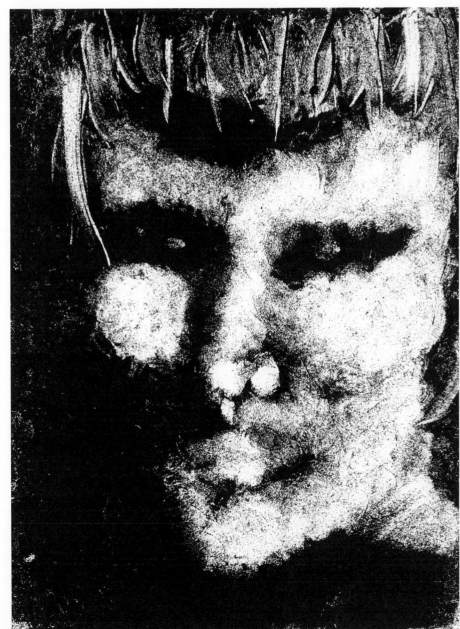

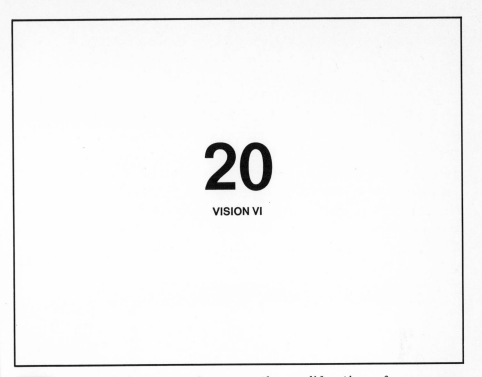

**20**

**VISION VI**

The twentieth century has seen the proliferation of many new and strange art forms. We see a strong desire to experiment, to move away from all traditional and absolutist ideas about art, to shun conventional techniques and media, and to make something that springs directly from the constantly shifting values of a high-speed scientific culture in which man has still to find himself. The terms "op," "pop," and "neo-dada," and "kinetic" are applied to art movements growing out of our time; and you may go into a gallery not to see paintings or sculpture, but to be present at a "happening." These contemporary developments should be mentioned in this last chapter, even though we are not attempting to treat them as studio experiences.

It is my view that these new styles have a common root. They are the offspring of the first great art experiment of this century—that is, cubism. Therefore, I want to focus my discussion of "artistic simultaneity" in terms of both cubism and the above-mentioned contemporary art forms. Changes in our conscious attitude to time, and the psychological problems occasioned by these changes, have motivated a great deal of contemporary art. The cubists, led by Picasso and Braque,

**Fig. 20–1**
**Photogram producing an image
of the cube motif**
*(Herbert M. Rosenthal)*

# Artistic
# simultaneity

started by analyzing an object and presenting several aspects of it simultaneously. The pop artist analyzes our culture and makes an image which juxtaposes several aspects of it, or symbols of aspects of it. Hence, although cubism is fifty years old, it is still relevant for today's art student, for it is the shot that started the modern art revolution, as Einstein's mathematical theories started the new scientific era. Consequently, the practical work of this chapter will be concerned with cubist time and space, but the discursive and philosophical ramifications of the exercise are, I believe, relevant to the art of mid-century.

If I were to be asked what aspect of twentieth-century progress had most significantly affected human life, I would say the time factor. The mathematical theories of Einstein, which were published in 1905, and the 1901 quanta theory of Max Planck are generally taken to mark the commencement of the intrinsic life and attitudes of the twentieth century. The Theory of Relativity produced the realization that even the scientific method could not make absolute predictions about the dynamic universe—that any prediction was subject to a degree of uncertainty if applied universally to all time-space situations. To add to the confusion, the speed of travel has been increasing at a pace which, helped by the adjustments in time as one passes through the various zones, makes it possible for one to be in two places at once, so far as clock time is concerned. In the area of communications, first photography, then the cinematograph, and finally the television have brought the world to the individual. In the case of live television, a man can sit at home and simultaneously be present at a happening thousands of miles away.

Thus we see a culture developing in which the growing speed of movement and communication disrupts man's long-established attitudes toward past, present, and future time. The same culture heralds the birth of a new scientific age in which the presumed absolute truths of the Newtonian world become qualified and give way to a series of relative truths—there is really no one simple truth. Traditional certainties are drastically shaken, and man begins the difficult reappraisal of his position in a changing universe. Just as cubism represents the first artistic response to the bewildering situation at the beginning of the century, the so-called "happenings" represent the mid-century response. Our culture has moved a long way since 1905, and developments in atomic physics and space travel, together with new and in-

ARTISTIC
SIMULTANEITY

**VISION VI**

232

credible astronomic predictions, have far outstripped any system of philosophy that satisfactorily relates man to the universe. The younger artists of our day find it difficult to relate to the past—to history and to the traditional modes of imagery. And they find very little cultural stability to augur well for the future. Movement and change are the keynotes of our society, and the most significant reality is the moment or the day which we live *now*. Thus the post-World War II generation accepts an existential attitude to life in which the qualitative moment rather than the quantitative flow of time is the main focus. This existential point of view is reflected in the immediate impact of light and movement with which the viewer is confronted in kinetic sculpture, in the cynicism and neo-cubist technique of pop art, in the chance discovery of relationships in neo-dada assemblage, and finally in the staging of a "happening" where something is going on before your very eyes.

The art of simultaneously showing both hidden and visible aspects of an object in the one image—a trend started by cubism—obviously creates a new time situation. Visual experiences which normally are "spread out" in time are presented as one simultaneous visual impact, and thus give the work an immediate sense of the "now."

Yet the question remains: What do we mean by artistic simultaneity? The word simultaneous is straightforward enough, meaning that several events are taking place at the same time, rather than in series or one after the other. As a spectator at the circus you may have experienced a situation when three or four acts are going on in the ring together. To see them you have to move your head and focus on each in turn; you do not, in fact, *see* them simultaneously. If we could widen our cone of vision at the point of focus, then we could receive more sensations in the same moment of time, and thus see more at once. But our visual experience is governed by the focusing of our eyes on one thing at a time, which means that seconds or even minutes can pass before we have seen all of a thing. As you watch the acrobat perform a handstand, you miss the clowns who are fooling about with the bucket of water; you will never see what they were doing at that moment. Consequently we realize that human visual experience is limited in its ability to take a comprehensive view of events, because of this linear sequence to our seeing. Our visual sensations occur in series, one after the other, even if by only a fraction of a second. We could other factors. We must now elaborate on the significance of perception as it relates to both time and movement factors, for this is essential to any understanding of cubism or artistic simultaneity.

Sensations result from light striking the surfaces of things, and the consequent revelation of their surface properties. Then, as we have seen, these light sensations occur in series as either we or the object shifts position, thus allowing new aspects of the surface to come into view. As each new aspect is sensed, it represents a transformation of the object because it adds to the previous sensory information received. Perception, however, is not limited to particular sensations of this sort; we can say that an act of perception is capable of replicating the object in the conscious mind as an instantaneous total entity, for the thing is not perceived as a collection of varied surface aspects but as a unified, single phenomenon. But perception goes further than this, for, as I have said earlier, it is capable of heightening our mental awareness of the object's whole form so that we may appreciate the subtle relationships between part and part, and gain insight into its essential structural nature. A series of visual sensations providing information about specific aspects of a thing are geared to a continuous "line" of time, but perception occurs when all of these exposures are

Fig. 20–3
Giacomo Balla
**Dynamism of a Dog on a Leash** (1912)
*(By courtesy of George F. Goodyear and the Buffalo Fine Arts Academy)*

mentally realized with apparent simultaneity. Consequently, one is hardly aware of the time factor in the sort of instant apprehension which characterizes a true perceptual experience. The situation remains the same when it is the object that moves while the viewer stays in a relatively fixed position. Here again, although sensory information varies as new aspects of the object are presented, our perception of the object remains invariable. The object is not distorted during violent movement, although it would be were perception to depend entirely upon sensory information.

It was inevitable that an interest in sensation and perception and their relationship to time and movement should occupy artists after art had freed itself from its twin masters, representational illusion (a concern with light sensations showing the visible surface properties of objects in space) and the perspectival method (use of a fixed viewing position). This interest in the object in motion is typified in Marcel Duchamp's *Nude Descending a Staircase, No. 2* of 1912 (Fig. 20–2), and Giacomo Balla's *Dog on a Leash* of the same year (Fig. 20–3). In both these works the artists are attempting to realize sensations rather than perceptions. Balla's painting is the less sophisticated of the two, for in attempting to show the motion of walking he resorts to the rather childlike method of drawing a series of legs in the different positions of backward and forward movement, which reminds us of figure-motion in an early movie. Duchamp's painting is much more subtle. The figure-object is distorted, not merely repeated, as it moves through space. The painting presents a series of momentary visual stimuli, or sensations, as a new aspect of the object is presented in each second of time. The result is a fluid and variable image, not at all like the image of perception which remains invariably solid despite time and movement. You can see what use the artist makes of the main mechanical axes of figurative movement, such as the vertical spine moving around the 360 degrees of a tilted, circular pelvis. The painting is a self-conscious attempt to reveal sensation per se, *before* the autonomous and more unconscious orderings inherent in such visual serialism give us the inviolated object we would normally perceive. But it should be pointed out that Duchamp's painting, despite its sciential exploration of visual experience, possesses what we have previously called painterly quality, whereas, in my opinion, the *Dog on a Leash* does not.

This has been a rather summary preamble to our main purpose, which is the drawing experiment itself. But I feel it is necessary because it sets the scene for the kind of visual exploration with which we shall be concerned. It is also important because it introduces the idea of an artistic simultaneity. By this I mean that although Marcel Duchamp's figure may have taken three or four seconds to move down the stairs, his painting presents a continuous event in time in an image in which everything can be seen happening at once. We are to experiment with a similar problem.

The various aspects of an object fall into two broad categories. There are those that cannot be seen from one particular viewing position, but which become visible as we look at the thing from all sides, either by walking round it or by turning the object. (Both movement and time are involved, whichever we do.) Secondly, there are those aspects of an object which are not externally visible: the hidden, internal aspects of the object. We may be able to deduce or to intuitively sense the interior shape of a thing from its surface appearance, particularly if it moves. Or we can dissect the object physically to discover this internal prospect. In the case of the *Nude Descending a Staircase*, for example, the artist reveals certain internal aspects of

the figure—aspects which are sensed by virtue of surface movement, and aspects which are known through actual anatomical study. It was the cubist and futurist movements that developed the practice of depicting in one painting what can be *seen* of an object (as either it or the viewer moves in space), together with what is *known* about an object as the result of analysis and study from many different viewpoints. This, of course, produced many difficulties for the viewer, who had been conditioned for so many centuries to an art concerned only with the appearance of things seen from a fixed viewpoint. Simultaneous projection of these serialist images in one design produced drawings of the head, for example, in which a profile was superimposed over a full face and a full face over a profile, as in Picasso's drawings shown in Figs. 20–4 and 20–5. The design that results from such a simultaneous projection of differing aspects is, of course, a new formal image in its own right. If you study Fig. 20–5 closely you will be able to pick out the various explored aspects of a head, even down to the skull-shaped front view with its one eye and large nose at center-left. Yet these differing "parts" are put together by the artist in such a way that they cease to be merely a series of differing sensations. The really significant thing about these drawings is that the new de-

**Fig. 20–5**
Pablo Picasso
**The Bust**
(©*Spadem 1967 by French Reproduction Rights Inc.*)

sign maintains a rigidity, order, and cohesion which satisfy the needs of normal perceptual experience. It would seem that when the artist self-consciously tries to treat visual sensations momentarily received, his ultimate design possesses all the unified and invariable characteristics of a perceived object. Although this cubist approach leads to the visual fragmentation of the object, a new unity is created in the work of art—an artistic unity which is an intuitively achieved, *new* perceptual reality. It is this intuitive re-creation of the object into a new cohesive image, after a series of sensations experienced in sequence, which I would describe as cubist vision.

The following experiment is intended to introduce you to time and movement in art, and to help you achieve an image in which particular things first seen in sequence are shown happening simultaneously.

**Fig. 20–6**
Pablo Picasso
**Violin and Grapes** (1912)
*(Collection, The Museum of Modern Art, New York. Mrs. David M. Levy Bequest)*

**THE DRAWINGS** The first drawings are to train the eye to concentrate on only one particular aspect of an object, consciously keep this sensation "in focus." Make a cone of stiff paper about 9" high. Do not make a base for the model as you will be required to look inside to see varying aspects of this space-defining object. The first step is to make a series of small drawings of the cone. First, make a straightforward drawing of the model as it appears at the normal eye level. Place this in the top left-hand corner of the sheet of paper, then produce about twenty 3" squares to the right of and beneath it in orderly rows.

The goal is to draw as many different aspects of the cone as you can. View it from many positions and draw each new presentation. Pick the model up and see it from every possible angle, inside and out. Fill about half of the squares with these drawings. Now try to visualize the object cut through and opened out. This imaginative fragmentation of the model is not easy. It requires a strong visual concentration—an X-ray-eye approach. Fill in the remaining squares with these deduced sectional aspects of the cone. Figure 20–7 shows a sheet of these drawings. All of these aspects of the cone resulted from concentrating visual attention on different parts of the object, and the fact that you could see inside it enabled you to reveal internal aspects of the thing. The drawings were made sequentially, each the result of a differing sensation as the object changed its position. If these disparate drawings were to become unified in a single design such as Picasso might achieve (Fig. 20–5), then you would have an image in which a cone is simultaneously fragmented and unified.

The second series of drawings is similar to those just completed, but instead of using a hollow geometric figure as a model we shall take a solid, organic fruit. One cannot see the internal aspects of a lemon, and so we must make an anatomical study of it. These drawings may be set out on a single sheet of paper exactly like the others, or they may be freely arranged. Start with a drawing of one external aspect of the fruit, and then cut into the lemon and draw its sectional aspects from several viewpoints. This dissection will enable you to examine the internal "organs" of the lemon and to draw them separately as well. Stop when you have a good selection of lemon parts.

The real test comes with the final drawing. The proposition now is to select approximately half-a-dozen of your aspect drawings of the lemon, bringing them together in a new black and white drawing. You can make this drawing any size you like, but I think the dimensions should not be less than 6″ x 6″ if you use a square format. Now you have a similar problem to that faced by Picasso in making his drawing *The Bust* (Fig. 20–5). How are you to put the pieces together so than an artistic and perceptual unity is achieved, and a lemon "happening" created? The new image, when it is realized, will obviously not be a representational illustration of a lemon; and yet it should evoke the essence of *lemonness*. The simultaneous presentation of so many differing

Fig. 20–7

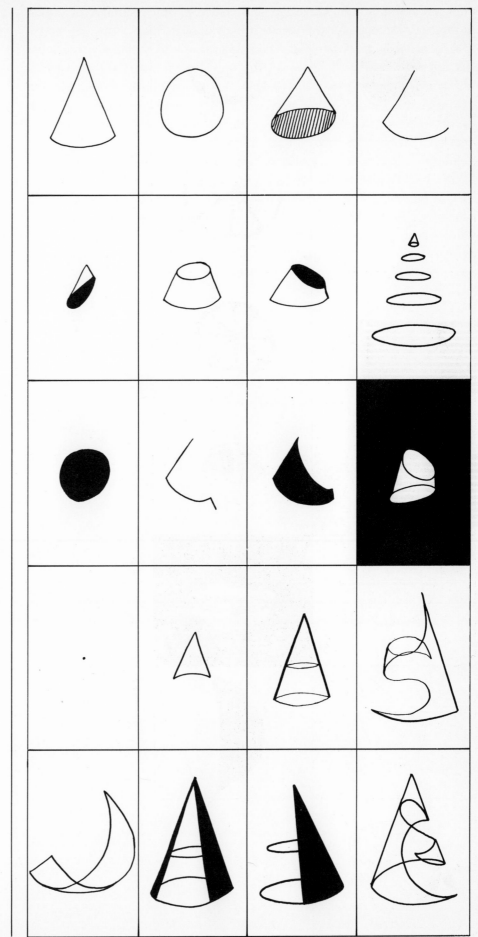

241

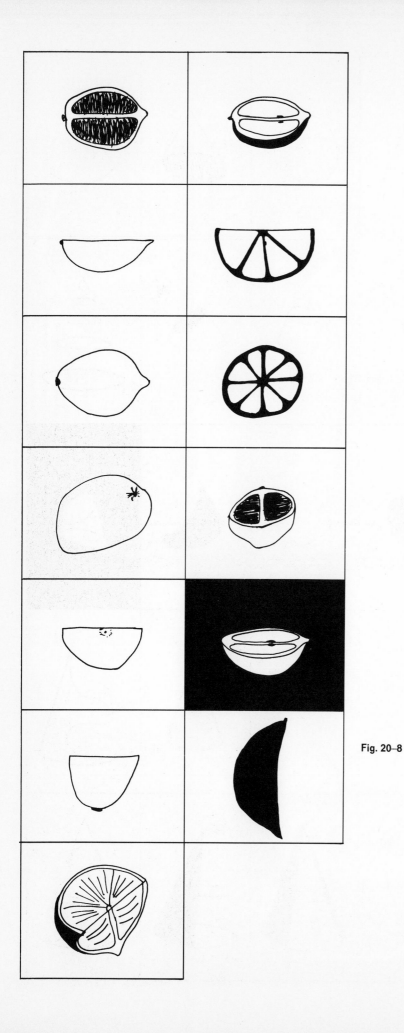

Fig. 20—8

lemon sensations can give the drawing an immediacy strong enough to suggest the occurrence of some event involving a lemon.

It should be stressed that this is not merely a question of formally organizing the parts in a pleasing "form-to-space" relationship. Both Picasso and Braque have always insisted on the intuitive, spontaneous, and unconscious nature of their cubist activity, as opposed to an intellectual or conceptual approach. Perhaps one could say that you should have an instinctive feeling for lemon shape or lemon quality, although I realize that this statement is too vague to be very helpful. Once again we must turn to a visual example in order to make the point clear. If you look at Pablo Picasso's *Violin and Grapes* (Fig. 20–6), you will notice that the artist has created a painting in which sensations of multifarious aspects of the violin dominate the whole image—even the space takes on a sympathetic violin-wood quality, and the grapes are interchangeable with the violin tuning pegs. The painting creates a violinlike world which one can enter and experience almost physically, or which one can observe as a spectator at an event. In your own drawing you should try to ensure a simultaneous presentation of lemon sensations, to create an image in which both space and form is "lemoned," so to speak.

In order to accomplish this, try to let this final drawing grow of itself and develop according to the feeling evoked in you by the tangible object. Perhaps suggesting that you surpass the transitory nature of sensation, and

Fig. 20–9

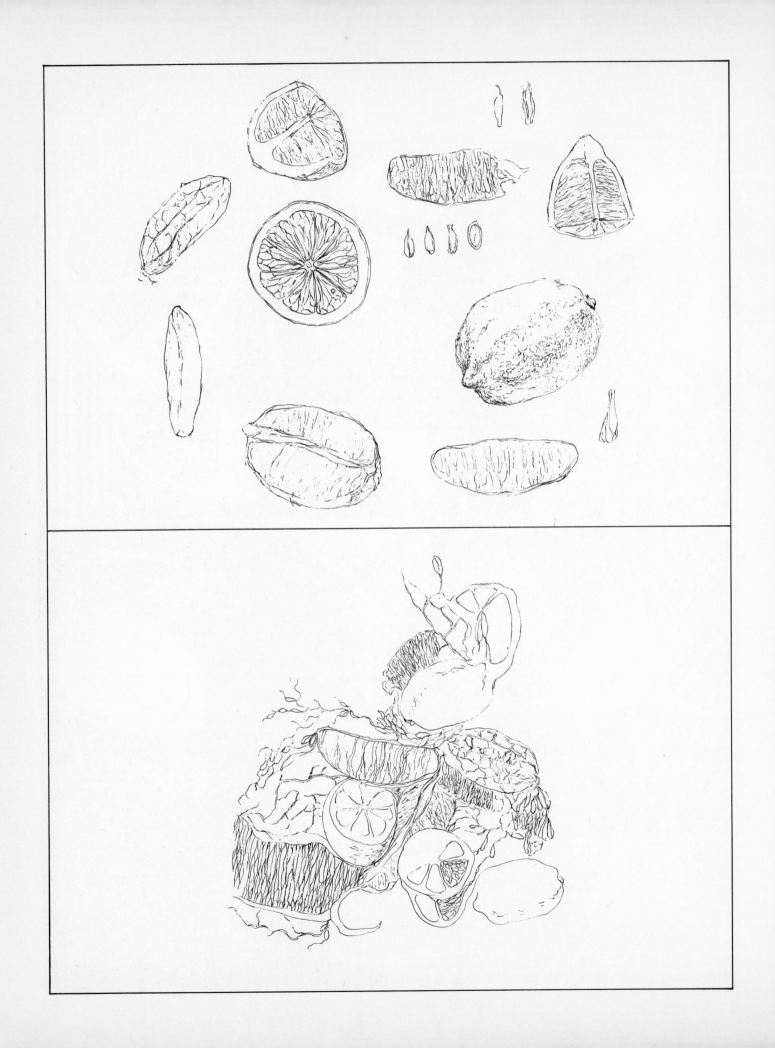

move nearer to the eternal principle of things, would be an excessively metaphysical request, but Sie Ho, a critic and painter in late fifth-century China, gives Six Laws of Painting of which the second, *The law of bones by means of the brush*, might also be a manifesto for cubism as we have described it. He suggests that it is only by simultaneously experiencing the essentials of both internal structure and external surfaces that the artist can evoke the true feeling of the object, or its real essence. And this is what perception is—the true feeling of the object. You should study Fig. 20–8 in company with Fig. 20–9. The former illustrates a student's response to the lemon dissection experiment, and the latter is the same student's composite drawing using these aspects of the lemon. Figures 20–10 and 20–11 are in complete contrast. The drawings here are less stylized and more organic. Again, the first of these reveals the several aspects of the lemon, and the second makes use of line only to create an image which is dominated by a feeling for the fleshlike tissue of the fruit's interior.

**CONCLUSIONS** From Cubism, one of the key movements of this century, much of our totally abstract art has been finally achieved. I have been describing what is loosely called "analytical cubism," which implies the presence of an object. But by 1910 Picasso and Braque were inventing cubist images without the help of objects, a development generally termed "synthetic cubism." The labels are not important, but the principles are. For in the later phase the artist realizes his complete freedom to create autonomously, emancipated from the tyranny imposed both by the object and the limitations of visual sensations. Although the traditional cubist images are now themselves part of art history and may well be considered old-fashioned by the contemporary student, the breakthrough they achieved is reflected in all the newer freedoms of the last decade. As I see it, the main difference between early cubist freedom and contemporary freedom in art, as found in such movements as neodada, pop, and "happenings," is that the stimulus for the artist has shifted. The avant garde artist today is not concerned with objects as things which are to be formally analyzed—the object itself is not the stimulus. Instead, he is spurred by the life of the culture itself, and the values (or lack of them) which it supports. Images of objects and the world are used as signs, and in some cases as symbols, to comment upon the ethos of our society. The pop artist or the neo-dadaist will use such cultural images in the same way as a cubist would use the varied aspects of an object. He will

Fig. 20–10
Adele Travisano
**Aspects of a lemon**

Fig. 20–11
Adele Travisano
**Final lemon drawing**

draw them from many sources, often far removed in origin and unrelated in time, and create his art by means of painting, collage, or construction, in any combination. Or he may take a familiar object, such as a nation's flag, and render it strangely unfamiliar by breaking it up and superimposing part upon part, creating both optical illusion and dadaesque oddity. Figure 20–12 is a painting by Robert Rauschenberg which uses photographs and reproductions by silk-screening them onto a canvas and then relates them spatially by painting. In the painting *Kite* there are photographic images of flag-carrying Scouts over which are superimposed fragmentary images of weapon-carrying soldiers. The result is deliberately ambiguous, vague, and difficult to date. The hovering helicopter however, is a sign of present war, while the eagle, enigmatic and detached, is a universal sign of power which was used as long ago as the days of Imperial Rome. There is a great deal more one could say about this painting, particularly in terms of its spatial qualities, for the changing planes of depth also relate to the differing phases of time which are evoked. There is a suggestion of infinite distance as well as of immediate and frontal space, which aids the aesthetic and psychological impact of the figurative motifs. But my prime reason for using this painting is to illustrate that the method employed by Rauschenberg in presenting such diverse images simultaneously has its roots in the cubist revolution. Instead of showing us aspects of an *object*, the painting shows us happenings in the life of society, but the painting telescopes differing events in time in the true cubist tradition.

At the beginning of this chapter I suggested that we were gradually acquiring an existential attitude to the qualitative moment of time, and that this attitude leads us to search for some significance in the happenings that are going on all the time, whether they be trivial or momentous. My reason for closing this book with an experiment in cubist simultaneity is to present a brief thesis showing that our changing evaluation of time lies behind some of our most radical art experiments. I have tried to show that the simultaneity of a cubist painting possesses an existential quality, and that cubism may thus be regarded as a major twentieth-century signpost to the art that happens before your eyes. You flick the switch, the colored lights come on, the construction moves, and you enjoy the changing colored aspects that kinetic sculpture presents.

Fig. 20–12
Robert Rauschenberg
**Kite**
*(Courtesy Ileana Sonnabend, Paris)*

Review
Section

**DRAWING MARKS |** A sensitivity to the quality of lines and marks, to degrees of tone, and to surface can be developed only by constant exposure to these aspects of drawing. Consequently, from time to time, further experiments must be suggested to call on the student's initiative in the selection of material and in the personal use he can make of them in both objective and nonobjective experimental drawing.

**SPACE |** Further work to continue the development of natural depth perception and spatial relationships can be accomplished in many different ways, but here are a few suggestions.

1.
Reproduce a complex grid taken from one of the linear structure drawings of Chapter 3 and fill in a minimum of six spatial regions with freehand vertical lines. Create six positions in depth by varying the concentration of lines in each space and by changing line weight and quality. The same exercise can be repeated by filling in the grid spaces with paint, moving from black to gray to lighter gray, etc., according to the depth position desired.

2.
Make a free charcoal drawing in a nonobjective composition that, once again, achieves spatial relationships through degrees of drawing weight and intensity of tone.

3.
Achieve variations on the "space-grid" idea in which surface textures create degrees of frontality or recession. Collage materials may be used as in Review Figure 2.

4.
Take a newspaper sheet containing type and photographs and allow your natural depth perception to operate over the areas of blackness, grayness, or comparative whiteness. Build up a grid with brush and line around these perceived areas of varying depth, allowing the grid line, by means of weight and quality, to emphasize and accentuate the depth positions of the perceived regions.

**FORM |** An awareness of skeletal form, an ability to express it in drawing, a realization of how summarily its limbs divide space, and a knowledge of when to use linear structure in drawing and design problems—all should be developed through further work. The drawing experiments suggested below provide opportunities for development.

1.
Consciously apply the skeletal structure of natural objects to the designing of screens, street lamps, wood and metal chair frames, or similar artifacts (see Review Figures 1 and 3).

2.
By means of articulated skeletal structures, experiment with the figure in action and repose, with or without the model.

3.
From observation of forms that are strongly skeletal and demand an appreciation and expression of linear structure, make still-life and plant drawings.

4.
Draw imaginatively from the stimulation of trees, plants, biological magnifications of organisms, and other natural objects whose skeletal form encourages linear abstraction and personal expression.

5.
Draw to give ideas for pictorial development; take your first inspiration from a linear organization of surface derived from some visual skeletal stimulus such as the tracery of floating pond weed, veins on the back of the hand, a bare vine in winter.

# Suggestions for Further Work

**FORM II** The many uses of the continuous surface directional line and tone as a means of expressing both space and mass volume are fairly obvious (see Review Figure 4), but further projects requiring their use are suggested as follows:

1.
Draw the figure, from the model if possible, in many positions, as a series of contour volumes, perhaps *over* an articulated skeleton, as suggested in the review to Form I.

2.
Try an expressive drawing of objects possessing strong mass form and/or holes, where both surface line and tone can realize the form. Experimenting with the dry brush and the finger as drawing instruments for both contour line and tone gives surprising results.

3.
Draw free, imagined forms expressed through surface line and tone—forms in significant juxtaposition possessing pictorial suggestions.

4.
Make free and imaginative drawings of space—of air formations, of smoke, vapor, steam, etc.—where form is moving and constantly changing.

5.
Make large charcoal drawings (5' x 3') of imagined wood forms, using the surface line to produce a sweeping rhythm of arm movement.

**SPACE II** The instinctive tendency to organize space into "regions of space" by the introduction of form has been shown in this chapter. Further work in space perception and in the "designing" of space is best carried out as suggested for Space I.

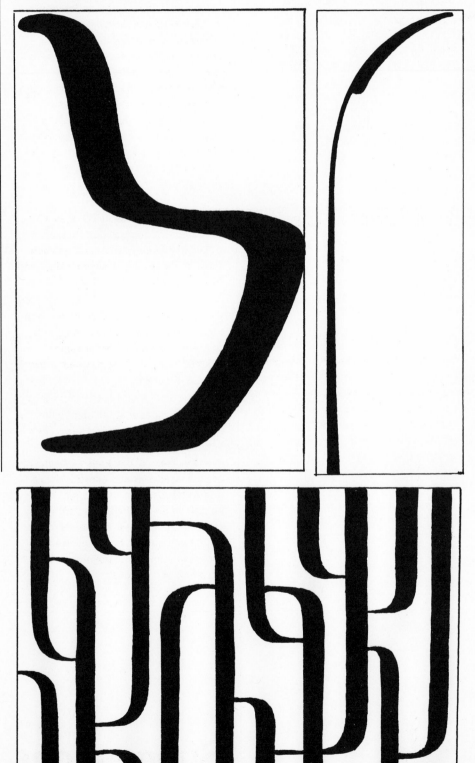

**Review Fig. 1**
*Drawings for a laminated wood chair frame, a concrete street lamp, and a metal screen. These drawings represent a development of the skeletal structure drawings. They reveal the student's increased awareness of space-to-form relationships in this type of object and his attempts to produce a linear form which possesses a strong organic structure.*

**SPACE III** Many experiments can be devised to attack the problem of deliberately having to express space perception through drawing. Here are three suggestions.

1.

Observe the operation of a water sprinkler on the grass in summer as it moves through a complete circle. Make a series of freehand sketches which indicate the height and curvature of the water jet's arc in perhaps fifteen or twenty positions throughout the complete circle of movement. In the studio, translate these sketches into one diagrammatic drawing which attempts to show the full circle of movement followed by the sprinkler, the constant or varying arcs of the jet in different positions on this circle, and the regions of space in depth created by the moving arc.

2.

Using a series of lines of differing weight and quality, design a space-grid in which some areas are almost entirely enclosed by lines and therefore project forward, while others, more open, recede at various depths. Separately, design a simple form which suggests a fast-revolving metallic body, and then draw this in four or five of the space regions. In the space which is most frontal, this body should be large and strong in line and weight; in the chosen space most receding, the revolving body should be small and light in drawing. In between these two extremes, the size and weight of the body should depend upon the relative space position of the region it is to occupy. The drawing, when complete, should suggest a space region of

infinite depth with materializing bodies flying in from outer space.

3.

"Draw" with different types of wire, using a line in the air to work out various problems three-dimensionally; for example, "The Disappearing Square," "The Square and the Round," "Space Compressed," "Diminution of a Theme," and so on.

**Review Fig. 2**
*Black and white collage using type and newsprint. The aim is to create many regions of depth dependent upon the "blackness" and size of the type used, and to develop some positive focal points. An exercise of this sort should follow the brush-dabbing experiment in Chapter 6.*

**FORM AND SPACE II** Many possible developments for this chapter are available in the drawings already made. These abstract sketches can be developed into full-scale abstract designs, incorporating tone, line, texture, and spatial depth, all of which have been previously discussed. Other suggestions would be

1.

Set up still-life groups which have a strong dynamic factor operating (a bottle right on the corner of the table, almost falling off, or objects supporting other objects rather tenuously). Translate such a group into a drawing revealing tension, equilibrium or stasis.

2.

Attempt to work out some design problems, such as possibilities for a six-light chandelier or a large water fountain. For a beginning express only the linear forces involved. See what *shapes* that might develop into the actual object are suggested by these line drawings.

**FORM AND SPACE III** Again, developments here can be made from the abstract and semi-abstract drawings already made, as suggested for form and Space II, above. Here are some other possibilities.

1.

Draw additional landscapes that treat space as solidly as form, to produce an integrated space-form pictorial structure.

2.

Thinking of the same space-form integration; and either the spatial extension of an object or its potential movement, work with still life, the figure, or the portrait, treating the space around the object or head, between the legs and arms, as shape positively related to the object, head or figure. Or draw from architecture and townscape with the same intention. (Study the paintings of Lyonel Feininger, for example.)

3.

Trees, particularly, make fine subjects for translation into spatial extension patterns, with integrated spatial regions. (Piet Mondrian's tree abstractions would repay study in this regard.)

**FORM III** The understanding and use of the structural unit is important principally to the designer. Some further experiments are as follows:

1.

Build a free-standing model, using one repeating unit of structure; for example, matchsticks, plastic hair curlers, nails, paper clips, etc.

2.

Make further imaginative drawings of "freaks" in nature, using an actual unit of structure taken from a natural object.

3.

Design an architectural unit from which to construct a screen wall.

4.

Examine some models of molecular structure—zinc or hemoglobin, for example. Select one that is not too complex and draw it simply as a system of lines and black blobs. Taking this drawing as the unit, create a complex pattern in a 9-inch square. At the same time, vary the line weight as the unit is repeated over the whole area to produce regions of depth in the spaces thus formed.

**FORM IV** All drawings of complex surfaces demand visual analysis of the organization of planes, curves, and angles, automatically making the artist aware of the pressure forces operating in and on the object. The following exercises are suggested to continue exploring this surface tension aspect of form.

1.
Draw the forms that develop in material other than paper after it is crumpled, bent, squeezed, or subjected to any other mechanical action. Use silk, aluminum foil, plastic sheeting, clay, etc., and notice the diverse surface formations created, owing to the different resistances of the various materials.

2.
Draw still life made up entirely of complex, folded materials, from pleated paper to folded textiles.

3.
Using a magnifying glass, make an enlarged drawing of wrinkled skin. There are several regions on the back of the hand and fingers that serve for this. Notice what happens to the surface when the skin is tensed by clenching the hand and when it is relaxed.

4.
Make five drawings which illustrate the development of a form to complexity. First make a simple, solid triangle from a sheet of aluminum foil, and then push into it once, with a finger. Draw the result. Push in the triangle again at another point and draw the result. Proceed in this manner until five drawings have been produced.

5.
Fill a drawing notebook with sketches of quarry walls, rock formations, rock surfaces, the wrinkles of cabbages and bark—anything, in fact, of interesting surface structure.

**FORM V: SURFACE TEXTURE** Some suggestions for further work to develop sensitivity to surface texture.

1.
Ink over surfaces possessing interesting qualities and take a print on sensitive paper; for example, take a print from the end of a cut log. Build up a collection of such prints for reference purposes.

2.
Experiment with the monoprint to produce textures (see Review Figure 5). Select several differing surfaces from the prints and put them together in the form of a collage.

3.
Select a poem that evokes mood, one that suggests laughter, sorrow, tranquility, anger, and so on. Attempt to make a translation of the poem in terms of textures, either by collage, or drawing, or both.

**Review Fig. 3**
*A sheet of quick sketches experimenting with a chair's skeletal structure, and some notes on line weight and projection to aid in seeing linear values on the chair frame.*

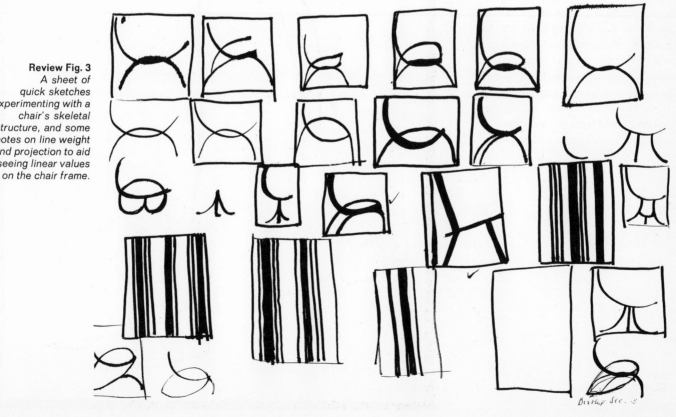

**FORM VI** Although Chapter 13 does not describe any practical work in its discussion on the aesthetic implications of form, I make a few suggestions here for some drawing experiences.

Perhaps it is not a good thing to develop too strong a conscious attitude to the aesthetic implications of form, as so much of this is intuitively present in a personal drawing. In any case, that which constitutes the aesthetic cannot be rigidly or even simply defined; but some awareness of it is helpful, and so the following suggestions for further development of this chapter are made.

1.
Select a flower or a leaf which has a strong aesthetic appeal as form. Draw it freely, deliberately exaggerating the particular aspect that appeals. Observe the drawing and decide if it appeals as much as the original object. Analyze why the answer is "yes" or "no." Determine why, and when, over-idealization defeats its own ends.

2.
To induce a mental and deliberate appreciation of form, take a simple cube, like the building brick, and draw it very lightly and quite large. Now work over this drawing by cutting into the cubic form and adding facets and more cubic volumes to produce a drawing of a sculptured brick form. Organize the design consciously and appraise it at each stage. Justify the design on intellectual grounds of proportion, symmetry, balance, etc.

3.
Repeat the second exercise, this time freely and as the spirit moves you, with very little deliberation about the way you modify the brick cube. Compare the result with the first drawing and determine whether the deliberate or the free attitude has produced the more satisfactory design.

**VISION I** Building up a nonobjective design through addition and subtraction can be carried out without using the linoleum block.

1.
Scratchboard can be used by scraping out a white shape first, putting part of it back with brush and ink, scraping out again and then inking back, until, by this give-and-take method, the area is eventually occupied by some arrangement of black and white forms.

**Review Fig. 4**
*Treatment of a draped shirt by outline alone, and then by means of the continuous surface contour line.*

**2.**
On a white sheet of paper, using two brushes—one for white paint and one for black—build up forms. First add free black forms, then modify them by breaking into them with white paint. Continue this process of alternate addition and subtraction until the design is complete.

**3.**
Work as in 2 above, with charcoal and kneaded eraser. Use the charcoal to lay in areas of black quite freely on the paper and use the eraser actually as a drawing tool, to take off in the black regions. Build up until the design is complete.

**VISION II** The following experiments are suggested to develop a stronger realization of common qualities of "shapeness" between forms and of how small a change in form is required to produce a new aesthetic implication.

**1.**
Draw freely with a brush and ink on a large sheet of paper to discover the transitions by which a square becomes a circle. Brush in a solid square at the top left, and working to the right, repeat this square, but make one change in its shape on each occasion. For example, the second square might lose a corner, the third another corner, and so on, until a complete circle results. Repeat this by going from cylinder to cone, square to triangle, etc. Notice the intermediate stages and realize how basically "near" each other are these forms. Try this shape metamorphosis by brush drawing transitions from free forms, and see what shapes result.

**2.**
Using an illustration from this book for reference, the Greek amphora (Fig. 13–1), make a series of drawings, each drawing attempting to exploit further the most personally attractive aspect of the original. The aspect might be the object's curvature, or its slim proportion, or its angularity. How far can this expressive change go before it degenerates into caricature or vulgar exaggeration and novelty? Is the original object already at a point of maximum aesthetic expression?

**3.**
Change unitary form into compound form. In a rectangle about 9″ x 7″, brush in a solid black circle occupying approximately one-fifth of the total area. Using the brush, extend this figure into the remaining area of the rectangle by pulling out limbs, protrusions, etc. Stop when the new form is sufficiently complex and when the empty area is satisfactorily occupied. This extension process can be done with many different types of unitary form.

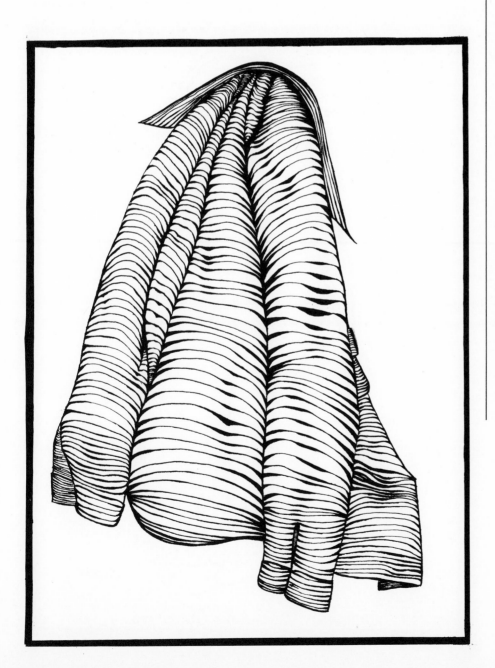

**VISION III** Sensitivity to painterly quality is most effectively induced by a personal involvement with shape and with color, an involvement demanding value judgments of a personal nature. Here are two suggestions for work in this chapter.

1.
Try abstracting from great paintings. Select some prints of paintings by El Greco, Rubens, Titian, Raphael, or other great artists (magazine reproductions are quite suitable for this). Pick out the main forms of the design and the main rhythms which hold the design together. Attempt to express these forms and these rhythms in a black water-color drawing with a full range of tones, one which will be an expressive abstract of the original.

2.
Collect a whole range of possible collage material centered around a specific color range—reds to browns or blues to greens—and consider textures and forms as well as color. Select from a wide range of sources. Assemble a design using this material, bearing in mind the phrase, "a significant and expressive combination of shapes and colors." Remember the complementary function of black and white to color. When the assemblage is complete, varnish it. This will give a homogenous quality to the color and the forms of the design.

**VISION IV** A constant exercise of the imagination must always be sought in art. The following work is suggested as an appendage to the chapter on the visual imagination.

1.
Select some large, full-page black-and-white photographs from books or magazines and using four pieces of paper, mask out areas of the picture, thus allowing concentration on one small region. After some experimentation, select one such region and enlarge it into a black-and-white drawing which will almost certainly be abstract, and which may begin to intrigue the imagination.

2.
Spatter some blots, large and small, onto a sheet of drawing paper. What do they suggest? How would you draw into them? Will the finished drawing suggest a landscape or a figure? Find some reproductions of "blot drawings" made by Alexander Cozens, the English eighteenth-century landscape painter.

3.
Observe surfaces in nature, stained and molded surfaces of rocks, leaves, tree bark, and similar things. What suggestions of forms are to be found in these variegated surfaces; what do they suggest to the pictorial imagination? Draw!

4.
Observe some highly magnified illustrations of biological cross sections. Here is a complete new world of form. Once again, what will the pictorial imagination find here? Make more drawings.

**VISION V** For further imaginative drawing from the observed object:

1.
From the figure, make a dozen quick drawings of diverse, five-minute poses by the model. Place the figures thus drawn in a new imaginative context in one design. It will be a help to study some of the figure compositions of Nicolas Poussin, the seventeenth-century French artist.

2.
From nature, draw a cabbage. Transform this into a face of old, old age.

3.
Set up some drapery, three or four separate lengths, having varied organizations of folds, in vertical formation against a wall. Keep about three feet of space between each length. Draw these vertical lengths of cloth using wide paper, and fill in the gaps by introducing an imaginary *draped* figure. This figure should not intrude, but should belong naturally among the folded material and result in an extravaganza of figure and fold.

**VISION VI** Further experiments in the breakdown of the object and the revelation of its several aspects in one composite design should be carried out in several different drawing mediums. The subject matter can extend from the natural object to the mechanical one. (Think of the aspects of an engine cylinder block, for example, as a subject for a composite design involving simultaneous projection.) It is also possible to move from the single object to the group, which presents imaginative and organizational problems of some magnitude. Development of the chapter in this way challenges one's creative and technical resources.

After this, you could become involved with a moving object, and find your own way to show the movement of a form through space. And finally, you may attempt a "time project." By drawing, painting, and collage, using motifs and images all possessing differing time connotations, make a composite image capable of disturbing the viewer's time sense of "the present," through the simultaneous presentation of image-events.

**Review Fig. 5**
*Experimental monoprints from the glass to discover new textural possibilities. A drop of glycerine was added to the ink in this case, thus retarding the drying of the ink and creating these blot-like shapes.*

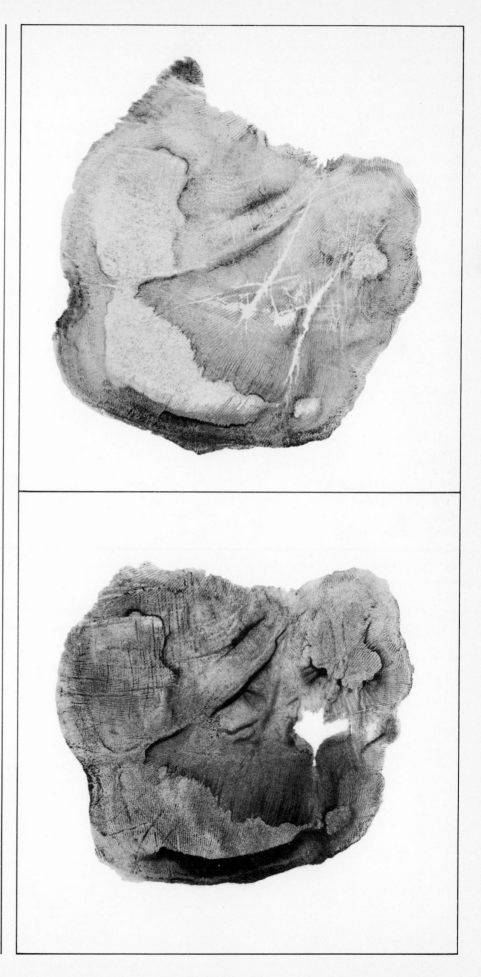

257

index

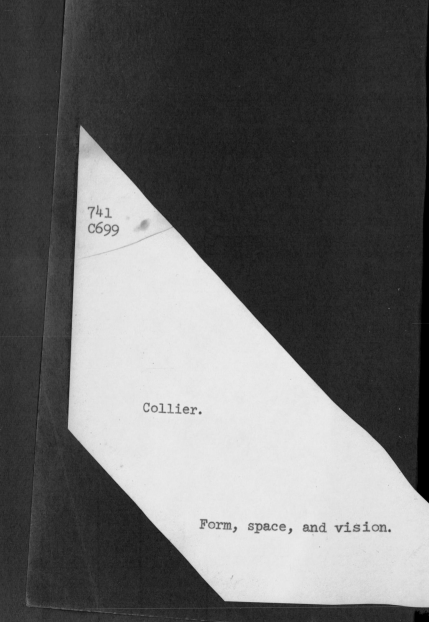